PEOPLE *of* *the* WORD

FIFTY WORDS THAT SHAPED JEWISH THINKING

MENDEL KALMENSON

ZALMAN ABRAHAM

PEOPLE OF THE WORD
Copyright © 2022 by Chabad.org
Second Printing—January 2023

718-735-2000
editor@chabad.org

Published by
Ezra Press
770 Eastern Parkway, Brooklyn, New York 11213
718-774-4000 / Fax 718-774-2718
editor@kehot.com / www.kehot.org

Order Department:
291 Kingston Avenue, Brooklyn, New York 11213
718-778-0226 / Fax 718-778-4148
www.kehot.com

All rights reserved. No part of this publication may be reproduced, stored in a retrieval system, or transmitted in any form or by any means, electronic, mechanical, photocopying, recording, or otherwise, without prior permission from the copyright holder.

 Ezra Press is an imprint of Kehot Publication Society.
The Ezra logo is a trademark of Kehot Publication Society.

2 4 6 8 10 11 9 7 5 3

ISBN: 978-0-8266-9013-5

Printed in China

*"Behold how good and how pleasant it is
for brothers to dwell together!"*
—Psalm 133

Dedicated to

David (Vadim)
and Sara Elka (Stella)
Aminov

on the occasion of his
50th birthday

Sacha and Tanya

Praise for People of the Word

"*People of the Word* beautifully illustrates how words create worlds and how concepts conceive. If you'd like to learn more about Judaism, and no less so about yourself, this splendid book is a must-read."

—TAL BEN SHAHAR, *PhD*
Best-selling author
Happiness Studies Academy
Potentialife

"This book is filled with information and mind-expanding insights that will deepen your knowledge of Hebrew and your understanding of life. Rabbis Kalmenson and Abraham's wisdom is prodigious, and they have produced a book that the Jewish community really needs both for its erudition and its compelling readability."

—JOSEPH TELUSHKIN
Bestselling author of more than 15 books on Jewish ethics and literacy

"Nice happiness chapter. I agree with your conclusions...."

—MARTIN SELIGMAN, *PhD*
Zellerbach Family Professor of Psychology
Director, Positive Psychology Center
University of Pennsylvania

"Mendel Kalmenson and Zalman Abraham have produced a work that should sit on every Jewish bookshelf and enrich the lives of countless readers, whatever their faith and affiliation."

—LEWIS GLINERT, *PhD*
Author of The Grammar of Modern Hebrew, The Joys of Hebrew,
and The Story of Hebrew

"...a very successful attempt at bridging the gap between Jewish traditional lore and academic knowledge."

—CYRIL ASLANOV, *PhD*
Chairman, International Center for University Teaching of Jewish Civilization
Hebrew University of Jerusalem
Member, Academy of the Hebrew Language

"*People of the Word* condenses decades of learning into a clear roadmap for spiritual, ethical, and positive living. The Rabbis open up a dimension of human potential for a broad readership that has been held deep within Jewish wisdom. In short, an invitation to see and live in an added dimension."

—LISA MILLER, *PhD*
Professor, Columbia University and NYT
bestselling author of The Spiritual Child *and* The Awakened Brain

"*People of the Word* is filled with insightful life lessons from major works of the Jewish tradition that inspire and attest to the richness of Jewish teachings."

—CAROL BAKHOS, *PhD*
Professor, Jewish Studies
Director, Center for the Study of Religion
University of California, Los Angeles

"With deep knowledge and thoughtful attention to contemporary concerns, readers find clear and lively explanations of key concepts of Judaism."

—SUSANNAH HESCHEL, *PhD*
Eli M. Black Distinguished Professor of Jewish Studies, Dartmouth College

"I highly recommend this new book "People of the Word" to anyone interested in discovering the secrets of life from a Jewish perspective."

—YITZCHOK DOVID GROSSMAN
Chief Rabbi of Migdal HaEmek
Founder and Dean, Migdal Ohr
Member, Chief Rabbinate Council of Israel

"Never before in history has there been such a widespread need for practical spiritual wisdom. *People of the Word* delivers with both wit and scholarship."

—DAVID H. ROSMARIN, *PhD*
Associate Professor, Harvard Medical School
Founder, Center for Anxiety

Table of Contents

Introductions vii

CHAPTER 1:	שמחה Happiness	1
CHAPTER 2:	אהבה Love	9
CHAPTER 3:	נסיון Challenges	17
CHAPTER 4:	צרה Suffering	25
CHAPTER 5:	מצרים Inhibition	35
CHAPTER 6:	נער Youth	43
CHAPTER 7:	רב Teacher	51
CHAPTER 8:	חינוך Education	59
CHAPTER 9:	הורים Parenting	67
CHAPTER 10:	לגמול Providing	73
CHAPTER 11:	נתן Giving	79
CHAPTER 12:	הצלחה Success	85
CHAPTER 13:	צדקה Philanthropy	93
CHAPTER 14:	חכמה Intelligence	101
CHAPTER 15:	ידע Intimacy	111
CHAPTER 16:	לחם Food	119
CHAPTER 17:	גוף Body	127
CHAPTER 18:	ענוה Humility	135
CHAPTER 19:	מזל Luck	145
CHAPTER 20:	חיים Life	153
CHAPTER 21:	כסף Money	159
CHAPTER 22:	מעשה Action	167
CHAPTER 23:	שנאה Antisemitism	175
CHAPTER 24:	אדם Humanity	183

CHAPTER 25:	דיבור	Speech	191
CHAPTER 26:	רגע	Time	199
CHAPTER 27:	עולם	Reality	207
CHAPTER 28:	דומם	Still Life	213
CHAPTER 29:	טבע	Nature	219
CHAPTER 30:	שם	Names	227
CHAPTER 31:	נשמה	Soul	235
CHAPTER 32:	אמונה	Faith	241
CHAPTER 33:	עברי	Hebrew	249
CHAPTER 34:	ישראל	Israel	257
CHAPTER 35:	יהודי	Jew	263
CHAPTER 36:	תורה	Torah	271
CHAPTER 37:	עדות	Reminders	277
CHAPTER 38:	מצוה	The Commandments	285
CHAPTER 39:	כהן	Priesthood	291
CHAPTER 40:	עבודה	Worship	299
CHAPTER 41:	תשובה	Repentance	307
CHAPTER 42:	בית הכנסת	Synagogue	315
CHAPTER 43:	תפילה	Prayer	325
CHAPTER 44:	שבת	Sabbath	333
CHAPTER 45:	מועד	Festivals	343
CHAPTER 46:	חטא	Sin	351
CHAPTER 47:	מותר אסור	Prohibitions	359
CHAPTER 48:	חזיר	Pork	367
CHAPTER 49:	שטן	Satan	373
CHAPTER 50:	גאולה	Messianic Era	381
APPENDIX:	יובל	Jubilee	389

Acknowledgments 423

INTRODUCTIONS

Introduction

British author Adam Jacot de Boinod spent five years researching over seven hundred dictionaries from different languages, culminating in a book titled, *The Meaning of Tingo and Other Extraordinary Words from Around the World*.

His findings suggest that a nation's dictionary says more about its culture than does its guidebook.

Indeed, you can tell a lot about a people by analyzing the prevalence and prominence of certain words in their language.

For example, Hawaiians have sixty-five words to describe fishing nets, one hundred eight words for sweet potato, forty-two for sugarcane, and forty-seven for bananas, all staples of a Hawaiian diet. In Albania, where there is a fascination with facial hair, there are twenty-seven words to describe mustaches and another twenty-seven for eyebrows. And in Persian there are numerous words to describe recalcitrant camels, including, for example, *nakhur*, a Persian word meaning "a camel that gives no milk until her nostrils are tickled."

Notably, in the same way that Inuits have many words to describe the subtle differences between different types and textures of snow, the Talmud employs a wide range of words to describe different types and categories of inquiry, reflecting the centrality of asking questions in Jewish culture and tradition.

Another telling example about Jewish culture is the fact that there are many words in Hebrew that describe joy and happiness.[1] To name a few, there are *sason, simchah, gilah, rinah, ditzah, chedvah,* and *tzahalah*, each of which describe a different shade of joy, from spontaneous joy (*gal* means wave) to the kind of exuberant joy expressed in song (*rinah*) and dance (*ditzah*), as well as the bittersweet joy that is tinged with sadness (*sason*), such as when a parent walks their child down the aisle.

As is evidenced by the numerous, nuanced descriptions of joy in Hebrew, despite the many humorous stereotypes to the contrary, Jewish people take their joy very seriously.

This brings us to an ancient question vigorously debated over millennia: Does the language we use merely *express* our worldview and values, or does it *shape* them?

Do the words we use merely *convey* our thoughts and emotions, or do they *influence* the way we think and feel?

As a growing body of research suggests, language does more than *communicate* our perception of reality, it *creates* it.

Indeed, according to Professor Lera Boroditzky,[2] a cognitive scientist who specializes in the fields of language and cognition:

"One of the key advances in recent years has been the demonstration of precisely this causal link [between language and perception]. It turns out that if you change how people talk, that changes how they think. If people learn another language, they inadvertently also learn a new way of looking at the world. When bilingual people switch from one language to another, they start thinking differently, too."

In the words of Charlemagne: "To have a second language is to have a second soul."

Boroditzky offers numerous examples[3] to showcase just how vital a role language plays in shaping the way we view and interface with the world around us.

For instance, in Pormpuraaw, a remote Aboriginal community in Australia, there are no words for "left" or "right." Instead, Indigenous Australians speak only in terms of cardinal directions (north, south, east, west). If one wants to tell a friend that they have an ant on their pants, one would say something like, "There's an ant on your southwest leg." Hello in Pormpuraaw would translate more accurately as, "Which direction are you going?" If you don't know which way is which, you may find yourself stuck, both conversationally and physically.

INTRODUCTIONS

"About a third of the world's languages rely on absolute directions for space," writes Boroditzky. "As a result of this constant linguistic training, speakers of such languages are remarkably good at staying oriented and keeping track of where they are, even in unfamiliar landscapes. They perform navigational feats scientists once thought were beyond human capabilities."

Yet people rely on spatial knowledge for much more than geographic orientation; it helps with time management, mathematics, musical pitch, interpersonal relations, and even causality.

For example, Boroditzky points out that in English, events are most often described in terms of agents doing things. English speakers will say things like, "John broke the vase," even if it was by accident. Speakers of Spanish or Japanese would say, "The vase broke," omitting the guilty party.

These linguistic differences have acute consequences in terms of the speaker's view of cause and effect, and the role that agency plays. This, in turn, affects the blame and accountability of those involved,[4] even within the criminal justice system itself.

Since English sentence structures focus on agents and causality, American justice emphasizes finding and punishing the perpetrator rather than aiding the victim.

Beyond the above examples, linguistic patterns have also been shown to shape perception and thought, to fascinating ends. The Russian language's many descriptors for shades of blue enables its speakers to better visually identify those colors. The Piraha, an Amazonian tribe in Brazil, use a language that favors terms like "few" and "many" rather than exact numbers. This results in a lower ability to keep track of precise quantities.[5]

"Likewise," according to Professor Antonio Benítez-Burraco,[6] "the way people think about time is encoded deeply in the grammar of most languages. In some languages, like English, time is tripartite: past, present, and future. However, in a language like Yimas, spoken in New Guinea, there are four types of pasts, from recent events to remote past." On the other extreme, "there are languages like Chinese that lack grammatical tense" altogether.

The Pormpuraawans of Australia tell time according to the sun's daily journey from east to west. Mandarin centers time around gravity, so that when something falls, the past is where it was—above—and the future is where it will be—below. The South American dialect of Aymara uses basic human reasoning: What's in front of us is the past, since it's already known, and what's behind us is the future, the unknown.

In sum, the patterns, structures, and particular words used in each language not only offer a window into a culture's sensibilities, dispositions, and priorities, they help shape them, as well.

Hence the title of this book: *The People of the Word: Fifty Words That Shaped Jewish Thinking*.

In the pages that follow, we aim to provide insight into fifty key Hebrew words and the big ideas embedded in their etymology, which have helped shape Jewish thought and values, and, in many instances, have led to measurable, real-world impact.

For example, one could argue that the emphasis on happiness and joy in the Hebrew language and Jewish tradition (as mentioned above and elucidated in the chapter titled, "*Simcha*" (page 3)) has contributed to the phenomenon that, according to the Gallup-Healthways Well-Being Index,[7] Jews score the highest of any faith and non-faith group in the US when it comes to happiness and well-being.

One could also posit, as did Nobel Prize winner Robert Aumann during a conversation I had with him while researching this book, that the great emphasis in Jewish tradition and culture on scholarship, curiosity, critical thinking, and *tikkun olam* (as elucidated in the entries on "*Rav*" and "*Chochmah*" see page 53 and 101) have led to the disproportionate representation of Jewish people among Nobel Prize winners.[8]

A final example of the link between the Jewish way of thinking, speaking, and behaving can be drawn between the Hebrew word *tzedakah*, often mistranslated as charity, and its true meaning as elucidated in Chapter 13.

If, as Salman Rushdie once said, "A culture can be defined by its untranslatable words," the word and concept of *tzedakah* has much to teach about the unique Jewish understanding and culture of giving.

To quote R. Lord Jonathan Sacks, of blessed memory: "The Hebrew word *tzedakah* is untranslatable because it means both charity and justice. Those two words repel one another in English, because if I give you a hundred pounds because I owe you a hundred pounds, that's justice. But if I give you a hundred pounds because I think you need a hundred pounds, that's charity. It's either one or the other, but not both. Whereas in Hebrew, *tzedakah* means both justice and charity. There's no word for just charity in Hebrew. Giving is something you have to do."

According to author Paul Vallely, who spent six years researching the history of Western philanthropy, from the ancient Greeks and Jews to modern times, culminating in a book titled, *Philanthropy: from Aristotle to Zuckerberg*[9]:

"It is, therefore, perhaps no coincidence that throughout the history of philanthropy, Jews have been consistently generous givers, and disproportionately so. A survey in Britain in 2019 showed that ninety-three percent of British Jews gave to charity compared with fifty-seven percent of the rest of the population. In the *Sunday Times Giving List* in 2014, more than twelve percent of the most charitable givers were Jewish, though Jews constitute less than half of one percent of the UK population according to the last census."

In the US, as well, Jews give charity in quantities far disproportionate to their numbers.[10]

For example, in 2010, nineteen of the top fifty-three US donors recorded in *The Chronicle of Philanthropy* were Jewish, including five of the list's top six.[11]

The point of the above examples and observations is not to suggest that Jews are *naturally* happier, smarter, and kinder, but that Jewish culture, as shaped and molded over the millennia by the Jewish ideas and values expressed in the Hebrew language, provides a universal paradigm shifting toolkit and template that can be emulated by all.

More than merely a thought-provoking read, we hope this book, like the fifty words upon which it is based, will inspire readers to concrete action that reflects their highest ideals and values.

To conclude where we began, in case you were wondering about the meaning of the word Tingo, mentioned at the beginning of this introduction: Tingo is an invaluable word from the Pascuense language of Easter Island (near Chile) meaning "to borrow objects from a friend's house, one by one, until there's nothing left."

And this, dear friend, perfectly describes the way we'd like this book to be read. We invite you to borrow these words, one by one, and make them your own—in thought, word, and deed.

Mendel Kalmenson
London, 2022

What's in a Name?

*The words a person speaks are deep waters,
a flowing stream, a fountain of wisdom.*
—*Proverbs 18:4*

We generally think of language as a convention of words arbitrarily chosen for the purpose of communication, to ensure that our speech or writing is understood by others. The names of things, however, are of little significance to what they really are. As Shakespeare puts it: "A rose by any other name would smell as sweet."

Usually, an object precedes its name—first it exists, then it is given a name. However, regarding creation, the Torah tells us, *G-d said*: "*Let there be light," and there was light*—the name not only predates the object but is the means through which it is created. A rose by any other Hebrew name, therefore, wouldn't quite smell as sweet.

Hebrew words and names are not arbitrary. They are definitive and expressive of the true nature of things.[12] The Biblical word for rose, *shoshanah*, is rooted in the word sheshoneh, "that changes," communicating that its beauty is in its delicate suppleness, its softness and responsiveness, and its ability to change (*shoneh*) in response to touch.[13]

Hebrew words are therefore understood to provide insight into the nature and meaning of things. This means that Jewish understanding of a particular object or idea is embedded within the Hebrew word used to describe it.

In Genesis,[14] the Torah tells us about Adam naming the animals. The Midrash[15] describes this act as an incredible feat that is even beyond the capability of angels. If names were arbitrary, there is no reason why this would be deemed a supra-angelic skillset. There must be deeper existential truths to be uncovered within a name.

Mystics explain[16] that our purpose in this world is to utilize our unique gifts of comprehension and creativity—gifts that are unique to the human race and do not exist among the angels—to uncover the Divine source and purpose of every created being that is embedded in their name and to assist in utilizing all things in service of their ultimate purpose.

Before G-d gave His laws at Sinai, our mission as humans was to bring the wisdom of each creation to fruition by recognizing and actualizing the purpose of its creation, which is buried within its name.

In G-d's language, words are portals through which we can discover the meaning of things from the Divine perspective.

When looking to make sense of ourselves, our world, and everything that transpires within it, the key to unlocking this deeper meaning can be found within the language of G-d's book, the Bible.

As mentioned earlier, words do much more than just communicate the nature and meaning of things; in Jewish thought, they occupy a creative and generative function. *Sefer Yetzirah*, the earliest book of Jewish mysticism, asserts that the twenty-two letters of the Hebrew alphabet constitute the "DNA" of the entire cosmos, "the letters with which G-d created the universe."

"Twenty-two letters, He drew them, hewed them, combined them, weighed them, interchanged them, and through them produced the entirety of creation and everything that is destined to come into being."
—*Sefer Yetzirah, Ch. 2*

Hebrew words, particularly those of Biblical derivative, provide a portal into the essence of things. They allow us a glimpse into G-d's mind, to peer at G-d's intent and gain insight into the purpose and meaning of everything in our world. Hebrew words are thus a key that can unlock the hidden meaning and significance of whatever is called by their name, including its philosophical, psychological, and theological significance. The purpose of this book is to help open this mysterious world of meaning.

When compiling this work, we searched for contrasts between Hebrew words and their counterparts in other languages, seeking to identify the unique outlook embedded within them.

Another critical factor that went into determining our choice of words for inclusion was the novelty of the big idea that the word expresses and its relevance to our lives.

This book is more than a book of words. It provides windows of insight into Jewish history, thought, culture, meaning, and practice. In writing it, we attempted to capture the unique spirit of Judaic thought that sets it apart from its counterparts and from popular society. We incorporated many themes that are relevant to our lives, to provide a glimpse of the profound depth of Jewish philosophy by unpacking fifty Hebrew words to uncover their deeper meaning, significance, and insights into life.

Zalman Abraham
New York, 2022

Happiness

simchah שמחה

CHAPTER 1 | HAPPINESS

HAPPINESS IS A THOUGHT

IF ONLY WE WERE more successful, more comfortable, or more respected, if only we had a perfect bill of health, less to worry about, and more to look forward to, then we would most certainly be happy. Or so we think. We tend to see happiness as a result of our circumstances, relegating it to the distant realm of "if only, then...," leaving us with little we can do to influence its actualization.

Accordingly, the word "happiness" is derived from the Middle English word *"hap,"* as in happenstance or haphazard, implying random chance or luck. If you were lucky enough to be born into ideal circumstances, you have the conditions needed to be happy. If not, it seems there isn't much you can do to impact your sense of satisfaction in life.

On the other hand, *b'simchah*, the Hebrew word for being in a state of happiness, shares the same letters as the word *machashavah*, thought.[1]

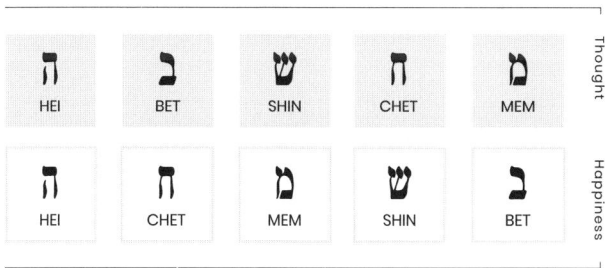

3

Judaism views happiness as a way of thinking, which is something that we can consciously direct, as opposed to a state of being that results from a specific set of circumstances outside our control.

From this perspective, happiness does not derive from our objective state of affairs but from our subjective state of mind. Put simply by Plato: "Reality is created by the mind. We can change our reality by changing our mind."

Meaning, it isn't luck or happenstance that ensures our attainment of happiness; rather, it is the way we think about and process the circumstances we encounter along our path.

This simple idea has huge implications. It means that we can instantly achieve the happiness we seek by adjusting the focus of our thoughts.

This deceptively simple idea reveals that the greatest obstacle to our happiness is the mind's tendency to fixate on the limitations of our circumstances and to regulate and take for granted the myriad good things we experience every day.

Each time we have a positive experience, we raise our expectations, sometimes exponentially, constantly needing more and more stimulus to achieve the same level of satisfaction.

In the words of our Sages: "He who has one hundred wants two hundred, and he who has two hundred wants four hundred."[2]

As a result, we never reach the satisfaction we seek, and happiness remains an endless pursuit, a never-ending hedonic treadmill, always just beyond our reach. From this perspective, fulfillment becomes a frustrating illusion that never materializes.

Judaism's solution to the "happiness problem" is to view happiness as a thought, making it an infinitely renewable resource, always at our disposal, rather than an existential lottery ticket.

All it requires is a minor investment of mental energy and an enhanced awareness to stop thinking only about what's missing in our lives and focus instead on what is present. In the words of the Mishnah: "Who is wealthy? He who is satisfied with his lot."[3]

True satisfaction in life comes not from having the things we want, but from *wanting the things we have*. To this end, there is a Jewish practice of reciting at least one hundred blessings each day, to seek out every opportunity to remember and verbally acknowledge our gratitude for the basic amenities of life. For in life, the only things we *truly* have are the things that we *appreciate*.

The letters that make up the word *simchah* also spell *shemachah*, which means erasure, teaching us that a key component to happiness is our ability to live fully in this moment, erasing, at least temporarily, any painful thoughts about the past or anxious thoughts relating to the future. Now is where true happiness is found.

The Baal Shem Tov taught that: "You are where your thoughts are."[4] Meaning that one's true location is where their mind is focused. The letters of the word *samei'ach*, happy, also spell *sham moach*—the location of one's thoughts. When we do not recognize that we are in control of our own happiness, we live in a near-constant state of anxiety and discontent, and that becomes a defining feature of our lives.

But when we realize that we have the capacity to choose and change our thoughts at any moment, we come to appreciate that the key to enduring happiness lies entirely in our hands.

The Big Idea

Happiness is a product of our subjective state of mind rather than our objective state of affairs.

It Happened Once

A MAN ONCE CAME TO R. DovBer, the Maggid of Mezritch, with a question.

"The Talmud tells us that 'a person is supposed to bless G-d for the bad just as he blesses Him for the good.' How is this possible? Had our Sages said that one must accept without complaint or bitterness whatever is ordained from Heaven, I would be able to understand. I can even accept that, ultimately, everything is for the good, and that we are to bless and thank G-d also for the seemingly negative developments in our lives.

"But how can a human being possibly react to what he experiences as bad in exactly the same way he responds to what he experiences as good? How can a person be as grateful for his troubles as he is for his joys?"

R. DovBer replied: "To find an answer to your question, you must visit my disciple, R. Zusha of Anipoli. Only he can help you in this matter."

R. Zusha received his guest warmly and invited him to make himself at home. The visitor decided to observe R. Zusha's conduct before posing his question. Before long, he concluded that his host truly exemplified the Talmudic dictum that so puzzled him. He couldn't think of anyone who suffered more hardship in his life than did R. Zusha—a frightful pauper, there was never enough to eat in R. Zusha's home, and his family was beset with all sorts of afflictions and illnesses. Yet, R. Zusha was always good-humored and cheerful, and constantly expressing his gratitude to the Almighty for all His kindness.

But what is his secret? How does he do it? The visitor finally decided to pose his question.

"I wish to ask you something," he said to his host. "In fact, this is the purpose of my visit to you—our Rebbe advised me that you can provide me with the answer."

"What is your question?" asked R. Zusha.

The visitor repeated what he had asked of the Maggid. "You raise a good point," said R. Zusha, after thinking the matter through. "But why did our Rebbe send you to me? How would I know? He should have sent you to someone who has experienced suffering..."[5]

ahavah אהבה
―――――――――

Love

I GIVE, THEREFORE I LOVE

THERE ARE FEW EXPERIENCES in life as powerful and transformative as love. And yet, there are few words as hard to define.

Contemporary Western culture is obsessed with love, particularly romantic love. Movies, books, songs, advice columns, talk shows, tabloids—our collective consciousness and media marketplace is saturated with images and stories of such love lost, won, renewed, and unrequited.

And yet, when one compares the idealized version of love glorified in popular culture with the facts on the ground—the sharply increasing divorce rate, the broken families, the millions of chronically lonely people—it seems that there is a profound disconnect between our idyllic expectations and actual reality.

The Jewish tradition has a lot to say about love. Love of G-d, love of one's neighbor, love of the stranger and the dispossessed, love of oneself, and of course, romantic love.

As different as these loves may be, they are all called by the same name, alerting us to the fact that love is multifaceted and complex, not just the stuff of fairy tales or happy endings of Hollywood.

The Hebrew word for love is *ahavah*, which is rooted in the more molecular word *hav*,[6] which means to give, revealing that, according to Judaism, giving is at the root of love.

What does this etymological insight teach us both about the function of love and about how love functions?

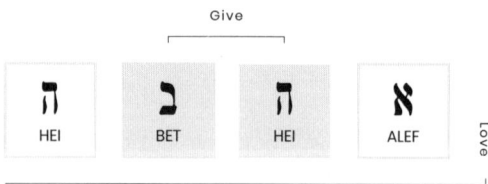

First, love is not all about you, the lover, but about the other, the beloved. Love calls us out of the confines of ourselves and into the wilderness of relationship. It is a transformative experience that dethrones the ego and puts it to work in the fulfillment of the needs and desires of another.

This is beautifully expressed in a teaching of R. Levi Yitzchak of Berditchev, who said that he learned the meaning of love from a drunk.

He once passed two drunks drinking in the gutter and witnessed one saying to the other, "I love you," to which the other drunk replied, "No, you don't." "Yes, I do," the first protested, "I love you with all my heart." "If you love me," the second insisted, "why don't you know what hurts me?"

Perhaps, what the second drunk was telling his drinking partner was that if he really loved him, he would know that the reason he drank was that he was hurting inside and simply wanted to escape his inner pain and turmoil. The second drunk was rebuking the first for his self-centered approach to their friendship, asserting that: "You don't really love me at all; you just love how you feel when we're drinking together…"

True love, then, is not about how you feel in someone else's presence; it's about how you make them feel in yours.

A well-known Chasidic parable relates the story of a fisherman who once caught a pike and exclaimed, "This will be for the baron; the baron loves pike!" The pike was extremely relieved to hear this, because he had been afraid his life was about to end. The fisherman then brought the pike to the baron's head chef, who looked at the pike and exclaimed: "The baron will be so excited; he loves pike!" This brought even greater relief to the fish, along with a surge of anticipation to meet his apparent admirer. However, as soon as the chef brought him into the kitchen and lifted a giant knife to chop the fish into pieces, the pike finally realized, "The baron doesn't love pike at all; he only loves himself and how I make him feel."

True love is other-centric and enduring—the opposite of infatuation, which tends to fade quickly. Infatuation is transactional, based primarily on what a person gets out of it, and thus most often leads to relationships of convenience, where every encounter is narrowly focused on what one can take or receive rather than on what they can offer or provide.

Love, on the other hand, is strengthened and prolonged with every act of thoughtfulness and selfless giving.

This leads us to a second major premise of Jewish love: Love is not primarily about how you *feel* but about what you *do*.

Famously, the Torah[7] commands us to *Love your neighbor as yourself*. In relation to this verse, many ask: How can we be commanded to feel something for those we don't have feelings for? One answer is that the command is not focused on internal feelings at all, but on external actions.

In the words of Maimonides[8]: "It is a commandment to love one's fellow as oneself, as stated in the Torah. Therefore, one must speak in praise of his fellow and be concerned for his property, as one is concerned about one's own property and honor."

It is worth noting that nowhere in this teaching does Maimonides mention how one is supposed to feel about their neighbor *emotionally*. Instead, he interprets the commandment *behaviorally*, as a call to action: speak well of your neighbor, be concerned for their property, and so on.

In framing the commandment this way, Maimonides echoes the famous teaching of Hillel, who interpreted the same commandment to mean: "That which is hateful to you, do not do unto others."[9]

According to both Hillel and Maimonides, when it comes to loving our neighbors and fellow citizens, our feelings are secondary. What matters most is our actions and how we treat and relate to others in our midst. What is true for the so-called stranger or neighbor is especially true for those closest to us, including family, friends, and even G-d: In love, feelings keep us focused on the self; actions are what connect us to others.

Accordingly, the *ketubah*, the Jewish marriage document, does not contain a single declaration of love. Rather than a compilation of love poems, it is in fact a legal contract that clearly spells out the material marital obligations between a husband and a wife. It is written in Aramaic, which is the legal language of the Talmud, rather than in Biblical Hebrew, the holy tongue.

Though not "poetry," per se, this ancient document, which frames love and marriage as a binding commitment with concrete behavioral implications and responsibilities, expresses ethically relational poetics of its own.

It is less of a promise to always only feel a certain way and more a promise to always uphold a higher standard of presence and action in relation to one's beloved. The "poetry" of the *ketubah* is ultimately expressed through the couple's life itself, lived as an expression of love beyond the four corners of the *ketubah* and the four poles of the *chuppah*.[10]

Beyond merely conveying the importance of prioritizing actions over feelings, the word *ahavah* (based on the root "to give") also communicates a subtle but profound psychological insight into how feelings actually work.

From the romantic perspective, we tend to think of love as a necessary prerequisite to giving—the more we love someone, the more we are capable and willing to give of ourselves to them. In this paradigm, our actions flow unidirectionally from our passion and feelings. From the Jewish perspective, however, the opposite is true—*the more we give, the more we love*. The act of giving itself is what opens the channels for the feelings to flow and even to grow. In the words of the Sages,[11] "One's heart is drawn after their deeds."

All that is not to say that one must never base their actions on their feelings, or that feelings are irrelevant. According to the Torah, love—whether of G-d, one's fellow, oneself, or one's partner and family—is so important that we are encouraged, instructed, and even commanded to act in ways that will ensure that this most paramount of emotions is consciously cultivated.

In the final analysis, the emotional sensation we commonly call love is, in fact, a collaborative creation generated by our thoughts, words, and deeds in concert with each other. In this light, love is measured not simply by how much feeling you get from thinking about or being in the company of your beloved, but by how much of yourself (care, consideration, desire, pleasure, and support) you are willing to offer them on the altar of your actions.

The Big Idea

True love is not about how you feel in someone else's presence; it's about how you make them feel in yours.

It Happened Once

AS A YOUNG, UNMARRIED woman, Chana Sharfstein was discussing with the Lubavitcher Rebbe some prospective matches that had been suggested to her, and she explained why none of them appealed to her.

The Rebbe smiled and said:

"You have read too many romance novels. Love is not the overwhelming, blinding emotion found in the world of fiction. Real love is an experience that intensifies throughout life. It is the small, everyday acts of being together that makes love flourish. It is sharing, caring, and respecting one another. It is building a life together, a family and a home. As two lives unite to form one, over time, there is a point where each partner feels they are a part of the other, where each partner can no longer visualize life without the other."

This quality of love is illustrated beautifully by R. Aryeh Levin, known as the *tzaddik* (righteous person) of Jerusalem, who once accompanied his wife to the doctor. He explained to the doctor: "Doctor, my wife's foot is hurting *us*." He loved his wife so much that he truly felt at one with her to the extent that he felt her pain as his own.

Challenges
nisayon

נסיון

CHAPTER 3 | CHALLENGES

NEW LEVELS, NEW DEVILS

LIFE IS FULL OF tests and challenges. No one escapes this fact. The deeper question is: Why? What is the purpose of all of these tests? Is there a way to prepare for them? And what is the rubric for "passing" them? The answers to these questions can be found within the very language we use to construct and consider them.

A test or trial is typically understood as a means to determine the state of development someone or something has achieved prior to taking it. This can be gleaned from the etymology of the words themselves. Test, or *teste*, is a Middle English word that was borrowed from Old French, which refers to "an earthen vessel, especially a pot in which metals were tried." Similarly, the word trial is based on an Anglo-French word *triet*, meaning an "act or process of testing, a putting to proof by examination, experiment, etc." In either case, the subject or object being tested was viewed with a necessary degree of doubt. The test or trial was thus administered as a way for an outside party to verify the integrity or acuity of the one being tested.

In Judaism, however, a test is not meant to assess or establish the current qualities of the one being tested; rather, it is meant to elicit and evoke the dormant strengths and unique talents that lie within!

Notably, the Torah[12] tells us that *G-d tested Abraham*. Our Sages[13] enumerated ten Divinely orchestrated tests that Abraham encountered. The first[14] was when Nimrod forced him to choose between renouncing his belief in the one Almighty G-d or be thrown into a fiery furnace. The tenth and final test was G-d's instruction to bind his son Isaac on an altar.

What was the purpose behind such a series of unremitting spiritual challenges?

Along these lines, the *Zohar*[15] asks: "If G-d is all-knowing, why did He need to test Abraham?" Didn't G-d already know the outcome? The answer is that G-d tested Abraham to provide him with an opportunity to activate the latent potentials for courage and commitment that G-d knew already existed within him.

In other words, these ten tests were not for G-d to see how faithful Abraham was; they were for Abraham to actualize the depths of his own spiritual potential.

Appropriately, the Hebrew word for a challenge or test, *nisayon*, is rooted in the word *nes*, which means to raise up. As the *Zohar* explains: "G-d tests the righteous only to elevate them to greatness." But for such elevation to occur, we must rise above our natural fear and aversion to challenges, which is alluded to in the related word *lanus*, meaning to run away.

Judaism teaches us to lean into our challenges instead of running from them, because our personal and collective trials and tribulations are designed to help us unlock hitherto untapped energies and abilities, empowering us to exceed our own expectations of our capabilities. This realization itself is an integral part of the process of unlocking the infinite potential hidden within.

Daunting as our struggles often feel, defeatist attitudes must not prevail. G-d is never against you. In fact, according to the Jewish view, any test or trial you may experience is not an expression of G-d's *doubt* in your capacity, but of His *faith* in your ability.

As the Talmud[16] poignantly teaches: "G-d does not make impossible demands of his creations." Just as it is inconceivable that loving parents would knowingly give their child a task that is beyond their abilities, G-d, our loving Father, would not present us with a challenge that exceeds our capabilities or is not for our own good.

Accordingly, whenever a person encounters one of life's many tests, it is actually a sign of G-d's trust in them and their potential.

Rather than being an expression of Divine reservation, every test in life is actually a cosmic vote of confidence.

In fact, our personal struggles can even be seen as signs of favor, *for G-d chastises those He loves.*[17] A test is G-d's way of saying: You're ready for the next level.

Interestingly, the word *nes* also refers to a banner, because each person's unique tests in life are like a badge of honor that represents their particular journey of personal growth and achievement. In other words, our struggles are what shape and form us, giving us our distinct stamp and signature based on how we respond to them.

This empowering idea is expressed in the paradoxical Talmudic statement[18]: "The more righteous one is, the more powerful their inclination to evil." This is counterintuitive. One would think that a person's level of righteousness is determined by, and should directly correspond to, the degree to which they have managed to diminish or uproot their evil inclination. Yet, according to the Talmud, the contrary is true—the more one grows spiritually, the greater their struggle with ego and temptation becomes. This is because the more righteous one becomes, the more capable they are at overcoming ever subtler and more substantial challenges.[19]

In other words, serious moral and spiritual struggles are not a sign of weakness but of strength and latent potential that we might unlock and activate through our productive perseverance in the face of life's challenges.

Significantly, another meaning of *nes* is miracle, implying the elevation of the supernatural over the natural. Indeed, Chasidut[20] teaches that, from the Divine point of view, every test in our lives provides the exact conditions conducive for us to surpass our own "natural" limitations, thus enacting a "miracle" within our own personal sphere.

As such, no situation in life, no matter how challenging, should be seen as impossible to deal with in a constructive manner. We always have the opportunity to exercise free choice in the way we respond to any circumstance.

Every test of our faith or character is thus a potential portal of transformation for our own, as well as the ultimate good; it all depends on how we approach, process, and pass through it. As the great Chasidic master R. Nachman of Breslov famously taught[21]: When you search for G-d and encounter an obstacle, do not try to avoid it or seek to go around (or even over) it, for G-d Himself is to be found within that very obstacle.

This perspective is deeply rooted in the concept of Divine Providence, *hashgachah pratit*, the belief that G-d is in charge of our world and oversees its minutest detail with deliberate intent.

The knowledge of such a Divine design behind reality compels us to overcome our naturally instinctive feelings of fear and despair when faced with any challenge, especially one we thought we were above or beyond. Instead, it empowers us to find the hidden blessing built into every hardship.

G-d, like our own personal trainer, is intimately aware of both our perceived limitations and our true abilities. He therefore strategically orchestrates our unique obstacle courses in order to help us access our deepest strengths and achieve our highest potentials. For, truly, each and every one of us is nothing less than a miracle in the making. Our tests and struggles in life are but the dark backdrop against which our inner light might shine.

The Big Idea

Tests and trials in life are an indication of inner strength, not weakness; they are G-d's way of letting us know we are ready for the next level.

It Happened Once[22]

A TRADITIONAL JEW WHO FOUND himself in the grips of a spiritual struggle once visited the Lubavitcher Rebbe to discuss his religious quandary.

He desperately wanted to live his life according to Jewish law, yet his heart was persistently leading him in a different direction.

After presenting his situation to the Rebbe, the man fell silent. He braced himself for a strong rebuke, expecting to be told in no uncertain terms how spiritually compromising his passions were.

The Rebbe, too, remained silent for a while.

"I envy you," the Rebbe finally said. Caught off guard, the young man did not quite grasp the Rebbe's meaning.

The Rebbe continued: "There are many ladders in life, and each person is given his or her own. The ladders present themselves as life's challenges and difficult choices. The tests you face are the ladders that elevate you to great heights—the greater the challenge, the higher the ladder. G-d has given you these difficult tests because He believes you can overcome them, and He has endowed you with the ability to do so. Only the strongest are presented with a ladder as challenging as yours. Don't you see, then, why I envy you?"

Suffering *tzarah*
צרה

CHAPTER 4 | SUFFERING

FROM WALLS TO WINDOWS

A GROUP OF FRIENDS WERE discussing what they would do differently if they were running the world instead of G-d. One said: "I would eradicate disease, hunger, and poverty." Another said: "I would get rid of natural disasters." A third suggested: "I would abolish bigotry and prejudice of all kinds!" The last of the group, who had sat silently listening to the others, finally said: "I would keep the world exactly as it is, except, I would understand why."

It is physically impossible for the human brain, with its limited abilities, to grasp an infinite G-d, or, for that matter, to understand His ways. Put plainly in a well-known idiom first cited by medieval Jewish philosopher R. Yosef Albo[23]: "If I knew Him, I would be Him."

As a result, we have great difficulty coming to grips with the inevitable pain and suffering of life, primarily because we only have access to a partial view of the big picture. We are thus left with only a portion of the story in which we are playing an integral part.

This can be compared to a patient who goes in for a surgery and suddenly wakes up on the operating table with no recollection of the procedure for which they came in. All they see is their body opened on the table and a bunch of masked people hovering over them and wielding knives. Of course they are horrified! Until the doctor explains to them the purpose of this painful process, after which they can calm down and allow the doctor to finish his job, which saves or at least improves their life after the fact.

Simply put, our finite perspectival limitations hinder our ability to understand the deeper significance of our painful experiences, which then leads to a feeling of affliction. It is no exaggeration to say that few things in life cause more suffering than the feeling that our pain is in vain.

This existential predicament is alluded to in the Hebrew word for misfortune, *tzarah*, which is etymologically rooted in the word *tzar*, narrow. In Jewish thinking, we are prone to psychological and spiritual suffering on account of our painful or challenging experiences because we can only see a narrow sliver of the bigger picture. Therefore, the antidote to *tzarot*, the existential feeling of misfortune, is to zoom out and try to see life and the world from G-d's perspective, so to speak.

Learning to view reality in this light is not easy. It requires a firm trust that G-d is in control of everything—including the minutiae of one's daily life—that G-d is ultimately good, that G-d only wants good for us, and therefore everything that G-d does is intended to bring us closer to the ultimate good that awaits us. The idea that there is inherent good in all that G-d does is powerfully reflected in the Talmudic dictate[24] that "One should recite a blessing for the bad that befalls him just as he does for the good." Indeed, the words "Blessed is the true Judge" are recited upon hearing bad tidings—for example, when receiving news of someone's passing[25]—emphasizing the Jewish belief that even when we don't understand why certain things occur, we have faith that there is a Divine purpose behind it all.[26]

That, in a nutshell, is the foundation of the Jewish worldview.

This worldview teaches that we each have the ability to overcome or transform any hardship or adversity we may experience by actively choosing to find the meaning and the good that is concealed within it.

This certainly does not mean that we won't ever experience discomfort or even excruciating, seemingly intolerable pain. However, when we are able to contextualize our pain as part of a greater good, even if it is beyond our understanding, it can empower us to endure such suffering, or even inspire us to harness it as fuel for future growth and evolution. As Victor Frankl puts it[27]: "In some ways, suffering ceases to be suffering the moment it finds a meaning."

Indeed, the very same letters in the Hebrew word for why, *lamah*, also spell *l'mah*, which means for what? or towards what end? This conveys the Jewish approach to strife and challenge, which is not to ask, "Why me?" but "What now?" In other words, how can I use this setback as a springboard for growth and self-development?

Interestingly, the letters of the word *tzarah* also spell *tzohar*, a window.[28] In other words, suffering opens a window into our deepest recesses, allowing us to become aware of and gain access to dormant potentials and deeper reservoirs of energy and insight that might have otherwise remained unrealized.

This is one of the hidden blessings of pain and challenge in life—they give us the opportunity to pause, reflect, dig deep, and grow beyond what we ever thought was possible. Pain pushes us out of our comfort zone and goads us to do the hard work of adaptation and evolution. Without it, we might simply stay safe in our own status quo and never risk becoming who we were ultimately meant to be.

Moreover, pain can create a window into other people's experiences, as well. Therefore, another blessing of pain is that it can serve as an agent of empathy, enabling us to connect, relate, and understand suffering and situations other than our own, thus expanding our heart and worldview. An interesting example of this is found in the Midrash.[29] After the sale of Joseph by his brothers, his older brother Judah—who was, in some way, responsible for selling Joseph into slavery—marries and has multiple children, who then die at a young age. The Midrash comments that this series of painful events in his own life was intended to give Judah a deeper understanding of what his father, Jacob, had gone through following Joseph's sudden disappearance—the pain of losing a child.

This idea is deepened and reflected in the Hebrew word for feelings, *regesh*, which is composed of the same letters as the word for bridge, *gesher*. The intense feelings we experience during difficult times not only provide us with empathetic insight into what others have endured, but they can also build a bridge between our experience and theirs, revealing the commonalities we share with so many whom we may think of as being very different.

So pervasive is this redemptive, process-oriented approach to pain and suffering in Judaism that one may find traces of it encoded within various letter-root structures throughout the Hebrew language.

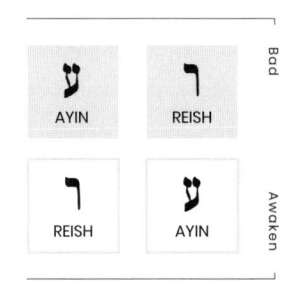

For instance, the letters of the Hebrew word for bad, *ra*, also spell *er*, which means to awaken. In other words: When bad, difficult, or painful things happen, they are meant to awaken us, to activate something deeper within us, and to connect us with ourselves and others in more profound ways.

ע	ר	Bad
AYIN	REISH	
ר	ע	Awaken
REISH	AYIN	

Similarly, the word *avak*, which means to wrestle, shares the same letters with *avukah*, bonfire, indicating that our existential wrestling with life and its obstacles is what ignites our inner flame. This exact dynamic is reflected in the single word *ptil*, meaning both wrestling and wick, as in the wick of a torch or candle.

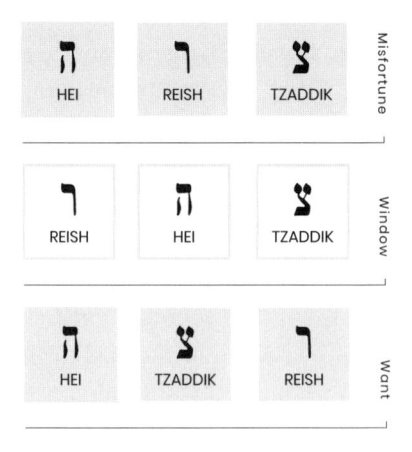

Amazingly, all of these can be found yet again within the word *tzarah* when you permute its letters to form the word *ratzah*, meaning want or desire. Experiencing misfortune can help us clarify what we truly want in life. Furthermore, *ratzah* is also connected to the word *ratz*, running, which is similarly related to the word *ratzon*, willpower. When we desire something, we will exert our willpower to run after it.

ה	ר	צ	Misfortune
HEI	REISH	TZADDIK	
ר	ה	צ	Window
REISH	HEI	TZADDIK	
ה	צ	ר	Want
HEI	TZADDIK	REISH	

Taken all together, we can say that grappling with our personal challenges ignites the wick of our soul with the fire of our desire and the will to change, grow, and evolve our life for the better.

This idea that there may be something positive hidden within

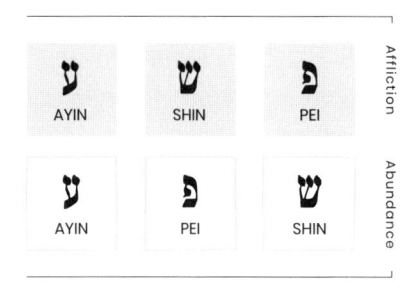

CHAPTER 4 | SUFFERING

suffering itself is alluded to in the letters that comprise the word *pesha*, affliction, which, when rearranged, spell *shefa*, abundance. Depending on the way we respond to the trials of our life, every ordeal has a potential blessing for us, if we can but unlock it by awakening our hidden reserves of energy, faith, love, strength, etc. This is reflected in the exchange between Jacob and the angel he wrestled, when Jacob refused to let the angel go until he blessed him. Jacob's seemingly eccentric insistence in the midst of such a charged moment demonstrates a profound lesson—we must never move on from a struggle or challenge without putting in the effort to extract its hidden blessing.

In addition to accessing previously untapped capabilities, rising to meet the challenges we encounter also has the potential to yield a unique kind of existential pleasure or delight. This, too, is reflected in a pair of words that share identical letters—*nega*, affliction, and *oneg*, pleasure. Concealed within what feels like a plague, we may unearth a rare spiritual pleasure, even if it is just the satisfaction of overcoming our seemingly insurmountable challenging circumstances.

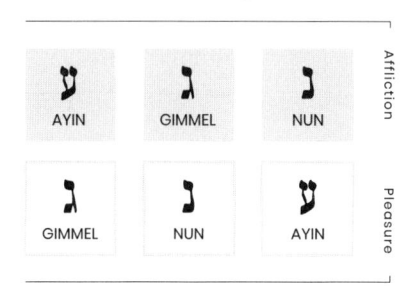

When we do not succumb to our own suffering but instead strive to rise above it, we are able to reverse the letters of the word *mar*, meaning bitter, and transform them into *ram*, uplifted.

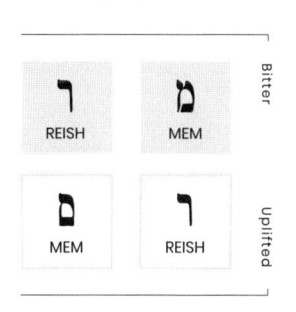

Poetically, the Talmud[30] compares suffering to crushing an olive in order to access its oil. It is only through the painful

31

process of being plucked, tossed, stored, and squashed to the point of dissolution that the inner oil—which provides rich flavor, nutrition, lubrication, and illumination—emerges from within its previously bitter, hard, and inaccessible encasement.

Herein lies the difference between being broken and being *broken open*. When one's heart is simply broken, they are fragmented, in pieces, destroyed. In this state, many fall into deep depression and are unable to carry out even the most basic functions. When one's heart is broken open, however, they become more receptive, empathetic, and expressive. From this place, new realizations and connections can be made that would have been impossible in their previous state of being—a new world and reality are now able to emerge.

This paradigmatic process of purposeful brokenness is illustrated poignantly within a single Hebrew word: The words for both broken and birthstool share the same root, reminding us that within every breakdown lies the potential for birth and breakthrough.

In fact, it is often the very stories we tell about ourselves that end up confining rather than defining us. Similar to contractions during labor, the discomfort we experience in painful or challenging situations has the power to push us out of our self-contained comfort zones, giving us the space to become more than we ever dreamed possible.

Ultimately, we may never grasp the mystery of all mysteries—why pain exists and why good people suffer—but we can learn how to respond to pain, choosing to heed its call to peer more deeply into ourselves, make changes in our lives, and reclaim the greater good and pleasure that G-d intended for us. As Leonard Cohen put it so poignantly: "There is a crack in everything; that's how the light gets in."

The Big Idea

The spiritual approach to strife and challenge is not to ask, "Why me?" but "What now?"

It Happened Once

"It was taught in the name of R. Akiva that one must always accustom oneself to say: Everything that G-d does, He does for the best.

"R. Akiva was once walking along the road [with a small band of travelers]. They came to a certain city, and he inquired about lodging, but they did not give them any. He said [to his distraught companions], 'Everything that G-d does, He does for the best.' They all went and slept in a field. R. Akiva had a rooster with him, as well as a donkey and a candle. A gust of wind came and extinguished the candle; a cat came and ate the rooster; and a lion came and ate the donkey. He said again, 'Everything that G-d does, He does for the best.' That night, an army came and took the city into captivity. It turned out that R. Akiva and his companions alone, who were not in the city and had no lit candle, noisy rooster, or donkey to give away their location, were saved.

"R. Akiva said to [his traveling companions], 'Didn't I tell you? Everything that G-d does, He does for the best.'"[31]

מצרים

mitzrayim   Inhibition

LEAVING THE EGYPT WITHIN

J EWISH TRADITION SEEMS TO be fixated on Egypt; specifically, with leaving Egypt.

Much of the Five Books of Moses tells the story of the events leading up to and following the Israelites' enslavement and subsequent exodus from Egyptian bondage. The impact of these events frames and fashions the formative stages of Jewish history.

In fact, the exodus shows up repeatedly in the Torah as the rationale behind many of the *mitzvot*, including the major Jewish festivals (not just Passover), all of which commemorate different aspects of the exodus.

There is even a specific mitzvah to remember the exodus every single day![32]

Based on the above, one may be justified in asking: Why does the flight from Egypt, which occurred over three thousand years ago, occupy such a central place in Jewish consciousness? Why haven't the Jewish people moved on from this ancient enemy as they have from so many other tyrannic oppressors that have since come and gone? Why keep returning to this particular trauma from their distant past?

According to Chasidic teaching, like all parts of the Torah, the exodus is not just an isolated episode from ancient history; rather, it is a perpetually relevant paradigm for life in the present. As our Sages teach[33]: "In every generation (and, indeed, every day), one is obligated to see themselves as if they had personally left Egypt."

Egypt and the exodus thus exist within the Jewish psyche not only as a particular geographic location and historic event but also as a state of mind and central focus of self-awareness.

To understand this more deeply, we must go down to Egypt ourselves.

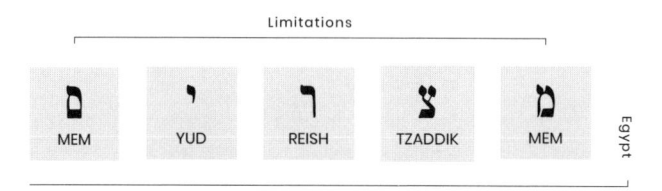

Limitations					Egypt
מ	י	ר	צ	מ	
MEM	YUD	REISH	TZADDIK	MEM	

The Hebrew word for Egypt, Mitzrayim, is made up of the same Hebrew letters as the word *meitzarim*, which means limitations,[34] symbolizing the areas in our lives where we feel stuck or constricted. In a personal sense, then, the exodus from Egypt implies an internal process of liberation, moving us beyond our own emotional, psychological, and physical limitations, which are often self-imposed.

The first step out of such internal bondage is the recognition and acknowledgment that our circumstances and capabilities are not fixed and that a different reality is always possible.

For example, since the 1990s and until recently, most psychologists believed that willpower was a limited resource that is subject to fatigue and is depleted with repeated use. Experiments consistently demonstrated the veracity of this hypothesis, until a new study[35] showed that those previous observations held true *only for those who already believed that willpower was limited.*

Those with a "growth mindset"[36] never exhibited any signs of dwindling self-control or motivation, regardless of how much willpower they exerted in working towards their goal.

This supports the idea that the beliefs we bring to a particular situation have the power to either create self-imposed boundaries or to break down the walls of existing assumptions.

As the saying goes: "Whether you think you can or you think you can't, you're right!"

CHAPTER 5 | INHIBITION

In addition to such perspectival elasticity, the quality of emotional receptivity is also crucial to the exodus story.

For instance, the Hebrew letters of the name Pharaoh, who enslaved the Jewish people in Egypt, can be rearranged to spell *oreph*, the neck.[37] In Jewish mystical sources, the narrow channel of the neck represents a precarious place of potential constriction and blockage between the mind and the heart.

Healthy people generally form emotional reactions to acquired knowledge and understanding, which is what motivates them to act and change. Pharaoh is stuck; his heart is impenetrable and incapable of reacting meaningfully to the inescapable truths unfolding before his very eyes, even to the point of self-destruction and the ruin of his country! This blockage is reflected in the Torah's description of Pharaoh's heart as "hardening,"[38] a peculiar expression that isn't found in reference to anyone else in the Torah.

Pharaoh's inflexibility, despite witnessing the ten plagues, which brought Egypt to its knees, reminds us of Earl Landgrebe's quip at the Watergate hearings: "Don't confuse me with the facts! I've already made up my mind."

In contrast, Pharaoh's daughter, Batya, was moved by the cry of an endangered infant and was unable to stand by idly in the face of injustice. In violation of her father's genocidal decree, she retrieved the Israelite baby from the water and called him Moshe (Moses) because *from the water* meshisihu—*I drew him out.*[39]

True to the spirit of his name, time and again, Moses, too, was emotionally impacted by the injustices he witnessed around him, leading him to "draw out" and rescue those suffering persecution.

Unlike Pharaoh, Moses' heart was open and receptive to the truth before his eyes, regardless of how that truth might impact his personal life. Therefore, Moses is not just the political opponent of Pharaoh, he is his psycho-spiritual nemesis, as well. His mission to bring the Jewish people out of Mitzrayim (Egypt) represents our personal struggle to liberate our soul-potential from the grips of our own *meitzarim* (constrictions).

The overarching theme of escaping one's limitations reaches its crescendo in the climax of the exodus,[40] at the Splitting of the Sea. This miraculous episode has come to symbolize the notion that many of the obstacles we perceive in our lives that seem impossible and impassable are not truly insurmountable and can be overcome with faith, fortitude, and forward movement.

If Egypt represents the tyranny of self-limiting beliefs and behaviors, the exodus signifies our spiritual journey towards expansive perception and limitless potential.

Therefore, we return to the story of the liberation from Egypt year after year, and day after day, in order to remind ourselves of this essential truth and translate it into practice.

We must never stop striving for freedom, because yesterday's peak can become today's prison cell.

This is the essence of what it means to leave Egypt.

The Big Idea

In Jewish thought, Egypt is not merely a geographical location but also a limited state of mind that we must continually strive to transcend and leave behind.

CHAPTER 5 | INHIBITION

It Happened Once

A BUSINESSMAN WHO WAS BECOMING close to Chabad once told the Lubavitcher Rebbe: "I don't see myself growing a beard or wearing Chasidic garb. Is there still a way I can call myself your Chasid?" The Rebbe replied with a smile, "Anyone who wakes up each morning and asks himself, 'How can I become better today than I was yesterday, and better tomorrow still,' I am happy to call my disciple."

Youth

naar נער

YOUTHQUAKE

Children are the promise of a future. This is the way many view the young: they are worthy of our time and attention insofar as they will be the next generation. In the words of King Ahaz of Judah[41]: "If there are no kid-goats, there will be no he-goats. If there are no he-goats, there will be no flock."

This perspective is vividly illustrated in a Midrashic account[42] that provides the backstory to the giving of the Torah. When the Jewish people stood at Mount Sinai, before revealing the Torah, G-d asked them to provide a guarantor to ensure it would be faithfully kept into the future. They replied, "Our ancestors will be our guarantors." When this proposition was rejected, they offered, "Our prophets will be our guarantors." This offer was also refused by G-d. Only when they said, "Our children will be our guarantors" did G-d reply, "Indeed, these are good guarantors. For their sake I will give it to you."

As true and functional as the above perspectives are, Judaism's perspective on youth goes beyond merely seeing children as a means to an end; it is founded on a profound appreciation for the unique spiritual energy and capacity of youth itself.

In 2017, the Oxford Dictionary selected the word Youthquake, defined as "a significant cultural, political, or social change arising from the actions or influence of young people," as the word of the year. This socio-linguistic phenomenon is reflective of the psycho-spiritual fact that there is a fire inside young people that adults often negatively characterize as a rebellious spirit.

Yet, at its core, it is not merely an immature sense of angst that drives youth, but tremendous energy and a refusal to settle for less when more can be achieved. In the words of the Lubavitcher Rebbe[43]: "The rebelliousness of young people is not a crime. On the contrary, it is the fire of the soul that refuses to conform, that is dissatisfied with the status quo, that cries out that it wants to change the world and is frustrated with not knowing how."

Such fiery passion and disruption is a constituent element of young people's experience and awareness, as evidenced in the Hebrew word for youth, *naar*. For instance, in the mystical Shabbat hymn *Lecha Dodi*, we find the passage, *hitnaari mei'afar kumi*, meaning, shake off the dust, arise. The word *hitnaari* (shake off) is formed from the same root-letters as *naar*, reflecting the revolutionary energy of youth that allows them to shake off the dust of contentment in order to see life anew.

As we grow, we become accustomed to life's ways, and complacency sets in. We start questioning our ability to change the world. Youth are free of this baggage; their seeming naivete works to their advantage. Children can therefore bring about what adults see as improbable, even impossible.

Furthermore, beyond their innate ability to throw off the shackles of social conformity in their quest for truth, children have a special spiritual sensitivity as well. This, too, is reflected in the word *naar*, which is etymologically connected to the word *uri*, meaning to wake up.

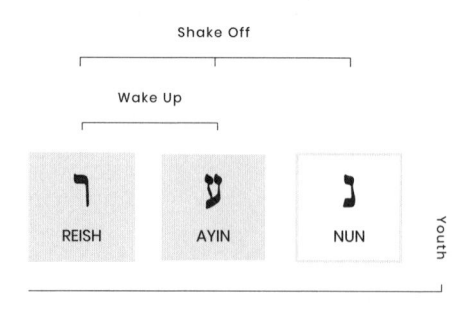

| Shake Off |
| Wake Up |
| ר REISH | ע AYIN | נ NUN | Youth |

In Jewish tradition, children are seen as symbolically representing and naturally embodying this state of spiritual awakeness that adults must consciously cultivate and seek to regain.

Such an inborn spiritual sensitivity in children is referenced numerous times by the Sages, such as in the assertion[44] that it was the children who first recognized G-d's presence at the Splitting of the Sea, even before Moses, Aaron, and the elders!

A further illustration of the elevated spiritual level of children is found in the Talmud[45]: Reish Lakish said in the name of R. Yehudah the Nasi: "The world endures only for the sake of the breath of schoolchildren [emitted during Torah study]." R. Papa asked Abaye: "What about mine and yours?" Abaye replied: Breath in which there is sin is not like breath in which there is no sin." According to the Talmud, not even the greatest Sages of our tradition are seen to be on the spiritual level of a simple child!

This idea is further expressed in the teaching that[46] "From the day the Temple was destroyed, prophecy was taken from the prophets and given to...children." King David, too, says as much when he declares that[47]: *Out of the mouth of the babes and sucklings You have established strength, in order to put an end to all enemies and adversaries.*

The reason children are more spiritually awake is that they are more pure and sensitive to the presence of the Divine within all. They are not yet corrupted by the wiles of egoic self-consciousness or held prisoner by the hubris that often accompanies increased knowledge and experience, and, therefore, they can receive and transmit the word of G-d more faithfully.

A fascinating Midrash[48] on the Purim story relates an episode in which Mordechai, after learning of Haman's decree to annihilate the Jews, asked three young school children what they were learning. The first boy promptly recited the verse he had learned at school that day: *Do not fear sudden terror, nor the destruction of the wicked when it comes.*[49] The second boy said, *Contrive a scheme, but it will be foiled; conspire a plot, but it will not materialize, for G-d is with us.*"[50] And the third boy said,[51] *To your old age I am [with you]. I have made you, and I will carry you; I will sustain you and deliver you.*"[52]

When Mordechai heard these responses, he smiled with a happy heart. Haman asked him: "What makes you so happy about what these children said?" Mordechai replied: "I am happy because of the glad tidings they told me—that I should not be afraid of the evil plot that you contrived against us."

We see here an example of an exalted Sage relating to the words of children as a form of prophecy. As R. Yehudah said in the name of Rav: "What is meant by the verse, *Do not touch my anointed ones?*[4] *My anointed ones* refers to *tinokot shel beit rabban*—school children."

In our liturgy we ask G-d: *Chadeish yameinu k'kedem*, renew our days as of old.

How, then, might we maintain youthful optimism and idealism even as we grow older and become accustomed to, even disillusioned by, life's ways?

The Biblical term for aging gives us insight into the secret to staying young. When the Torah describes Abraham and Sarah's elder years, it uses the term *ba'im bayamim*, which literally translates as entering their days, teaching us not only how long they lived (quantitatively) but how deeply they lived (qualitatively). They *entered* each day *fully* with curiosity and openness, never thinking they had it all figured out or holding onto expectations of how things were *supposed* to be.

Similarly, we find that in the Torah,[53] Joshua was still referred to as a *naar* even when he was fifty-six years old.[54] The Midrash[55] explains that this was because he possessed a youthful and energetic drive even at that age.

It is human nature that the older a person becomes, the less he tends to be affected by events around him, either because he has become more mature and settled or because he has already lived so many years that he is not so easily fazed by events—life holds fewer and fewer surprises.

When we "enter our days" with a fresh pair of eyes, we are spiritually awake and attuned to discover the unique expression of Divine unity in every moment.

In meditation practice, this is called "beginner's mind," and it is seen as an ideal state to cultivate; to see things simply as they are instead of as we are, to be open to whatever arises, and to believe in the possibilities of change and growth while remaining a perpetual student of life's mysteries. Children effortlessly embody this awareness. Since they are less experienced in life, everything appears to them as new and miraculous.

It is this same understanding of the spiritual advantages of youth that led some of the great masters of Jewish spirituality and meditation to offer the following humble and breathtaking prayer to G-d before they began their prayers[56]: *"Ani mitpallel l'daat zeh hatinok,"* asking G-d to grant them the ability to address Him with the innocence of a child.

In Jewish tradition, the most spiritually mature viewpoint, as expressed by these mystics, is that intellectual sophistication can be an obstacle to fully receiving or encountering the Divine Presence. Philosophical arguments, mental gymnastics, and lofty meditations, no matter how subtle and breathtaking, can get in the way of our direct connection with G-d.

Such intellectual pursuits can be likened to standing on the shore waxing poetic about the sea rather than diving in and immersing oneself in the water. In order to re-enter a childlike state, we must simply open ourselves up to the Divine all around and within us instead of spending all our time thinking about encountering it. Children exemplify this ability to faithfully leap into life, and, therefore, from the spiritual point of view, the innocence of a child is not something to grow out of but something to grow into.

The Big Idea

Physically speaking, children are potential adults; spiritually speaking, adults are potential children.

It Happened Once

ONCE, DURING THE *NE'ILAH* prayer at the end of Yom Kippur, the Baal Shem Tov cried more than usual. His closest disciples understood that he must have sensed a negative heavenly decree looming, and they responded by intensifying their own prayers and supplications. When the rest of the congregation witnessed this, their hearts moved them to join in the impassioned pleas.

There was a young boy from the neighboring village who had come to the synagogue for the Days of Awe. He was completely uneducated in Jewish practice.

As a village dweller, the boy knew the sounds of all the different farm animals, and he especially loved the rooster's crowing. When he heard the weeping from the rest of the congregation, his heart was also shattered, and he cried out loudly, with pure exuberance and youthful sincerity, "Cock-a-doodle-do! G-d, have mercy!"

The worshippers in the synagogue were disturbed to hear a child crowing like a rooster, and a few of them even scolded the boy. They would have thrown him out if he had not protested, "I am a Jew and I also belong here."

The confused cacophony was pierced by the prayerful voice of the Baal Shem Tov, whose face shone brightly as he concluded *Ne'ilah* with a special melody.

After Yom Kippur ended, the Baal Shem Tov related to his disciples that there had, in fact, been an accusation leveled in heaven against the boy's village for their lack of connection to Jewish life and spiritual practice. Try as he might, despite using all of the mystical powers at his disposal, the Baal Shem Tov was unable to avert the decree.

Until, suddenly, the sound of the village boy's fervent call rose to Heaven, and its heartfelt sincerity brought great pleasure Above, nullifying the decree at once.[57]

רַב ~~rav~~

Teacher

CHAPTER 7 | TEACHER

THE ART OF SPIRITUAL WAR

J UDAISM IS A RELIGION that doesn't just encourage respect but mandates it as a religious obligation and duty—respect for one's parents, elders, spouse, siblings, employees, even adversaries. Yet, once you step into the study hall, all reverence is left at the door.

While there are many laws concerning the proper reverence accorded to one's teachers,[58] when it comes to the actual process of learning, students are encouraged to put all inhibiting etiquette aside. In fact, polite manners and common courtesy were sometimes suspended altogether for the sake of Torah study. For example,[59] "Members of the house of R. Gamliel would not say 'in good health' (the equivalent of 'bless you') when someone sneezed in the study hall, so as not to disrupt their study."

Shockingly, we even find instances of Sages hiding in their teacher's bathroom or bedroom to learn firsthand about the spiritual approach to the private and intimate matters of life. When caught, the excuse they gave was always the same: "This too is Torah, and I must learn."[60]

Certainly, respect for one's teacher is a core value in Judaism, because teachers are a repository of learning, even considered to be akin to a "walking Torah scroll," as the Talmud states, "How foolish are those who stand up for a Torah scroll but not for a great man

53

[teacher]."[61] However, when deference stands in the way of truth, such formalities must be discarded.[62]

This is because, at its root, learning is a journey of truth-seeking that requires a degree of ruthlessness. One Talmudic passage[63] even makes this approach to study personal:

"What is the meaning of the phrase 'enemies in the gate' with regard to Torah study? R. Chiya bar Aba says: Even a father and his son, or a teacher and his student, who are engaged in Torah together in one gate become (temporary) enemies with each other due to the intensity of their studies."

The Talmud[64] even goes so far as to characterize Torah study as a kind of war, repeatedly referring to it as "the war of Torah." This is because Torah study involves a combative dance of *shakla v'tarya* (Aramaic for give and take), a constant back and forth, a choreographed dialectical process intent on deconstructing old ideas and introducing new realizations.

This approach to learning is powerfully captured by the Hebrew word for teacher, *rav*, which is etymologically linked to the word *riv*, meaning battle. The function of a teacher is thus defined as creating and curating a constructive space for cognitive conflict and dissent, which is how we learn best.

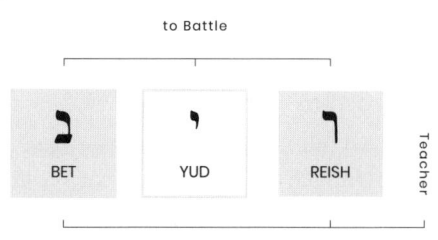

Homeostasis, the natural tendency to seek out a stable equilibrium, is a deep-seated human trait. As such, we crave the comfort of closure and thus often settle for the most readily available answer. But such "closure" does just that—it closes us off from further questions as well as the curiosity behind them. This, in turn, makes it difficult to discover new insights, since an exploratory process requires us to first uproot our attachments to any previous understanding in order to consider new viewpoints and possibilities. In other words, to learn, we need to *open* our mind, the very opposite of "closure."

Instead of quietly accepting what they are told, a good student should be taught to think critically and independently. Only after one has honestly grappled with an issue can they truly absorb it and make it their own. A good teacher is therefore not one who allows the student to remain comfortable, but one who proactively engages them in constructive provocation, inspiring them to question their assumptions and not take anything for granted.

Education expert James Nottingham describes the education process as "a learning pit," where the teacher's objective is to push the student into a proverbial pit by challenging them to confront and grapple with issues outside of their comfort zone that don't necessarily fit neatly into their worldview. This is achieved by asking questions that shake up and poke holes in a student's perception of reality. Such perspectival disorientation makes a person productively puzzled and unsettled, provoking them to actively wonder and wander outside their own box. Only once the student realizes how their thinking is stuck or has reached its limits does the teacher gently guide them out of the pit by providing the tools to help them arrive at a new realization—a eureka moment of sorts—which enables them to entertain a more nuanced and expansive picture of reality.

In many ways, traditional Torah study stands in stark contrast to the "safe space" environment that our modern culture now expects teachers and schools to provide. Of course, no student should ever feel like they are in any physical or emotional danger in the classroom. Indeed, the verse states: *The words of the wise are heard when they are spoken gently*,[65] and the Sages teach that "an impatient person is not one who can teach."[66] However, they also add that "a timid person cannot learn." Over-emphasizing a cognitive "safe space" and reinforcing a student's dependence on a so-called comfort zone can engender intellectual laziness and overregulation, which are the enemies of learning.

In this spirit, R. Chaim of Volozhin suggests a novel interpretation of the passage in *Ethics of Our Fathers*[67] that refers to a student's regard for their teachers: "*Vehevei mitavek baafar ragleihem*," which is usually translated as "sit at the dust of their feet." However, the word *mitavek* more literally means "to wrestle." Students are wrestlers, and study is a form of battle. Students are thus discouraged from blindly accepting the words of a teacher. If they have a valid question, it must be raised. Sometimes, it even turns out that the truth lies with the student, not with the teacher. In the words of R. Chanina in the Talmud, "I have learned much from my teachers, more from my colleagues, but most from my students."[68]

This horizontally structured, battle-like approach to learning extends beyond the teacher/student relationship and applies to interactions between students as well. For almost three thousand years, from the Babylonian Talmudic academies of old to modern-day *yeshivot*, pairs of students, or *chavrutot* as they are called, engage in a dynamic process of collaborative learning, with each party challenging their partner's thinking to break down previous assumptions in order to arrive at new and innovative ways to understand the subject matter. To someone who is unfamiliar with this style of learning, the *chavruta* system can appear to be competitive and combative. The seeming chaos and ruckus of multiple pairs of students yelling across a pile of open books can be unsettling to the uninitiated. However, as those who have experienced the intellectual urgency and spiritual camaraderie of *chavruta* learning know, it is also electrifying and extremely effective. Notably, the word *chavruta* shares a root with the Hebrew word for friend, *chaver*. This alludes to the crucial fact that such intellectual sparring stems from a place of fellowship. Just as in martial arts, where one's sparring partner is a trusted companion, meant to help them learn, grow, and acquire new skills.

As it says in the Talmud[69]: "A prisoner cannot free themselves from prison." We are each prisoners of our own perceptions. We need other people to help break us out of our limiting paradigms in order to glimpse a new horizon. Left to our own devices, we will forever return to our old ways of thinking and rigidified patterns of understanding. As R. Yosei son of R. Chanina teaches[70]: "Those who study alone grow foolish."

As individuals, even if we may be willing to consider a new or different perspective, it is usually only within very specific parameters of association with which we already feel comfortable. To truly break out of an old paradigm and embrace a completely new reality, we need another person—a teacher, a sparring partner, a friend—someone who is unafraid to question our premises at their foundations and help us open our eyes to a whole new way of understanding Torah, ourselves, and the world. The war of Torah thus yields a love of learning in which all sides are victorious.

The Big Idea

The role of a teacher is not to teach his students what *to think, but* how *to think.*

It Happened Once

THE TALMUD RELATES[71] THAT R. Eliezer was once debating a matter of Jewish law with his colleagues:

...R. Eliezer cited all sorts of proofs [that his view was correct], but they were rejected. He said to them: "If the law is as I say, may the carob tree prove it." The carob tree was uprooted from its place a distance of one hundred cubits. Others say it was four hundred cubits. They replied: "One cannot prove anything from a carob tree."

[R. Eliezer] then said to them: "If the law is as I say, the stream will prove it." The water in the stream began to flow backwards. Again they replied: "One cannot prove anything from a stream."

He then said to them: "If the law is as I say, may the walls of the house of study prove it." The walls of the house of study began to cave in. R. Yehoshua rebuked them [the walls] saying, "If Torah scholars are debating a point of Jewish law, what are your qualifications to intervene?" The walls did not fall, in deference to R. Yehoshua, nor did they straighten up, in deference to R. Eliezer. They still stand there at a slant.

[R. Eliezer] said to them: "If the law is as I say, may it be proven from heaven!" A heavenly voice then proclaimed: "What do you want of R. Eliezer? The law is as he says..."

R. Yehoshua stood up and cited the verse: *"The Torah is not in heaven!*[72] ...We take no notice of heavenly voices, since You, G-d, have already, at Sinai, written in the Torah to *follow the majority*."[73]

R. Nattan subsequently met Elijah the Prophet and asked him: "What did G-d do at that moment?" [Elijah] replied: "He smiled and said: 'My children have triumphed over Me; My children have triumphed over Me.'"

Education
chinuch

חינוך

CHAPTER 8 | EDUCATION

MADE TO MEASURE

MANY SCHOOL SYSTEMS TODAY function like factories, with standardized curricula that act as an assembly line for every student. This industrialized approach to education does not take into account the individual learning styles or interests of each student, leaving little room for developing their innate potential and particular gifts. As Einstein succinctly put it, "Everybody is a genius, but if you judge a fish by its ability to climb a tree, it will live its whole life believing that it is stupid."

In place of such a homogenizing method of teaching, King Solomon writes in the Book of Proverbs[74]: *Educate a child in his own way, so that even when he grows old he will not stray from it*. This more personalized approach is reflected in the Hebrew word for education, *chinuch*, a variation of which is used in the Mishnah[75] to describe the act of hewing out stone inside a catacomb, fit specifically to size. Similarly, education is meant to be tailored and responsive to each individual student.

Judaism therefore supports a more child-centered, rather than top-down, paradigm of education, in which each child is seen to possess both their own unique way of learning as well as their own wellspring of wisdom. As we learn in Proverbs,[76] *Counsel in a man's heart is like deep water, but a man of understanding will draw it out.* Targum Yonatan[77] explains that the man of understanding in this

61

PEOPLE OF THE WORD

verse refers to a teacher who "draws out" the wisdom from within each student by asking them the right questions.[78]

Fittingly, a common Hebrew word for teacher, *melamed*, is etymologically related to the word for midwife, *meyaledet*.[79] A good teacher will aid the student in "giving birth" to their own innate wisdom and ideas.

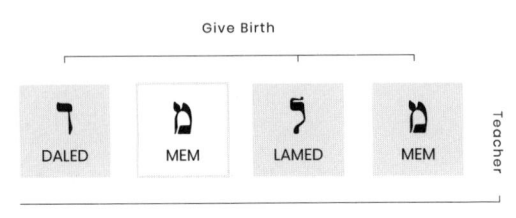

Notably, the two-letter root of the word *chinuch*, *chein* (usually translated as grace), is translated by the *Targum*[80] as *rachamim*, meaning compassion, which is related to the word *rechem* or womb. A classroom is therefore like a womb—a place filled with a *ruach cham*, a warm spirit of nurturing and burgeoning new life.

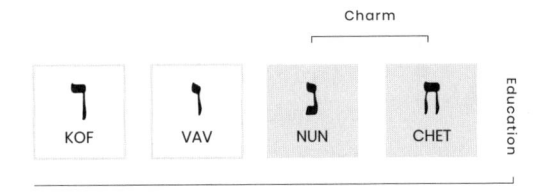

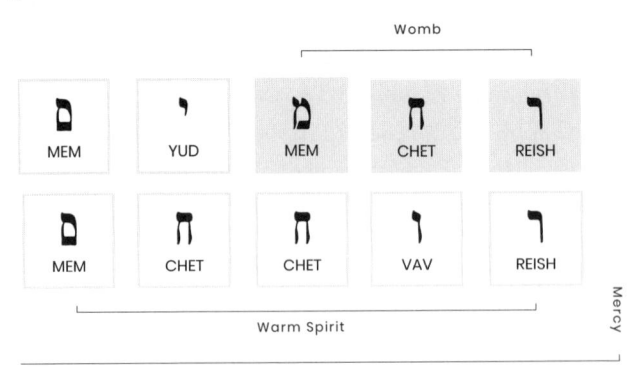

Accordingly, a teacher must be a person of kindness, warmth, and sensitivity, so that their manner of teaching will be infused with these qualities. As our Sages say[81]: "The words of the wise are heard when they are spoken gently."

Furthermore, our Sages caution that one who easily loses patience is not fit to be a teacher.[82]

In addition to its personalized approach to education, Judaism is ultimately focused on the development of the whole person. Contrary to the current focus of many schools, in Jewish thought the ideal result of education is not limited to the acquisition of knowledge and information; rather, it is integrally concerned with the more holistic formation of a *mentch*—a fully developed person with refined moral character. Jewish education is therefore not just about the honing of the intellect; rather, it is about the development of the person in their entirety.

In this sense, the goal of education is to set the student up for life. As Rashi writes,[83] "*Chinuch* refers to a person's entrance into a trade that they will eventually take up."

Ideally, education provides the training that will help students develop the ability to think independently and act with integrity.

Accordingly, our Sages teach[84]: "*Derech eretz kadmah laTorah*," meaning that common decency and dignified behavior is a prerequisite to higher knowledge.

In the words of R. Schneur Zalman of Liadi[85]: "...there can be no Torah without fine character."

Regarding this, the sixth Lubavitcher Rebbe, R. Yosef Yitzchak, writes[86] that "the main effort of an educator lies chiefly in transforming the base and ignoble traits of his pupil."

Expanding on this, the Lubavitcher Rebbe writes[87]: "Children, by nature, do whatever they see fit, without any restraints...[and] must therefore be trained to set boundaries and change their habitual natures, until they attain sovereignty of mind over heart."

This philosophy is based on a verse in Job[88] that states: *A human is born as a wild donkey.* Meaning, a person's natural tendency is to follow their most base and animalistic instincts, with no consideration for the deeper meaning or long-term impact of their appetites and actions. The work of the teacher, therefore, on a deeper level, is to help their students develop a more refined character by instilling in them a spiritual worldview, which includes a set of positive habits and values.

Such a process of character refinement is not as simple as conveying information; rather, it must be taught by example—the teacher must be a *mentch*[89] and someone the child can respect.

It is for this reason that the word *chinuch* is understood by some scholars[90] as a derivative of the word *chein*, which means charm or rapport—referring to an invisible bond, an emotional connection and mutual appreciation, that exists between the teacher and student. To describe this invisible connection, the Steipler Gaon quotes from Proverbs,[91] *Just as a person's face is reflected in the water, so too a person's heart is reflected in that of their fellow.* This is yet another indication of how deeply relational and effective meaningful education truly is.

It follows that the essence of the teacher-student relationship and the internal work of the teacher is to connect to his student. In this sense, a more accurate translation of *mechanech*, teacher, is a connector. In this spirit, the Talmud[92] relates that the Sage Rabbah would begin his class with a light-hearted remark to get his students to laugh and create an air of camaraderie, and only then would he turn to more serious matters and begin the lesson. Commentaries explain that he did this to open the hearts of the students so they would become more receptive to learning.

Elsewhere,[93] the Talmud advises that an educator should teach their students subjects that genuinely interest them. To quote our Sages: "A person should learn Torah (only) from a place [topic] that the heart desires."

This is because *wanting* to know something is essential to any intellectual process. Conversely, disinterest and indifference dull the mind and its faculties of comprehension. Those who genuinely seek to understand a subject will apprehend it, no matter how difficult.

Put simply, *the mind doesn't just open the heart, the heart opens the mind.*

Such an approach requires a teacher to be both perceptive and sensitive to where each of their students' interests lie. Such fine attention is a subtle but clear communication to a student that their teacher cares about what captivates them.

All of this points to a single essential truth: For education to be truly effective, the most important component is the quality of the relational connection that exists between teacher and student. The student needs to feel that the teacher sincerely cares—not just about the subject matter, but about *them*. Only when the student is made to feel loved, respected, and cherished will their hearts be opened and the environment be ripe for real learning and growth to take place. As the saying goes: People don't care how much you know until they know how much you care.

A moving example of such care and devotion is illustrated by a story in the Talmud.[94] Rav once found his colleague, R. Shmuel bar Sheilat, who was a schoolteacher, tending to his garden. Seeing that he was not with his disciples, Rav asked: "Have you abandoned the children entrusted to your care?" R. Shmuel replied: "I have not seen my garden for thirteen years, yet, even now, I cannot stop thinking about the children!"

Teaching isn't just another nine-to-five job; a great teacher is one for whom teaching is a lifelong calling. And it is from such a dedicated midwife, *mentch*, and role model that students learn most and best.

As the Hebrew word *chinuch*, which literally means inauguration, suggests, the ultimate objective of a teacher is to initiate a student on the path of lifelong learning. For, ultimately, to quote Socrates: "The purpose of education is not to fill a vessel but to kindle a flame."

The Big Idea

"Education is what remains after one has forgotten what one has learned."[95]

It Happened Once

A MAN ONCE SHARED HIS parenting frustrations with the Lubavitcher Rebbe, saying, "Rebbe, I don't understand! Despite raising all of my children exactly the same way, one of my kids chose to leave the path of Jewish faith and practice! How could this be?! I raised them all exactly the same way!"

The Rebbe replied gently, "Perhaps raising all of your children in exactly the same way was precisely the problem... For when it comes to raising and educating children, it's absolutely essential to take each of their unique personalities, needs, and interests into consideration..."

Parenting *horim*

הורים

CHAPTER 9 | PARENTING

OF ROOTS AND FRUITS

THE LATIN WORD *PARENTE*, the origin of the English word parent, means to bring forth, to give birth, or to produce, highlighting the physical role parents play in the creation of a child. The Hebrew word for parents, *horim*, on the other hand, means teachers, emphasizing the fact that Jewish tradition sees parents not only as progenitors and guardians but also as educators tasked with empowering their child with the knowledge and tools they need to live healthy, wholesome, and independent lives.

Being a parent is thus not merely defined by bringing a child into the world, but equally, if not more importantly, by preparing them for a successful future. Towards this end, the Talmud[96] teaches that a parent is obligated to instruct their child in the following three areas of life: 1) A belief and value system to help them navigate the complexities of life; 2) a trade, to ensure their financial independence; and 3) basic survival skills—an example of which is swimming.

Reflecting this point, Abraham is considered to be the father of the Jewish people, and to this day is called *avinu*, our father. A verse in Genesis[97] provides insight into why Abraham was chosen for this historic role. As G-d says: *I have chosen him because he commands his sons and his household after him that they should keep the way of the L-rd to perform righteousness and justice.* Abraham merited to father the Jewish people because of his exemplary focus on education in general and moral instruction in particular.

69

This idea is enshrined in the *Shema*, the central Jewish prayer, which instructs parents: *And you shall impress these words upon your children.*[98]

According to Jewish tradition, education is primarily considered the role and responsibility of a parent, not a teacher. In fact, in the entire Five Books of Moses, there is no word to describe a formal "teacher," because from the Biblical point of view, the ideal teacher is the parent!

Therefore, even if, as is most common today, parents send their children to school or other educational institutions, it is important to recognize the centrality of their influence in their child's education.

Indeed, this pedagogical paradigm of parental engagement, which has been a cornerstone of Jewish tradition for millennia, is now echoed in current educational research and even public policy. According to Waterford.org,[99] a national organization developing and providing free online early education for low-income families:

"What's the most accurate predictor of academic achievement? It's not socioeconomic status, nor how prestigious the school is that a child attends. The best predictor of student success is the extent to which families encourage learning at home and involve themselves in their child's education."[100]

Developing this idea even further in the *Shema*, parents are encouraged to, *teach these words to your children, and you shall speak of them when you sit in your house...when you lie down, and when you rise...and write these words upon your doorposts."*

These words convey the fact that, according to the Torah, not only is the parent considered a child's primary teacher, but the home is the primary classroom. From this perspective, ritual items placed and used within one's house can be functionally understood as educational materials, as well. Like an informative poster in a classroom, a *mezuzah*, for example, becomes a reflection point or inquiry prompt.

Ultimately, as parents, there are two endowments we can hope to bequeath to our children.

One is wings, the other is roots. Wings represent the academic and social opportunities that allow children to soar beyond their current station in life. Roots, on the other hand, represent one's deeper values and sense of belonging to a particular culture, tradition, history, and community.

Like a tree with large and far-reaching branches, a person can achieve great success and their impact can be vast. However, if their roots are shallow, their equilibrium is easily uprooted when the storms of life come their way.

Therefore, in addition to the upward mobility offered by powerful and expansive wings, providing children with the deep stability of sturdy roots is what supports them in offering up their highest fruits.

As Franklin D. Roosevelt famously put it: "We cannot always build the future for our youth, but we can build our youth for the future."

The Big Idea

In the Jewish tradition, parents are the ideal teachers, the home is the optimal classroom, and moral instruction and character development are the ultimate goals of education.

It Happened Once

A YOUNG GIRL'S PARENTS ALLOWED her to choose between two schools they had selected.

One school was academically superior, while the other placed greater emphasis on good character than on good marks.

She decided to consult the Lubavitcher Rebbe about her choice.

"First and foremost," the Rebbe replied, "you must look at which school will help you best develop as a human being and as a Jew."

לגמול

ligmol   Providing

THE GIFT OF INDEPENDENCE

EMBEDDED WITHIN HUMAN NATURE is the inclination to help others in need. But what is the ultimate goal of such giving?

The urge to give can sometimes be self-serving, especially when it leaves the recipient in a state of interminable dependence. To give someone the gift of independence, however, is to set them free, allowing them to stand on their own two feet.

This subtle distinction is reflected in the Hebrew word for providing for others—*ligmol*, which is the same word used for weaning, when a mother stops nursing a child. The Torah[101] tells us that *Abraham held a great feast on the day that Isaac was weaned.* Judaism sees weaning not just as a significant change in a child's diet, but as a crucial developmental milestone worthy of celebration.

In child-rearing, it is tempting for a parent to want to keep providing for their child as much as possible, for as long as possible. In the words of the Talmud,[102] "More than the calf wishes to suck, the cow wants to suckle."

However, this parental impulse to constantly tend to a child's every whim and want is not in the best interests of the child. The job of the parent is not to focus on what *they* want to give to their child, but on what their child truly needs in order to develop the necessary skills to succeed in life on their own. After all, we won't always be around to care for them.

As mentioned in the previous chapter, a parent's obligation to their child includes the following three criteria: 1) A Jewish education, to help provide them with a value system and moral compass with which to navigate the complexities of life; 2) a trade, so they can earn a livelihood; and 3) basic survival skills—such as how to swim, for example. In all of these parental obligations, the Sages are teaching us not only the criteria but the actual objectives of successful parenting—the raising of well-adjusted, independent human beings![103]

In Judaism, it is understood that the epitome of what we can do for another person is not just to give them what we have or what they currently need, but to help them be able to support themselves. As the famous saying goes: "Give a man a fish, and you feed him for a day; teach a man to fish, and you feed him for a lifetime."

Maimonides[104] famously lists eight ascending levels of being charitable, the highest of which is to help a person become self-reliant. In Maimonides' words: "The loftiest degree, exceeded by none, is that of the person who assists someone by providing him with a loan or by accepting him into a business partnership or by helping him find employment in order to strengthen his hand so that he will not need to be dependent upon others."

One might think that a gift is nobler than a loan; after all, a loan is returned, while a gift requires one to part with their money forever. This may be true from the perspective of the donor, but from the perspective of the receiver, a loan has a far greater impact because it keeps them on—rather than off—their feet in order to repay it.

Additionally, the greater benefit of a loan or a job, as opposed to a handout, is that it helps preserve the dignity and agency of the recipient as they work to achieve financial independence and stability.

Maimonides continues: "With reference to such aid, it is said, *You shall strengthen him, whether he be a stranger or a settler* (Leviticus 25:35), which means to strengthen him in such a manner that his falling into further want is prevented."

In his commentary on this same verse, Rashi gives a similar explanation and then quotes a parable from the Midrash:

"Do not leave him alone so that he descends and falls, for it will be hard to raise him back up. Rather, support him from the time his hand slips. To what might this be compared? To a burden on a donkey. While it is still on the donkey, one person can hold it up and set it straight. But if it falls to the ground, even five people cannot put it back on." Our responsibility to help others thus begins well before they are no longer able to help themselves.

Put differently: "An ounce of prevention is worth a pound of cure." This is the socio-economic version of "preventive medicine" rather than the "emergency room" approach practiced in many countries and communities.

Such an empowering approach to self-sufficiency also extends to education, another form of giving. In the Jewish understanding of education, the goal is not to convey information simply so that the student is able to repeat and regurgitate what they heard. Rather, the goal is to provide them with the critical skills that enable them to become independently proficient, empowering them to study and acquire knowledge on their own.

This applies spiritually as well. Our Sages teach[105] that Aaron the High Priest was instructed to kindle the lights of the menorah in the Holy Temple "until the flames ascended and stayed lit on their own." Chasidut[106] explains that the same holds true when kindling the spiritual flame in others. It is not enough for those we seek to inspire to merely retain what we give them, passively reflecting another's luminescence; they need to be empowered to acquire and generate their own insight and inspiration in order to independently shine their own unique light.

All of these insights underscore the same basic truth. Whether we are talking about someone's financial, educational, or spiritual needs, the greatest gift one can give another is the resources and skills necessary for them to provide for themselves and take charge of their own destiny.

It Happened Once

LATE ONE NIGHT, TWO hours into an audience with the Lubavitcher Rebbe, Israeli diplomat Yehuda Avner asked, "Rebbe, what is it that you seek to accomplish?"

"Yehuda," said the Rebbe, "look there, on the shelf. What do you see?"

"A candle," he replied.

"No. It's not a candle; it's just a lump of wax with a string down the middle. When does this lump of wax become a candle? When you bring a flame to the wick."

His voice rising, the Rebbe continued in a Talmudic singsong: "The wax is the body of the human being, the wick is the soul, and the flame is the fire of the Torah. When the soul is ignited by the flame of the Torah, that's when the person becomes a candle, achieving the purpose for which he was created.

"This is what I try to do—to help every man and woman achieve the purpose for which they were created."

An hour later, with the sun about to rise and the meeting drawing to a close, Avner asked, "So, has the Rebbe lit my candle?"

"No," the Rebbe replied quietly. "I have given you the match. Only you can light your own candle."

The Big Idea

Judaism's idea of helping others is to put them on their feet, not on your shoulders.

Giving

natan נתן

CHAPTER 11 | GIVING

GIVING IS RECEIVING

T HE Hebrew word for giving, *natan*, is a palindrome, which reveals a deep truth about the reciprocal dynamic of giving: When one gives, they also receive in return.[107]

נ ת נ
NUN TAV NUN

Giving

In a recent study,[108] researchers discovered that those who spent more of their income on others rather than themselves enjoyed significantly greater and longer lasting happiness. In fact, as little as a five-dollar gift was enough to produce measurable increases in one's happiness. Overall, the self-reported happiness of those who regularly give charity is forty-three percent higher than those who don't.

Other findings[109] include lower depression rates among those who donate more than ten percent of their incomes.[110] Giving away money isn't the only way to enjoy the benefits of generosity: People who are very giving in relationships—being emotionally available and hospitable—are much more likely to be in excellent health (forty-eight percent) than those who are not (thirty-one percent).

Indeed, according to current research, the positive energy that you feel when you do a good deed has a tangible impact on your body. In much the same way that exercise releases endorphins into your brain that make you feel good,[111] acts of charity generate what scientists call the "helpers' high."

In other words, human beings are hardwired to give.

Hence, according to Professor Elizabeth Dunn and her colleagues,[112] who surveyed data from one hundred thirty-six countries: "In contrast to traditional economic thought—which places self-interest as the guiding principle of human motivation—[our] findings suggest that the reward experienced from helping others may be deeply ingrained in human nature, emerging in diverse cultural and economic contexts."

This is consistent with the Torah's teaching that humanity was created in the image of G-d. According to the Kabbalists, G-d created the world primarily in order to express his loving-kindness. As the Sages teach: *"Teva Hatov l'heitiv*—it is in the nature of He Who is Good to do good."

The human propensity for giving is thus a natural reflection of the Divine image in which we were created.

Interestingly, in addition to getting feel-good returns, giving also has its financial advantages.

The Talmud promises wealth to those who give charity, interpreting the verse, *Tithe [aseir] you shall tithe [t'aseir]*[113] as: "Tithe *[aseir]* in order that you will become wealthy *[titasheir]*."[114] Unlike most *mitzvot*, where the reward is received in the World to Come, G-d promises us a more immediate reward in this lifetime for charitable giving, namely that our wealth will be increased the more we use it for the benefit of others.

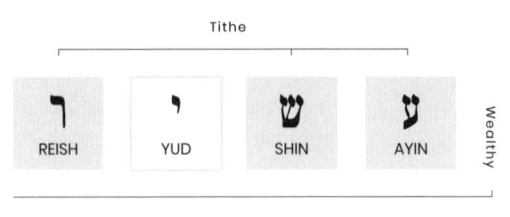

Accordingly, the Hebrew word for wealth, *osher*, is etymologically related to the word *aseir*, to tithe, which teaches that what we receive is reflective of what we give. Wealth comes to those who are active and effective allocators of their resources, who demonstrate an understanding that the purpose and function of wealth itself is to invest it where it is needed most. When we are humble philanthropic agents with a proven record of supporting worthy causes, G-d entrusts us with even greater wealth to enact even greater investments on His behalf. In the words of R. Yaakov ben Asher:[115] "Let not evil counsel arise in your heart that says: 'How can I reduce my own wealth by giving it away to the poor?' Know that the wealth *is not yours*; it is only a deposit given on condition that you use it as the Depositor desires, giving a portion of it to the poor."

Giving is getting doesn't just apply to material wealth; whenever we act for the sake of others, we also end up benefiting ourselves. For example: The Talmud teaches,[116] "One who prays on behalf of another when in need of the same deliverance, he is answered first."

Ultimately, notwithstanding the tremendous rewards and benefits that accompany giving, what is most important is not what we get for ourselves but what we give to others. In the words of Winston Churchill: "We may make a living by what we get, but we make a life by what we give."

The Big Idea

When we give of ourselves to others in need, we are not diminished but enriched.

It Happened Once

Sir Moses Montefiore was an outstanding Anglo-Jewish philanthropist of the nineteenth century, and the first Jew to attain high office in the United Kingdom. On his one-hundredth birthday, *The London Times* devoted editorials to his praise, noting that "he had shown that fervent Judaism and patriotic citizenship are absolutely consistent with one another."

He was asked, "Sir Moses, what are you worth?" Sir Moses thought for a while and named a figure far too small for an international merchant prince of his magnitude.

"But surely," pressed his astonished interviewer, "your wealth must be much more than that!"

Sir Moses gently replied, "You didn't ask me how much I own. You asked me how much I am worth. So I calculated how much I have given to charity this year.

"You see," he explained, "we are only worth what we are willing to share with others."

hatzlachah הצלחה

Success

CHAPTER 12 | SUCCESS

REDEFINING SUCCESS

To be successful is a universal aspiration. But what is the definition of success?

In the Oxford Dictionary, success is defined as "the attainment of popularity or profit," or, according to Merriam-Webster, it is "the attainment of wealth, favor, or eminence."

Interestingly, the English word success comes from the Latin word *succeden*, to "follow after," implying a mimetic approach to success—as if success means to become more like someone else—or "to take the place of another," inevitably pitting us all against each other in a state of perpetual competition. According to such a view, one is constantly comparing themselves to others and measuring their success by how well they match up against them.

In Scripture, the word *hatzlachah* is used in a number of different contexts to describe various processes of fulfillment. For instance, we find it used in reference to a fire that consumes,[117] the act of forging across a river,[118] and a person receiving a promotion.[119] Regarding the

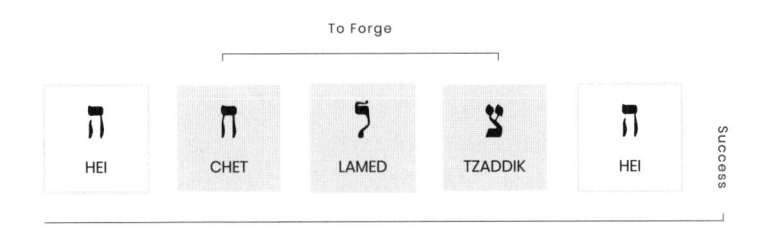

To Forge

ה	ח	ל	צ	ה	Success
HEI	CHET	LAMED	TZADDIK	HEI	

87

term's diverse application, the commentator and Hebrew grammarian R. Meir Leibush Wisser, known as the Malbim, writes[120] that "the word *hatzlachah* refers to anything that serves its unique purpose…"

Accordingly, *hatzlachah* means to identify your own personal path and realize your unique purpose; in other words, to achieve whatever you alone were created to accomplish.

As the Chasidic master R. Menachem Mendel of Kotzk famously said: "If I am I because you are you, and you are you because I am I, then I am not I and you are not you. But if I am I because I am I, and you are you because you are you, then you are truly you, and I am truly I." In other words, the first step towards living a successful and fulfilling life is determining who you are *in relation to yourself rather than in contrast to others.*

Unlike the conventional view of success, which is determined by certain objective criteria, in the Jewish view, success is not one-size-fits-all. G-d created each person with a distinctive purpose in life, and He gave each of us the necessary tools and talents to achieve that purpose. The identification of that mission is what establishes our particular definition of success. Achieving those goals in practice is what determines our level of success.[121]

Such a highly individualized approach to success requires first and foremost that we do the necessary work of rigorous self-examination in order to clarify what our personal path and purpose truly is. Such a realization can happen in a lightning flash of illumination or it can gradually dawn on us over many years. Regardless of how we arrive at our self-understanding, it is imperative that we remain true to ourselves to the end and invest our full selves into accomplishing what we were sent here to do.

The following anecdote illustrates this point.

On the occasion of her birthday, a woman wrote a letter to the Lubavitcher Rebbe, mentioning some of her efforts over the past year to share the beauty of Judaism with uninitiated Jews. After warmly noting her achievements, the Rebbe wrote, "…bear in mind, however, that a person who was granted the ability to impact one hundred people and reaches only ninety-nine has not yet fully realized their

G-d-given potential."[122] We must never confuse doing a great deal with doing all we can. According to the Rebbe, this fully invested approach to whatever we are doing is *the* rubric of true success.

This twofold focus of a personalized approach to defining success—i.e., that we each have an individual soul makeup and unique purpose to pursue, and that our efforts are measured solely in relation to our own capabilities—does not completely discount the productive role of healthy competition in determining success; however, it does reframe exactly who we are competing against—namely, ourselves.

If we have given our all, if we have exceeded our past attempts, if we have put our whole self into achieving our purpose, whatever that may be, then we can, and should, consider ourselves a success.

A well-known Chassidic story captures the essence of this perspective. As the last hours of R. Zushe of Anipoli's life drew near, his students found him crying bitterly as he pondered his life achievements. Puzzled, they asked, "Surely our teacher has led a righteous and worthy life. What does our teacher fear?" R. Zushe replied, "When I am summoned to heaven, I am not afraid they will ask me, 'Why were you not like our patriarch Abraham or our great leader Moses?' For if they would ask that, I would respond: 'Was I blessed with the courageous spirit of Abraham or the humility and vision of Moses?' What I am afraid they will ask me is, 'Zushe, why were you not more like Zushe?' What will I answer them then?"

Another fundamental feature of success according to Judaism is defined by how one responds to life's challenges and setbacks. From this perspective, failing or falling is not only unavoidable, but it is, in fact, built into the system of life. It is how we learn, grow, evolve, and become who we were meant to be.

The question is: How does one comport oneself in the face of defeat? Does one see failure as a dead-end or as part of a learning curve? Does one give up, throw in the towel, blame others? Or does one collect themselves, learn from their mistakes, and rededicate themselves to their goals? According to Judaism, the answers to these questions weigh heavily on the scales of success.

Ultimately, success is not an achievement, it is an attitude. It is not defined by the outcome of one's efforts, but by the effort itself. To not be deterred or deflated by life's inevitable disappointments and obstacles is what Judaism defines as success.

This way of thinking is also encoded within the Hebrew word for success. The word *hatzlachah* is etymologically linked to the Hebrew word for "forged," as in the verse,[123] *tzalchu et haYarden—they forged across the Jordan River*. Success is thus characterized by the fortitude and perseverance to make it through challenging situations and difficult circumstances.

In fact, throughout the entire Bible there is only one character who is specifically referred to as successful—Joseph. Incredibly, the Torah refers to Joseph as an *ish matzliach*, a man of success, not at the height of his career and reign as the all-powerful viceroy of Egypt, but during the lowest points of his life, first as a slave,[124] and then again as a prisoner.[125] In other words, Joseph is considered successful not when he is at the top of the pyramid, so to speak, but when he is at the bottom. This is because, according to the Torah, success is not determined by the absence of defeat, but by the way one responds[126] to the inevitable setbacks and betrayals of life.[127]

In the words of Proverbs[128]: *Seven times the righteous person falls and gets up, while the wicked are tripped up by misfortune.*[129]

The righteous person doesn't just get up despite his fall; he is elevated precisely because of it.[130] In other words, it is by virtue of one's tenacity and faith in the face of momentary defeat that one grows in both strength and spirit. And that, according to Judaism, is the very definition of success.

The Big Idea

Success is not an outcome but an input. It's not what you get out of all your endeavors but what you put into them that ultimately counts.

CHAPTER 12 | SUCCESS

It Happened Once

THE LUBAVITCHER REBBE'S SECRETARY once contacted a school administrator from New Jersey with a message from the Rebbe: "It came to the Rebbe's attention that there is a Jewish day school in your area that is on the brink of closure due to low student registration. Since you are the administrator of another school in the area, the Rebbe requested that you work on increasing the enrollment in that endangered school."

"But it's not on the same religious level as mine," he protested to the secretary. "I do not feel that it is fitting for me to be involved with that school."

The secretary replied that he could make an appointment for an audience with the Rebbe to discuss the matter if he so wishes, "However, you should know that the Rebbe feels that you are the best person for the job..."

Not wishing to disregard the Rebbe's wishes, he made an appointment. He prepared a long letter that contained eighteen reasons why he felt that he could not fulfill the Rebbe's request.

After reading the letter, the Rebbe asked him: "Tell me, are these eighteen explanations sufficient reasons that eighteen—or more—children should lose the opportunity to have a Jewish education?

"If you accept the position, I am certain that G-d will broaden your resources—giving you more time and capabilities."

Leaving the Rebbe's office, he felt like a person on a mission. He threw himself into the task of increasing that school's enrollment. His efforts paid off, and enrollment tripled in a short time.

He wrote a very proud letter to the Rebbe, listing all his successes.

The Rebbe sent him a response. Between his blessings and remarks, the Rebbe also added one word: "Success?!"

The principal was stunned! A short while later, he visited the Rebbe again for a private audience.

"Can I ask what you meant with the comment you wrote on my letter?" he inquired.

The Rebbe gently asked whether one can herald as a success having a few dozen children enrolled in a school when there are so many more children who are still not receiving Jewish education.

"But I tripled the enrollment," the man protested. "Is that not considered success?"

The Rebbe explained that success means exerting effort; it's the continued struggle to do what is right and reach one's full potential.

The man left the encounter with a new perspective. He understood that while the Rebbe greatly appreciated his efforts, he didn't want him to rest on his laurels. There was so much more still to be done.

Philanthropy
tzedakah

צדקה

CHAPTER 13 | PHILANTHROPY

DO THE RIGHT THING

Jews don't believe in giving charity; they believe in doing the right thing.

There are two radically different perspectives on wealth that provide the basis for charitable giving. In the first, whether a person inherited their wealth or earned it through hard work, it is rightfully theirs. If they freely choose to give of their wealth to those in need, it is a praiseworthy and unexpected act of generosity. In this view, there is absolutely nothing wrong with some people having more, even much more, than others. Wealth disparity is seen as a natural consequence of various factors, such as individual effort, education, talent, life circumstances, or luck. The goal in such a worldview is to amass as much wealth as one desires, and, ideally, this opportunity is freely available to all who seek it.

The second perspective contends that the unequal distribution of wealth in society is a calamity that needs to be rectified. Those who possess more than their fair share are obliged to share their wealth with the less fortunate. If they do not, they are guilty of perpetuating an injustice. From this perspective, the accumulation of wealth by any individual at the expense of the collective is considered a crime. Following this line of thought to its logical conclusion essentially leads to some form of state-sponsored socialism or increasingly restrictive measures like earning caps to enforce an oppressively equitable socio-economic model.

The Jewish notion of *tzedakah*, often incorrectly translated as charity, rejects both of these views, choosing instead to combine elements of both. Unlike charity, a term derived from the Latin word *carus*, meaning to be kind and endearing, *tzedakah* comes from the

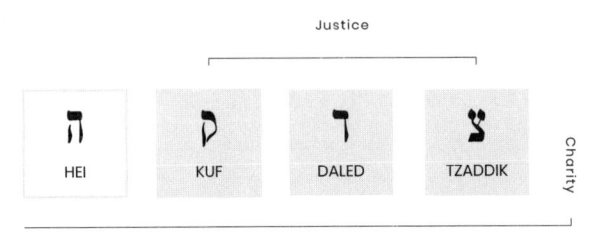

Justice

ה	ק	ד	צ
HEI	KUF	DALED	TZADDIK

Charity

word *tzedek*, meaning justice—something, according to the Torah, that we are obligated to pursue.[131]

Indeed, according to author Paul Vallely, who spent six years researching the history of Western philanthropy, from the ancient Greeks and Hebrews to modern times, culminating in a book titled, *Philanthropy: from Aristotle to Zuckerberg*:

"For the Greeks and Romans, *philanthrôpía* was always a voluntary [and even self-serving[132]] activity among the elite; by contrast, *tzedakah* is a religious obligation that falls, proportionally, on both the rich and those with smaller incomes."

However, rather than being externally enforced by the government or some other entity, *tzedakah* is a values-based responsibility, stemming from within. The specific ways in which we perform this act are entirely up to us; how much,[133] when, where, why, and to whom we give—these details are left in our hands and hearts to decide.

Ultimately, the giving of *tzedakah* is rooted in the organismic understanding that when there is a need expressed within the greater structure of which we are a part and we have the means to fill it, it is our sacred duty to do so. *Tzedakah* is therefore the socio-spiritual mechanism whereby each part bears responsibility for the well-being of the whole.

In Roman times, the notion of caring for the poor was not widely held. For instance, the Talmud[134] tells of the Roman consul Turnus Rufus, who questioned R. Akiva about Judaism's obligation to provide for the poor: "If your G-d loves the poor, why does He not support them Himself?" In Roman thought, the division between wealth classes was understood to be an essential, even providential, part of society's Divine design and was thus intended to remain that way, unaltered.

Thankfully, we have come a long way since then. The number of nonprofits, volunteer organizations, and food banks is living proof of this. In today's society, it is common for us to view ourselves as duty-bound to care for the welfare of every person, especially those less fortunate. This is much to the credit of the Jewish view being adopted into the mainstream and shaping the way we think about our social responsibilities today.

In contrast to the ancient Roman view, Judaism insists that if we see a person in need, it is because we have been given the opportunity to help them, and we are therefore obliged to do so. In fact, the Hebrew words for pauper, *ani,* and poverty, *aniyut,* are both derived from the root *laanot,* meaning to respond. This highlights that poverty is meant to elicit a response from those who have the means to give. Need, lack, disadvantage, and oppression are all G-d's invitations to us to fulfill our obligation to pursue justice through acts of *tzedakah.*

Rooted in a religiously ordained concept of social justice, the word *tzedakah* reminds us not to be overtaken by feelings of magnanimity and hubris as a result of our charitable deeds. Instead, giving *tzedakah* should elicit humility and appreciation for the blessing and opportunity to serve as G-d's trusted allocators on earth. As R. Yaakov ben Asher writes in *Arbaah Turim*,[135] "[Whatever] wealth [you have] is not yours[136]; it is merely a deposit given on condition that you use it as the Depositor desires, by giving a portion of it to the poor." In other words: we don't have what we have because it is ours—in some way owed to us—but because G-d has entrusted it to us to distribute where it is most needed. The wealth we possess is a deposit from G-d that we are given for temporary safekeeping; it is earmarked for us to invest purposefully where and when the need arises.

From this perspective, there is no reason for the recipient of *tzedakah* to feel ashamed or undignified. On the contrary, it is they who enable the giver to partner with G-d in completing creation!

As our Sages teach[137]: "More than the rich man does for the pauper, the pauper does for the rich man." This is a total inversion of the way we normally view the power dynamics between rich and poor, and a redefinition of who is really giving to whom.

From a Torah perspective, the reason that there is a wealth disparity in the first place is for people to choose to right this wrong. If they would be forced or coerced into it, they would not learn the vital lesson the Torah seeks to impart, which is that we each bear responsibility for the greater, interconnected whole of society. Yes, *tzedakah* is a mitzvah, but, ultimately, G-d does not want us to care for the poor just because we have to; rather, He wants us to do it because we truly believe it is the right thing to do.

The Big Idea

We don't help people in need because it's a nice thing to do; we do it because it's the right thing to do.

CHAPTER 13 | PHILANTHROPY

It Happened Once

A DISCIPLE OF THE BAAL Shem Tov once asked him: "You teach that there is a Divine purpose in everything, but what is the Divine purpose in atheism?"

The Baal Shem Tov replied: "When someone knocks on your door and asks for *tzedakah*, you, as a devout believer, must not tell him, 'G-d will surely take care of you.' You must, in fact, act as if there were no G-d and you were entirely responsible for this person's well-being. In such a moment, atheism impels one to act!"[138]

Intelligence *chochmah*
חכמה

CHAPTER 14 | INTELLIGENCE

THE ART OF NOT KNOWING

THE WORD WISE ORIGINATES from the German word wit, meaning keen and incisive intelligence. In Judaism, wisdom is not defined by intellectual acuity or even the ability to comprehend and store a wealth of information; instead, wisdom is characterized by an aptitude for curiosity and a genuine desire to encounter and explore new ideas and perspectives. Rather than having a tight grasp on a specific concept or subject, wisdom is more like an open palm, welcoming new insights beyond what one has previously attained.

In the words of best-selling author Professor Adam Grant, in his book *Think Again*, "If knowledge is power, knowing what we don't know is wisdom."

The Mishnah[139] teaches: "Who is wise? He who learns from every person."

Typically, we think of an intelligent person as someone from whom people seek to learn rather than someone who seeks to learn from others.

By defining the wise man as one who is perpetually open to learning more rather than an already established expert, the Mishnah democratizes what is seen to be the precious property of the few, placing the keys of wisdom in the hands of the masses, since anyone can learn something from another.

From this perspective, a clear link between wisdom and humility emerges.

For example, no less of a character than Moses himself is described in the Torah[140] as "the humblest of men."

Indeed, it was Moses' willingness to learn from everyone and everything that caused him to pause on his path through the desert to wonder at what appeared as a mere scrub fire. And it was his burning curiosity that qualified him to be chosen as Judaism's greatest teacher, lovingly referred to by all Jews as *Rabbeinu*, "our teacher," to this day.

The centrality of curiosity to the definition of wisdom is alluded to in the Hebrew word for wisdom—*chochmah*. The *Zohar*[141] points out that *chochmah* is a composite of two words: *koach* and *mah*, which means the power (*koach*) to ask "what?" (*mah*)—the ability to be humble and inquisitive.

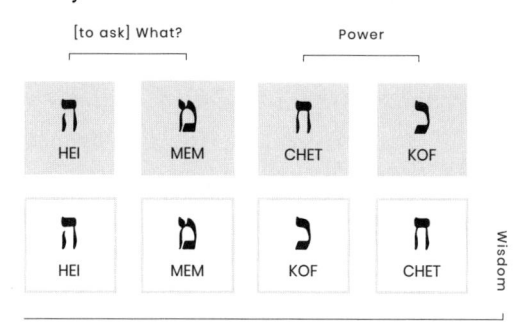

In fact, Jewish thought does not just tolerate questions, it celebrates them.

The Pesach Seder, for example, is a veritable feast of questions. The purpose of the Seder itself is introduced in the Torah[142] as a parent's answer to their child's question: *And it will come to pass when your children say to you, "What is this service to you?"*

Interestingly, the Torah says: *When your child will ask*, not if, since that's what Jewish education is all about—developing the art of asking meaningful questions.

Isidore Rabi, winner of the Nobel Prize in physics, was once asked why he became a scientist. He replied, "My mother made me a scientist without even knowing it. Every other child would come home from school and be asked, 'What did you learn today?' But my mother used to say, 'Izzy, did you ask a good question today?' That made all the difference."

Asking questions is fundamental to Jewish culture and consciousness.

In the same way that Eskimos have multiple words to describe the subtle differences between types and textures of snow, the Talmud employs a wide range of words to describe different types and qualities of questions.

In the words of R. Adin Steinsaltz[143]: "It is no coincidence that the Talmud contains so many words denoting questions, ranging from queries aimed at satisfying curiosity to questions that attempt to undermine the validity of the debated issue.

"The Talmud also differentiates between a fundamental query and a less basic inquiry, a question of principle and a marginal query."

In Judaism, therefore, wisdom is not measured by how much you already know, but by how much you are willing to learn.[144]

Such an approach, according to Professor Grant, favors curiosity over closure, doubt over certainty, and humility over pride.

"When psychologist Mihaly Csikszentmihalyi studied eminent scientists like Linus Pauling and Jonas Salk, he concluded that what differentiated them from their peers was their cognitive flexibility, their willingness to move from one extreme to the other as the occasion requires...

"We can even see [this pattern] in the Oval Office.

"Experts assessed American presidents on a long list of personality traits and compared them to rankings by independent historians and political scientists. Only one trait consistently predicted presidential greatness after controlling for factors like years in office, wars, and scandals... What set great presidents apart was their intellectual curiosity and openness...They were interested in hearing new views and revising their old ones. They saw many of their policies as experiments to run, not points to score."[145]

Interestingly, the Talmud[146] teaches that although the House of Shammai, a renowned school of Rabbinic thought, were known to have sharper minds and engage in more penetrating analysis, the law almost exclusively follows the House of Hillel. The Talmud explains that this is "because they [the House of Hillel] were kind and modest, they studied both their own rulings and those of the House of Shammai, and they were even so humble as to mention the teachings of the House of Shammai before their own."

In other words, the House of Hillel's insight was considered more refined because they took the time to consider and incorporate their opposition's analysis into their own point of view.

This expression of humble receptivity validated their rulings and decisions on Torah matters, because it revealed their commitment to listening to and learning from others besides themselves. This, according to Judaism, is the very definition of wisdom.

In contrast, the House of Shammai was known to be combative and defensive in their argumentation.

The Talmud[147] tells of a tragic incident "likened to the day the Israelites made the Golden Calf," in which members of the House of Shammai stood with spears at the entrance to the attic of Chananya ben Chizkiya ben Gurion, where all the great Sages of Israel were gathered.

According to the Jerusalem Talmud,[148] they even threatened to kill these Sages, whom they held hostage to ensure the law would be decided in accordance with their view.

Obstinate claims to exclusive "ownership" of the truth, or the "right" answer, are precisely what close one off to learning more than what they already know. One who assumes this mindset may indeed be smart, but according to Jewish thought, they are not wise.

Essentially, Judaism views wisdom as a character trait rather than an intellectual ability or achievement.

In *Ethics of Our Fathers*,[149] the Mishnah lists seven features of a wise person:

A wise person does not 1) speak before one who is greater in wisdom; 2) does not interrupt when others are speaking; 3) is not hasty to answer; 4) asks what is relevant and answers to the point; 5) speaks of the first [point] first, and of the last [point] last; 6) concerning that which he has not heard, he says: I have not heard; 7) and he acknowledges the truth.

None of the features mentioned here describe any specifically intellectual abilities. They are all characteristics of a humble and receptive disposition, the expression of which is a testament to the depths of one's wisdom.

Paradoxically, throughout Jewish literature, a scholar is referred to as a *talmid chacham*—not a scholar, but a "student-sage." Generally, the student and sage are thought to fill two different roles: the student seeks to acquire wisdom, whereas the sage has already accrued some measure of mastery, which he can then impart to others.

In defining the sage as a student, Judaism teaches us that to be considered a sage one must remain perpetually receptive and open to new knowledge. Simply put: When a person is full of themselves, they lack the requisite space to receive new wisdom.

In the words of the Talmud[150]: "A full vessel cannot receive."

The person who defines themselves by their prior knowledge confines themselves to it and is therefore not available for an influx of new insight.

An illustration of this idea is found in a poignant Talmudic vignette:[151] R. Zeira, a well-known Sage, once took upon himself a strenuous fast for one hundred days in order to actively remove decades of Babylonian Talmudic study from his mind in preparation for studying the Jerusalem Talmud, which employs markedly different paradigms and processes for interpreting Jewish text and tradition. In order to learn a new method of study, he first had to liquidate his old library, so to speak.

Normally, we think of knowledge as something that accumulates—when you've mastered one idea or discipline, it serves as a suitable foundation upon which to learn another. This is often true. However, there are times when pre-existing concepts or methods brought to a new field of inquiry or discovery impede one's ability to encounter a new subject, limiting them from experiencing the true depth and dimensionality of the new idea that is there, waiting to be discovered.

This is why R. Zeira felt the need to actively delete from his mind the Babylonian method of Talmud study, so that when he studied the

Jerusalem Talmud, his approach to the new way of thinking would not be tainted by his prior training.

This episode of R. Zeira offers a profound lesson in how we approach study. Instead of seeing continued learning as a process of reinforcing one's existing beliefs and opinions, the ideal approach to education is characterized by letting go of what one already "knows" in order to make way for new paradigms and perspectives to be considered without bias or preconception.

The idea that curiosity is the cornerstone of wisdom is what shapes Judaism's novel approach to study. Society increasingly views learning in utilitarian terms, as a means of acquiring knowledge and mastery in a particular subject or skill. Judaism values learning, not as a means to an end, but for its own sake. As we learn in the Mishnah[152]: "R. Meir would say: Whoever studies Torah *for its own sake* merits many things; moreover, [the creation of] the entire world is worthwhile for him alone."

In fact, Jewish tradition views study itself, like prayer, as a form of daily spiritual practice and religious obligation. As it says in Scripture[153]: *The Torah shall not leave your mouth; you shall study it day and night.* Accordingly, one's learning is never finished; each moment and encounter presents its own potential revelation.

Typically, the conclusion of a written manuscript is marked with the words "the end," striking a note of finality. In the Talmud, however, at the end of every chapter and every tractate you will find a declaration that begins with the words, *hadran alach*, "We will return to you."

This statement of intent underlines the concept that when completing a tractate, we do not regard it as having been learned in its entirety, because Torah is infinite. As the Talmudic Sage Ben Bag Bag would say[154]: "Turn it and turn it again, for everything is in it." It is thus not so much a statement of farewell but *au revoir!*

This is emblematic of Judaism's approach to learning in general, which is, ultimately, not to focus on how far you have already come, but to acknowledge and appreciate the never-ending journey of discovery that lies ahead.

CHAPTER 14 | INTELLIGENCE

It Happened Once

THERE WAS A GREAT sage who had a daughter of marriageable age and was looking for a suitable son-in-law. He went to the greatest *yeshivah* in the region and posed a question, wagering that any student who could answer the question would be given his daughter's hand in marriage. No students were capable of coming up with the answer. As the sage was leaving town, suddenly the wagon driver heard a young man calling out after them while running towards the carriage. They stopped and asked the young man what he wanted. He said to the sage: "Well, what is the answer to the question you posed?" The sage said, "Ah, this is the student who will become my son-in-law," and he proceeded to tell him the answer.

The Big Idea

In Judaism, wisdom is not measured by how much you already know, but by how much you are willing to learn.

ידע

yeda   Intimacy

CHAPTER 15 | INTIMACY

THE G-DLIEST ACT

IN MANY SPIRITUAL TRADITIONS, physical intimacy is associated with evil, sin, and human weakness. This has led numerous religious thinkers to either uphold celibacy as the ideal spiritual state, or to begrudgingly tolerate human sexuality as an inescapable weakness of the flesh.

Judaism never shared this sentiment. In the Jewish view, intimacy was always embraced and even viewed as sacred when occurring within the appropriate context and with elevated intentions.[155]

Whereas in certain faiths, priests, monks, and other religious functionaries are required to be celibate, the Jewish high priest is required to be married to fulfill his most sacred of duties in the Holy Temple on Yom Kippur.[156]

From the Jewish perspective, sexuality is the most volatile of human urges and can bring out the best or the worst in us. Accordingly, a sexual encounter can be the most sacred of human activities or the basest of sins—depending on how we approach it.

In his compendium of Jewish law and practice, *Mishneh Torah*, Maimonides incorporates the laws of sexual morality into the Book of Holiness.

There is a common misconception that traditional Judaism advocates a utilitarian approach to marital intimacy, viewing it solely as a functional activity for the purpose of procreation. This could not be further from the truth.

For instance, a verse in Genesis[157] describes King Abimelech peering out of a window and witnessing Isaac "jesting" or "making sport" with his wife, Rebecca; an observation that led Abimelech to believe that they must be married.

The Biblical word for jesting is *metzachek* from the word *tzechok*, laughter. Indeed, while some commentators[158] understood this to be a euphemism for the act of intercourse itself, others understood this to be a reference to endearing interactions between a couple before engaging in intimacy. For example, R. Eliyahu Mizrachi says that it may have been a reference to "kissing and cuddling," Chizkuni describes it as "the jest that precedes intercourse," and the Or Hachaim describes it as "the kind of affectionate behavior customary between man and his wife."

The fact that such "jesting" is part of the Biblical description of the act of intercourse indicates that Judaism does not treat intimacy as a cold, physiological act.

And this is not limited to Biblical sources. The Talmud[159] advises one to speak "endearing words" to create an emotional connection with one's partner before engaging in physical intimacy.

Similarly, Nachmanides[160] notes: "First one must cleave to his wife, and then they will become one flesh. There can be no true oneness of the flesh without first experiencing a cleaving together of the heart."

Fundamentally, Judaism views intimacy as a loving and even playful experience, in which both emotional arousal and sensual pleasure play integral roles.

Indeed, one of the marital obligations outlined in the *ketubah*, marriage contract, alongside the requirement for a husband to provide food and clothing for his wife, is a contractual obligation for a man to pleasure his wife on a regular basis.[161] Failing to do so even constitutes fair grounds for the wife to demand a divorce.[162] Indeed, the Talmud characterizes men who put their wife's pleasure before their own as meritorious and worthy of special blessing.

Moreover, the Jewish view of intimacy's potential for connection and holiness extends well beyond the selflessness that one brings to it and relates to the essence and nature of the act itself. To understand this more deeply, it would be helpful to analyze the word the Torah uses to describe sexual union.

The Biblical word commonly used to refer to physical intimacy is *yediah*, knowledge. For example, in Genesis[163] *Adam knew (yada) his wife Eve, and she became pregnant and bore a son.*

Referring to intimacy with the word knowledge suggests that Judaism views physical intimacy as a meeting of mind and heart rather than just a purely physiological act.

Indeed, Jewish teachings advocate a multidimensional connection that is deeper and more wholesome than just the pleasuring of the body. To this end, Judaism offers directives that guide a couple towards intimacy on all levels—mental, emotional, physical, and spiritual. This, in turn, not only makes for a deeper, more meaningful, and fulfilling union, but also a sacred one.

For example, in order to ensure there is no mental distance during intimacy, Jewish law instructs that the ideal time to be intimate is at night and in a place where no other voices can be heard so as to avoid distraction. Similarly, neither partner may be drunk, to ensure they are both fully present and mindful when they are with each other.[164]

To ensure there is no emotional distance, Jewish law states that one may not fantasize about another person during intimacy, nor be intimate when angry with their spouse or when they are contemplating divorce. There is even a view[165] that intimacy should be avoided altogether when a person is angry, even if their anger is not directed at their spouse.

To avoid any physical distance, Jewish law stipulates that both partners wear no clothing at all so that there is absolutely no separation between them. Couples should also face each other for the same reason.

The Sages' suggestion that Shabbat, the holiest day of the week, is an ideal time for intimacy further highlights the intrinsic potential for holiness within this form of union.[166]

Furthermore, the *Zohar*[167] teaches: "When is a person called 'one'? ... When a person is in the union of intimacy.... When male and female join, they become one. They are one in body and one in soul; they are one person. And G-d dwells in their oneness."

This is truly remarkable. Not only is the sexual act not forbidden or discouraged, but it is considered a sacred encounter that welcomes the Divine Presence among us!

Despite Judaism's emphasis on the sacredness of intimacy, the subject is, for the most part, treated with modesty and discretion and not discussed openly. In fact, Maimonides[168] writes that Hebrew is called "the holy tongue" specifically because it has no explicit words for the sexual organs or for the act of intercourse, only referring to them through euphemism. This is not because the act itself is not a sacred one; rather, it is because its sanctity is retained precisely by keeping it private rather than explicit.

Such sensitivity is reflected in the Holy of Holies, the innermost sanctum within the Holy Temple, wherein the high priest could directly encounter G-d in spiritual intimacy. Notably, within the Holy of Holies there were two cherubs perched atop the Ark of the Covenant. The Talmud[169] relates that when Jews would make pilgrimage to Jerusalem for the festivals, the *kohanim* would roll up the curtain for them and show them the cherubs intertwined in a loving embrace. They would say to the gathered people: "See how you are beloved by G-d, as the love between man and woman."

In sharp contrast, the Talmud relates: "When the invaders entered the Temple and saw the cherubim, whose bodies were intertwined with one another, they carried them out to the marketplace and said: 'These Jews . . . preoccupy themselves with such things!' Immediately, all who saw this display despised the Jews, as it is said (Lamentations 1:8): *All who honored her now scorned her, because they saw her disgrace*.[170]

Commenting on this episode, Chasidic luminary R. Tzadok of Lublin notes: "The invading army viewed sexual intimacy as debauchery and lustful obsession. They did not recognize its inherent holiness."[171]

However, as we have learned, Judaism sees sexuality in a radically different, holy light. For, "if sexual intimacy were shameful, G-d would not have commanded us to fashion the cherubim and place them in the holiest and purest place in the world!"[172]

From the Jewish perspective, sexuality is not a necessary evil to propagate the human race; rather, it is the ultimate expression of oneness humankind can achieve. Indeed, when we come together in love and holiness, there is no more sacred act and Divine invitation for G-d to dwell among us.

The Big Idea

In the Jewish tradition, the act of intimacy is not simply allowed or tolerated; rather, it is celebrated and sanctified.

It Happened Once

THE MISHNAH RECORDS A debate as to whether there was ever any doubt regarding the inclusion of the Song of Songs—which describes the love between G-d and the Jewish people, sometimes in very intimate terms—in the twenty-four books of the *Tanach*.

However, R. Akiva said, "G-d forbid to say that [its inclusion was ever in doubt]. For the whole world was never as worthy as [it was on] the day on which the Song of Songs was given to Israel. For all the writings are holy, but the Song of Songs is holy of holies."[173]

Food

lechem   לחם

THE SPIRITUAL PRACTICE OF EVERYDAY LIFE

Is Judaism a religion of heaven or earth? Is Torah preoccupied with this world or the next? Where is the locus and focus of spiritual endeavor and fulfillment to be found?

The Sages[174] teach: Without bread, there is no Torah. More than just communicating an inescapable fact of human existence, this teaching, when understood properly, can serve as the mission statement of Torah itself.

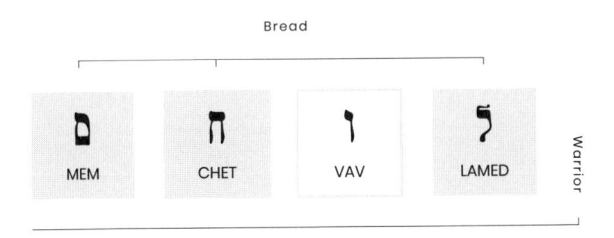

	Bread			
מ	ח	ו	ל	Warrior
MEM	CHET	VAV	LAMED	

The Hebrew word for bread, the foundational staple of the human diet, is *lechem*, a cognate of the word *lochem*, a warrior.[175] The *Zohar* teaches: "The time of eating is the time of battle,"[176] and "One who desires bread should eat it at the point of a sword."[177]

In Judaism, the spiritual battlefield is not limited to overtly "spiritual" moments, such as when one is wrapped in a *tallis* and absorbed in fervent prayer in the synagogue. Torah's true mission is to bring heaven down to earth, to suffuse the physical world with spiritual energy and light.

The Torah's ultimate concern extends beyond the prescribed bounds of ritual and worship, including also, and even especially, the seemingly "mundane" aspects of human existence and experience. Everyday activities such as getting dressed, eating breakfast, or doing business all fall under the purview of the Torah's mission to Divinize our lives.[178]

In fact, bread is used in Scripture[179] and Rabbinic writings as a symbol for various forms of physical engagement, including marital relations. Every moment of life is thus a "battle"—an opportunity to open ourselves to the Divine Presence in that experience.

In many religions, the highest ideal is to remove oneself from all worldly pleasures for the sake of spiritual enlightenment. Judaism, on the other hand, teaches that the real battle is not to withdraw from the material realm in order to avoid the obstacles it presents to spiritual devotion, but to engage and uncover the spiritual purpose within one's everyday activities.

An interesting example of this principle is found in the case of the nazirite. A nazirite was someone who chose to consecrate themselves to G-d by living a more reclusive, ascetic, and isolated lifestyle for a period of time. Surprisingly, these fervent spiritual seekers were instructed to bring a sin offering at the conclusion of their vow! In explanation of this curious law, the Talmud teaches that this was in order to atone for their misplaced self-imposed asceticism.[180] In the words of the Jerusalem Talmud[181]: "Is what the Torah forbade not enough that you must voluntarily forbid other things too?!"

Simply put: Completely withdrawing from the sensual world is not the Jewish way to live a spiritual life. To the contrary, one's true spiritual state is revealed precisely in how one integrates their physical and spiritual needs and desires. This path of integration is what ultimately resolves the seemingly intractable dichotomy between spirit and matter that has troubled so many mystics and philosophers from time immemorial. From the Jewish perspective, the holy work of the spiritual warrior is to acknowledge and amplify the sacred presence within all aspects of existence.

For instance, the Talmud[182] teaches: "A person's true character is ascertained by three things: his cup [how he eats], his pocket [his financial dealings], and his anger [how he treats others]." Notice that none of

CHAPTER 16 | FOOD

these examples include any specifically spiritual activities; they are, in fact, all about how one conducts oneself in material and social realms.

Moreover, when a person arrives in the World to Come, the first question he is asked is not about spiritual matters; rather, it is, "Did you engage in business with honesty?"[183]

Judaism teaches that one's spiritual state is expressed not only in their levels of learning or depth of prayer, but in how they conduct themselves on the most physical of levels.[184]

As Maimonides writes[185]: "Just as a wise man is distinct in his wisdom and his character traits, and he stands apart from others regarding them, so, too, he must be distinct in his deeds, in his eating, in his drinking, in his marital relations, in his use of the bathroom, in his speech, in his walk, in his clothes, in satisfying his needs, and in his business dealings. All such deeds of his should be especially pleasant and proper."

The Talmud[186] even goes so far as to compare one's dining table to the altar in the Holy Temple: "When the Temple stood, the altar effected atonement for a person. However, now that the Temple no longer stands, a person's dining table effects atonement for him."

How does eating become a spiritual experience, let alone comparable to the service of the altar in the Holy Temple?

Simply put, the "battle of bread," and by extension all permissible physical activity, is determined by our intention and approach. Eating can be an act of hedonism or an act of holiness, depending not only on *what* we eat, but on *how* we eat.

The Torah states[187]: *For not on bread alone will man live, but upon that which issues forth from G-d's mouth.* In the Lurianic mystical tradition,[188] this verse speaks of the spiritual potential hidden within the physical food we eat. The challenge is to recognize and consciously connect to the Divine energy present within the food, and all physicality. This is not so simple.

In overtly "spiritual" experiences, such as prayer, meditation, and fasting, we are focused entirely on the spiritual realm. When we eat, or engage in any other physical act, it is much harder to remain conscious of the spirit concealed within the material world, as our physical appetites, when given free rein, tend to dominate our awareness. However, by cultivating the awareness of the food's Divine origin and expressing that awareness by reciting a blessing before[189] and after eating, we are able to align and integrate the physical and spiritual dimensions of our lives into a unified whole.

Furthermore, beyond the initial act of articulated awareness, what we do with the indwelling Divine energy matters, too. For eating to be a truly holy act, we need to ensure that we utilize the energy we receive from the food[190] to grow morally and spiritually in study, prayer, and good deeds.[191]

The spiritual complexity of holy eating helps explain a curious Talmudic statement.[192]

R. Yehudah the Nasi says: "It is prohibited for an ignoramus to eat meat." He expounds: "Anyone who engages in Torah study is permitted to eat meat, and anyone who does not engage in Torah study is prohibited from eating the meat of animals or fowl."

In many traditions, the more spiritually sensitive one is, the more they are encouraged to abstain from eating meat. According to Judaism, however, the heights of spirituality are attained not by abstaining from foods like meat, but by enjoying and elevating them.

In fact, the spiritually delicate act of refining other forms of life is reserved specifically for those who are most spiritually sophisticated and therefore capable of this unique spiritual artform.

In other words, Judaism encourages us to engage the world more deeply and directly, not less, by finding ways to contextualize our material pursuits and engagements within a spiritual framework, thereby elevating them, and us.

Taking this spiritually embodied perspective even further, the Sages teach that if a person's home is compared to the Temple and their dining table to the altar,[193] their bedroom is considered the Holy of Holies![194]

As discussed in the previous chapter, in the Jewish tradition, acts of love and intimacy are not shameful activities that a couple engages in *despite* their religious devotions. Rather, they are considered acts of holiness when done in the right context and with the right intention.[195] The notion of becoming "one flesh" and experiencing such unity with another is sacred inasmuch as it mirrors G-d's oneness on high. Moreover, it is through marital relations that one comes closest to the act of creation itself, by bringing new life into this world.

In a broader sense, marriage itself is a holy practice. Unlike other monastic traditions that idealize abstinence and encourage celibacy among their clergy, in Judaism, the high priest was not allowed to perform the service of Yom Kippur, the holiest day of the year, if he was not married. In fact, so critical was it for the high priest to be married when performing the holiest service of the year that a woman would be designated before Yom Kippur as his wife-in-waiting should his current wife suddenly pass away on Yom Kippur.[196]

The celebration and sanctification of all aspects of life and the human condition is Judaism's response to the overwhelming urge to compartmentalize our lives into separate spheres—heaven and earth, soul and body, sacred and secular.

Similarly, many people perceive a separation between their religious and personal domains, leading them, for example, to see the synagogue as a place for spiritual life and their home as the personal space where they live out their mundane lives.[197]

Against such a dichotomization, Judaism teaches that spirituality is not just the "battle" to find connection during prayer or meditation; rather, it is equally, if not more importantly, expressed and experienced in how and why we eat, sleep, relate, and do business.

And, therefore, while the synagogue is the place where we gather with others for prayer, our homes are the "Holy Temples" where heaven meets earth in the totality of our lives.

The Big Idea

The aim of Jewish spirituality is to dissolve the false dichotomy between heaven and earth, soul and body, and the sacred and secular.

It Happened Once

IN HIS INTRODUCTION TO the classic work of R. Samson Raphael Hirsch titled, *Horeb: A Philosophy of Jewish Laws and Observances*, Dayan Dr. I. Grunfeld shares the history of an important debate over the center point of Judaism.

He writes that in an attempt to assimilate Judaism to the dominant faith, the German-Jewish Reformers of the nineteenth century introduced into modern Jewish thought the idea that worship of G-d in the synagogue is the central point in Jewish life; whereas, in reality, the laws of the Torah should inform and permeate the whole of life.

Against this fundamental error of "localizing" G-d in the house of worship instead of allowing Him to be the central force in our life, R. Hirsch wrote some of his most trenchant essays.

In one of those essays, he states:

"If I had the power, I would provisionally close all synagogues for a hundred years. Do not tremble at the thought of it, Jewish heart. What would happen? Jews and Jewesses without synagogues, desiring to remain such, would be forced to concentrate on a Jewish life and a Jewish home. The Jewish officials connected with the synagogue would have to look to the only opportunity now open to them to teach young and old how to live a Jewish life and how to build a Jewish home. All synagogues closed by Jewish hands would constitute the strongest protest against the abandonment of the Torah in home and life."

guf גוף

Body

CHAPTER 17 | BODY

HIGHER THAN THE SOUL

MANY RELIGIONS AND SPIRITUAL traditions view the body as an adversary of the soul that drags it down and distracts it from its true mission. It follows that the spiritual strategy employed by this worldview is to diminish the body's compromising impact on the soul.

The idea that the body must be tamed or even "beaten" into submission is a pervasive one. In his book, *Walking Words*, the Uruguayan writer Eduardo Galeano sums up prevailing contemporary views of the body succinctly: "The church says: the body is sin. Science says: the body is a machine. Advertising says: the body is business. The body says: I am a fiesta."

The Jewish perspective on the body is quite different. Whereas some traditions view corporeal life as an obstacle course—a series of challenges designed to test our spiritual resolve and integrity—Judaism sees the body as the interface and means of expression for the soul in physical reality. In this way, the body gives the soul a voice, and the soul provides the song.

Such a positive view of the body may strike some as counterintuitive from a religious perspective, but this is the basis of Jewish faith and practice. Judaism is a religion of action, not just good intentions. Towards this end, G-d desires the physical performance of *mitzvot*, which the soul is incapable of without the body. After all, it has no hands of its own to don *tefillin* or give charity, which is why it needs the body to give it form and expression, enabling it to achieve its raison d'être in the physical realm.

Accordingly, the Jewish approach to physicality is one of active engagement, not of avoidance or escape through ascetic practices and behaviors. While Judaism does not encourage indulgence, neither does it view abstention as the goal of bodily experience. The purpose of corporeal life is therefore not to negate but to embrace physicality and utilize it to achieve spiritual aims. As it says in Proverbs: *Know G-d in all your ways.*[198]

For instance, in the *Tanya*, R. Schneur Zalman of Liadi discusses reciting a blessing before eating a meal. The purpose is described as twofold: to spiritually elevate the physical substance of the food itself, whether plant or animal, and then to harness the energy gleaned from eating into *mitzvot*.[199] Thus, in the ideal world, the body is transparent to the soul—a suitable vehicle to assist it in carrying out its Divine mission.

This transformation from physical energy to spiritual action can and must begin with one's own bodily functions and habits. It is for this reason that Jews even recite a blessing after using the bathroom, thanking G-d for the intricate workings of the body and acknowledging that if even one opening were to close, it would be impossible to continue the mighty and sacred task of living in and Divinizing the world. And so, following what could be considered our most base activity, we say a blessing to acknowledge the Divine design of the body itself. Over time, these rituals, of which there are many in Judaism, help us develop a more refined nature and existential orientation that is in sync with the soul and better suited to acting on its behalf.

Indeed, the Hebrew word for body, *guf*, means a lid or cork,[200] signifying that the body serves as a container to encase and give form to the soul. Like software, the soul is immaterial and cannot function without the body's physical hardware to process and translate its instructions into tangible actions. The body is thus the vessel that enables the soul to inhabit physical life. Without it, the soul would be unable to interface with the physical world.

However, the body is not merely a means to an end, needed to facilitate the soul's aims and enable it to find physical expression; it also has its own unique contribution that transcends even the soul's greatest capabilities. King Solomon writes in Proverbs[201] that *a rich harvest comes through the strength of an ox*. The body, like an ox, possesses strength and passion that, when unbridled and untamed, has the potential to wreak havoc. However, it is this same fiery passion and brute strength that, when harnessed and directed towards spiritual aims, can be utilized to achieve what the soul could not accomplish on its own.[202]

From the soul's experience of reality, all is already one. Through embodiment, however, the soul experiences a more fragmentary perspective, giving rise to the drives and ambitions of earthly life. These psycho-emotional drives, such as jealousy, envy, and greed, which arise from life in the body, can potentially be harnessed by the soul to propel it beyond the heights it could reach on its own. For instance, the Sages teach: "Envy among scholars increases wisdom."[203]

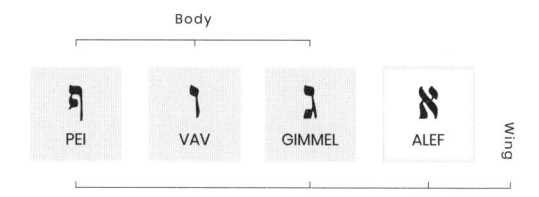

In this way, the body takes the soul to places it could not reach alone. This is alluded to by another Hebrew word that shares the same root letters as the word *guf* (body), *agapayim*—wings. Contrary to popular belief, it is the body that provides wings for the soul, not the other way around. Therefore, the body is not just a vessel for the soul, but its vehicle.

Ideally, like horse and rider, the body carries the soul with power and devotion, while the soul provides the body with direction. The body does not therefore simply allow the soul to operate in this world; it carries it further along its path towards fulfillment of its purpose.

The advantage of the body over the soul is thus not merely in its passion and brute force that enables the soul to soar; rather, Judaism views the body as more central to the purpose of creation than the soul. In fact, the soul is sent into this world with the express mission of transforming the nature of the body from a coarse, self-centered, and materialistic entity into a more refined and spiritually-attuned being.

The body is therefore not just a greater engine for achievement in this world than the soul, it is the ultimate purpose of the soul's descent from its heavenly, spiritual abode into mortal life.

Reflecting this spiritual perspective, Jewish law is very particular about how we treat the body, conferring upon it a degree of sanctity and holiness. For instance, the Torah prohibits harming the body in any way, as can be deduced from the verse,[204] *Guard your life exceedingly*, to the extent that "the danger of physical harm is treated with more severity than (ritual) prohibition."[205]

Additionally, *pikuach nefesh*—the halachic principle that preservation of human life overrides virtually[206] any other religious rule—is another powerful expression of Judaism's regard and even reverence for life in the body. In this way, the Torah frames our physical health and survival as a religious mandate of the highest order! For, as R. DovBer, the Maggid of Mezritch, once taught, "A small hole in the body is a large hole in the soul."[207]

In fact, even after death, when the soul has departed from the body, Jewish law requires that we treat the body with the utmost respect. As a tangible expression of this, a ritual purification is performed on a lifeless body before it is placed into the ground and returned to the earth. This indicates the spiritual value and sacredness that Judaism ascribes to the body, which extends well beyond its utility for the soul.

Remarkably, from a mystical perspective, the spiritual origins and potential of the body exceeds even that of the soul! Indeed, the fourth Lubavitcher Rebbe, R. Shmuel, writes[208] that "in the time to come, the soul will be nurtured by the body. Because, in truth, the body comes from a place that is immeasurably higher than the soul."

Based on the Kabbalistic teaching[209] that our forefather Abraham also serves as a metaphor for the soul and Sarah for the body, a striking textual allusion to the spiritual supremacy and wisdom of the body over the soul emerges from G-d's words to Abraham[210] (the soul): *Whatever Sarah [the body] tells you, hearken to her voice.*[211] This reflects the radical notion that, in potential and through the soul's activation, the body's unique spiritual intuition and insight[212] exceed that of the soul itself.[213]

Interestingly, there is a debate between Jewish philosophers as to whether the messianic era is one of corporeal reality, where the soul is vested in a body, or whether it is a spiritual state of heavenly ecstasy, entirely removed from any physical trappings.

Maimonides[214] maintains that the ultimate state is one of spiritual abstraction. The Kabbalists,[215] however, follow the view of Nachmanides[216] that the ultimate state is one in which the soul is embodied.[217] In this spirit, the Mishnah teaches that[218] "one hour of returning to G-d and performing good deeds in this world [i.e., in a body] is more precious than the entire World to Come[219] [in which one is totally disembodied]."

Accordingly, Judaism values life within the body over the highest spiritual experience; since G-d's ultimate desire is not for more ethereal spirituality, but for "an abode in the lowest realms."[220] G-d's greatest pleasure is therefore not in the negation of the body but in its elevation.

The Big Idea

The body is not just a friend of the soul or fuel to its fire; its refinement is the very purpose of the soul's descent into this world.

It Happened Once

THERE WAS ONCE A Chasid by the name of Yaakov Mordechai who, for many years, deprived himself of all physical comforts in order to achieve supremacy of soul over body. Before his passing, however, he expressed regret at having weakened his body with his unrelenting regimen and desire to put spirit over matter. Perhaps, had he not been so hard on his body, he could have lived to observe one more mitzvah. "For thirty years I slept on a bench (instead of a comfortable bed)!" he was later quoted to have said. "But to put on *tefillin* even one more time is far more valuable than to sleep on a bench for thirty years!"[221]

Humility
anavah

עִנְוָה

CHAPTER 18 | HUMILITY

PROUDLY HUMBLE

HUMILITY IS OFTEN UNDERSTOOD as the antithesis of arrogance. From this perspective, just as arrogance is an exaggerated sense of one's own importance or abilities, humility is a gross underestimation of them. In truth, however, the outlooks of both the exaggerator and the underestimator are fundamentally self-centered and focused on their own sense of importance and abilities, or lack thereof.

Both arrogance and false humility stem from the ego and are defined in relation and comparison to other people—either I am much better than my peers, or I am woefully worse. Regardless, such a perspective derives from deep insecurity and only serves to further separate one from their fellows, creating a false paradigm of competition between oneself and everyone else.

From a spiritual point of view, no human being is in competition with another.[222] We each have our own unique gifts and potential, as well as a purpose that only we can accomplish. This personal mission is the reason our souls descended into this physical world in the first place. Herein lies the antidote to arrogance and false humility—recognizing that we each have our own inimitable purpose and have been given the gifts to carry it out, and the same goes for everyone else.

Perhaps to help cultivate this mindset, the great Chasidic master R. Simcha Bunim of Peshischa would always keep a piece of paper in each pocket. On one was written, "The whole world was created for me,"[223] and on the other, "I am but a speck of dust."[224] These seemingly contradictory sentiments are the recipe for true humility—recognizing that each of us has a mission that only we can complete, and thus, in the words of the Chasdic masters, "The day you were born is the day G-d decided that the world could not exist without you"; and yet, each of us is just one small piece of an infinitely complex and grand design.

It is from such an empowered and empathic place that we are able to acknowledge and even celebrate ourselves, including our strengths and capabilities, without compromising the value of humility.

For instance, the Mishnah teaches: "When Rebbi (R. Yehudah the Nasi) died, humility...disappeared." In the ensuing Talmudic discussion, R. Yosef said, "Do not teach that humility disappeared, for I am still here (and I am humble—Rashi)."[225]

In the classical sense, to call attention to one's own humility seems outright hypocritical.

However, the Talmud suggests that the truly humble person is not one who shrinks from positive self-acknowledgment, but one who is confidently aware of their own value.

R. Yosef was aware of his virtues and did not shy away from them or try to deny them. He was brutally honest with himself and others, and, equally important, he was willing to stand up and declare his own humility because that was simply the truth. He nevertheless epitomized true humility because he did not credit himself for his own talents and achievements. Instead, he appreciated that they were gifts from G-d.[226]

Similarly, Moses, the greatest prophet and leader in Jewish history, is referred to in the Torah as *the humblest man on the face of the earth*.[227] Although he was aware of the incredible feats he had achieved—standing up to Pharaoh, leading the Israelites out of Egypt and through the desert, speaking to G-d face to face on Mount Sinai, etc.—he knew that his virtues and achievements were Divine gifts, and, furthermore, that if someone else had been in his shoes, they may have done a better job.

There is a crucial distinction here. The truly humble person recognizes the whole of who they are, including their abilities and achievements, not just their shortcomings. However, they don't take credit for their qualities and accomplishments.

They know that all creativity, ingenuity, and insight come *through* us, not *from* us. This is why a talented person is called "gifted," because everything is truly a gift from the Creator. Thus, to see oneself as worthless is not humility, it's ingratitude. G-d has blessed each one of us with unique qualities so we can utilize and make the most of them. In fact, it is only when we are aware of our self-worth that we can be truly humble. Then we can truthfully ask ourselves, "How am I using the Divine gifts that have been given to me? Am I reaching my own potential for greatness?"

This sentiment is powerfully encapsulated in the Hebrew word for humility, *anavah*. While the English word humility originates from the Latin, *humilis*, meaning meekness or lowliness,[228] *anavah* stems from the word *anu*, meaning "to respond." For in Judaism,

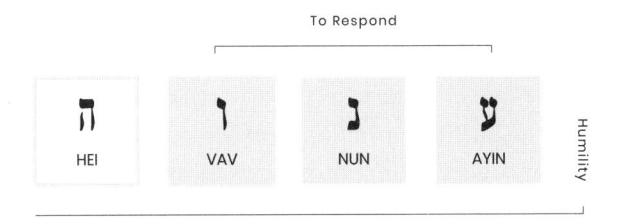

To Respond				
ה	ו	נ	ע	Humility
HEI	VAV	NUN	AYIN	

humility is rooted in a sense of responsibility and accountability. From this perspective, the awareness of privilege or proficiency does not perversely inflate one's sense of self-worth and supremacy above others; rather, it fills one with immense gratitude and indebtedness, generating greater dedication to one's mission.

In the words of American writer Frederick Buechner: "Your vocation in life is where your greatest talent and joy meets the world's greatest needs."

This is the work of humility.

In his book, *Good to Great*, Jim Collins describes his observations of the world's greatest executives and what they all have in common. He describes what he calls, "level five leaders," which are leaders who display a powerful combination of personal humility and indomitable will. They're incredibly ambitious, but their ambition is first and foremost for the greater cause—for the organization and its purpose—not for their own self-aggrandizement. In his experience, whenever there was a company that went from good to great, there was always an executive driving that transformation with this same alchemical mixture of qualities. Humility is, thus, the redemption of ambition. By directing one's striving towards something larger than the self and anchoring their pursuit of excellence in a sense of responsibility to the greater whole, one becomes an instrument for positive change in the world.

The humble person therefore asks, "Why? Why did G-d give me these talents or resources? What am I meant to do with them? What is the greater need or purpose towards which I can direct and dedicate my energy and passion?" All of life is spent refining the answers to these questions, while striving to utilize our gifts to the best of our abilities.

To quote American author Leo Buscaglia: "Your talent is G-d's gift to you. What you do with it is your gift back to G-d."

This sensibility, so intrinsic to the quality of *anavah*, is expressed not just intrapersonally, but interpersonally as well. Humility is not only defined by a deep feeling of responsibility for one's own gifts, but also by a heightened receptivity to the gifts of others.

In the words of R. Lord Jonathan Sacks: "True humility...does not mean undervaluing yourself. It means valuing other people."[229]

Those who are truly humble do not focus solely on themselves; rather, they set their sights on how their gifts can serve the greater whole. They are thus able to stand in awe of the greatness of others, and even to help others see the gifts they possess more clearly. Such an ability to recognize and draw forth the greatness in others is the hallmark of great leaders.

Genuine humility means knowing and accepting who we are and who we are not; what we can do and what we cannot do. With this sense of personal clarity, we are able to see how we fit into the grand scheme of life, moving beyond ourselves to recognize, reveal, and revel in the greatness in others. It follows that real honor is not the honor we receive, but the honor we give. As the Mishnah says: "Who is honored? He who honors others!"

To summarize, in the stirring words of R. Sacks, "Humility is more than just a virtue, it is a form of perception, a language in which the "I" is silent so that I can hear the "Thou," the unspoken call beneath human speech, the Divine whisper within all that moves, the voice of otherness that calls me to redeem its loneliness with the touch of love. Humility is what opens us to the world."

The Big Idea

"Humility is not thinking less of yourself, it's thinking of yourself less."[230]

It Happened Once

R. LORD JONATHAN SACKS SHARES the following reflections based on an encounter with the Lubavitcher Rebbe:

"As a young man, full of questions about faith, I traveled to the United States, where, I had heard, there were outstanding rabbis. I met many, but I also had the privilege of meeting the greatest Jewish leader of my generation, the late Lubavitcher Rebbe, R. Menachem Mendel Schneerson. Heir to the dynastic leadership of a relatively small group of Jewish mystics, he had escaped from Europe to New York during the Second World War and had turned the tattered remnants of his flock into a worldwide movement. Wherever I traveled, I heard tales of his extraordinary leadership, many verging on the miraculous. He was, I was told, one of the outstanding charismatic leaders of our time. I resolved to meet him if I could.

"I did, and I was utterly surprised.

"He was certainly not charismatic in any conventional sense. Quiet, self-effacing, understated, one might hardly have noticed him had it not been for the reverence in which he was held by his disciples. That meeting, though, changed my life. He was a world-famous figure. I was an anonymous student from three thousand miles away. Yet, in his presence, I seemed to be the most important person in the world. He asked me about myself; he listened carefully; he challenged me to become a leader, something I had never contemplated before. Quickly, it became clear to me that he believed in me more than I believed in myself. As I left the room, it occurred to me that it had been full of my presence and his absence. Perhaps that is what listening is, considered as a religious act. I then knew that greatness is measured by what we efface ourselves towards. There was no grandeur in his manner; neither was there any false modesty. He was serene, dignified, majestic; a man of transcending humility who gathered you into his embrace and taught you to look up..."[231]

"...It was an extraordinary gift. It was 'royalty without a crown.' It was 'greatness in plain clothes.' It taught me that humility is not thinking you are small. It is thinking that other people have greatness within them."[232]

Luck
mazal

מזל

WRITTEN IN HEAVEN, TRANSLATED ON EARTH

MAZAL TOV IS THE colloquial Jewish expression of congratulations, the traditional felicitation given at a wedding, bat mitzvah, or *brit*. It is also the standard response to hearing good news from or about another person. But what does this familiar Jewish expression really mean?

The word *mazal* is sometimes translated as "luck,"[233] something that happens perchance. According to this interpretation, *mazal tov* would mean good fortune or good luck.

In fact, the real meaning of *mazal tov* is the very opposite of luck. The literal translation of the word *mazal* means a constellation of stars. Instead of luck, therefore, *mazal* implies a kind of fate or some form of predetermination, alluding to the idea that what happens on earth is initiated and orchestrated by higher, cosmic forces.

Indeed, according to the Jewish view, everything that happens on earth is first articulated in the heavens. As the Midrash[234] teaches: "R. Simon said: 'There isn't a single herb or spice that doesn't have a constellation in the heavens that strikes it and tells it to grow.'"

There are a number of examples of Jewish astrological tradition throughout the Talmud. One fascinating passage[235] describes various temperaments likely to be found among people born during various hours of the day. These personality traits and dispositions are specific to the qualities associated with the dominant planets at the time of their birth.

"One who was born under the sun will be a radiant person; he will eat from his own and drink from his own, and his secrets will be exposed. If he steals, he will not succeed.

"One who was born under Venus will be a rich and promiscuous person. Why? Because fire was born [during the hour of Venus].

"One who was born under Mercury will be an enlightened and expert person, because Mercury is the sun's scribe [it is closest to the sun].

"One who was born under the moon will be a person who suffers pains, who builds and destroys, and destroys and builds. Who eats not from his own and drinks not from his own, and whose secrets are hidden. If he steals, he will succeed [like the moon, which constantly changes form, whose light is not its own, and which is at times exposed and at times hidden].

"One who was born under Saturn will be a person whose thoughts are for naught. And some say that everything that others scheme about him will be for naught.

"One who was born under Jupiter [*tzedek*] will be a righteous person [*tzadkan*]....

"One who was born under Mars will be one who spills blood. R. Ashi said: He will be either a bloodletter or a thief, a slaughterer of animals or a circumciser."

Furthermore, the Talmud tells of numerous Sages whose destinies were informed by Chaldean astrologers. For instance, R. Akiva was told by an astrologer that his daughter would pass away on her wedding day.[236] R. Yosef declined the position of head of the Rabbinic academy because astrologers informed him that he was destined to pass away two years after taking the position.[237]

The Talmud clearly associates the concept of *mazal* not with random luck but with a kind of astrologically-based predetermination, as in "The blessings of health, children, and livelihood do not depend on merit; rather, they depend on fate (*mazal*)."[238]

Indeed, the Jerusalem Talmud[239] recounts a fascinating custom practiced by the Amalekites that highlights the power of *mazal*. "They would place soldiers at the frontline on their birthday in the belief that a soldier would not fall easily on his birthday." From this the Talmud derives that a person's *mazal* is dominant on their birthday.

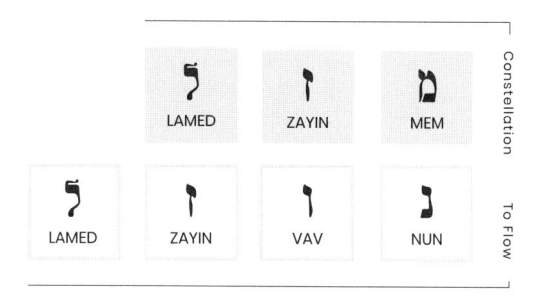

ל	ז	מ	Constellation
LAMED	ZAYIN	MEM	
ל	ז	ו	נ	To Flow
LAMED	ZAYIN	VAV	NUN	

Interestingly, *mazal* is an etymological cognate of the word *nozal*, which means a downward flow.

This follows the Jewish belief that every person has a reservoir of spiritual energy in the higher realms[240] that can either remain "above" in the ethereal realms as dormant potential, or descend "below" and translate into actual physical blessings in the form of children, health, wealth, or other blessings, depending on our actions and input.

For instance, Rosh Hashanah is the day of judgment when our annual allotment of good fortune for the coming year is determined. However, the Talmud[241] explains that although our future was already decided on Rosh Hashanah, we continue to pray each day of the year to assure that our allotted fortune will reach us and manifest in a concrete and positive manner. If it was decreed, for example, that a certain amount of rain would fall throughout the year, the same volume of rain could fall all at once as a destructive deluge, or it could be spread over time in a manner of blessing—meaning, in the right increments to ensure that the crops will flourish.

Herein lies the Jewish twist on ancient astrology: Our "fate" may be decreed "above," but our "destiny" is determined by our actions "below." The concept of *mazal* is the active mediation between these two dimensions, the manner in which what is decreed in the heavens is brought down and materialized on earth in the form of blessing or its opposite.

The idea that blessing is not a function of luck but of actualizing one's heavenly destiny is alluded to in many Jewish sources.

Blessing

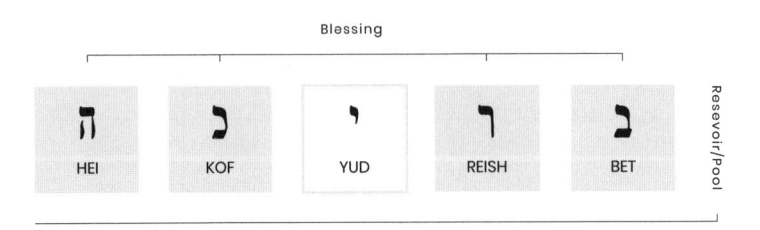

ה	כ	י	ר	ב	Reservoir/Pool
HEI	KOF	YUD	REISH	BET	

For instance, Chasidut[242] states that the Hebrew word for blessing, *brachah*, is etymologically associated with the word *hamavrich*, to lower down, as in,[243] "if one has lowered a vine down into the ground." Other Jewish sources[244] understand the word *brachah* to be a derivative of the word *breichah*, a reservoir or pool, referring to the above mentioned spiritual reservoir of potential blessing that exists in the upper realms and can be channeled into this world through our positive actions.

The expression *mazal tov*, therefore, is not an acknowledgment of one's good luck; rather, it expresses our wish that what is stored up in heaven should manifest on earth in a manner of revealed goodness.[245]

It is important to note that some Jewish sages reject the notion that Judaism subscribes to any form of astrology whatsoever. In the aforementioned Talmudic passage that discusses the temperaments determined by the planets under which one was born, R. Yochanan[246] concludes that, ultimately, "the Jewish people are not governed by *mazal*." Maimonides[247] seems to understand R. Yochanan's words to mean not only that "Jews are not governed (and their fate is not predetermined) by astrology" but that "there is no place at all for astrology in the Jewish faith."

Unlike Maimonides, however, the predominant stance among Talmudic commentators (see Rashi and *Tosafot*[248]) is that Judaism does accept the governance of astrology to a certain degree, with the caveat that while *mazal* does have an influence, we are not powerlessly bound by that influence and can, in fact, change the outcome or expression of that influence through prayer and by overcoming our inclinations. If one transforms themselves in some substantial way, they can transform their predetermined fate and manifest their higher destiny.

Based on this perspective, the accepted view is that, while there are natural and cosmic forces at play in our lives, we always retain the freedom and ability to choose our own paths and influence our own outcomes. Reflecting this idea, the Talmud[249] relates a conversation between Abraham and G-d, in which Abraham tells G-d, "I looked into my astrological destiny, and I am not fit to have a son." To which G-d replies, "Emerge from your astrology, for Israel is not governed by *mazal*." Appropriately, G-d then tests and refines Abraham's faith and character until he is given a new name by G-d, indicating that he has sufficiently transformed himself enough to change his destiny, at which point he does indeed have children.

Similarly, the Talmud tells us[250] that R. Akiva's daughter, mentioned above, did not end up dying on her wedding day, because, while everyone else was preoccupied with the wedding feast, she took notice of a poor person in need and gave up her own portion of food to feed him.

Based on the above, one's *mazal* is not something to be passively received but proactively achieved.

When we wish each other *mazal tov*, therefore, it is not an expression of surrendering to random luck or faceless forces beyond our control. Instead, it is a wish that our story, as written in the stars, translates on earth in ways that are positive, just, and life-enhancing.

The Big Idea

According to the Jewish take on astrology, one's mazal *is not simply a matter of chance but a matter of choice.*

It Happened Once[251]

R. Akiva's daughter once went to the market to buy things for the home. As she passed a group of stargazers and fortune tellers, one of them said to the other: "See that lovely girl? What a dreadful calamity is awaiting her! She is going to die on the very day of her wedding!"

On the night of her wedding, before retiring to bed, she removed her golden hairpin and stuck it in a crevice in the wall.

The following morning, she pulled her pin from the wall, and in doing so dragged a small but poisonous snake with it. Horrified, she realized that she had killed the snake that was lurking in the wall's crevice when she stuck the pin into the wall the night before. What a miracle!

She heard a knock on the door. "Are you alright, daughter? I heard you scream," her father said. Then he saw the dead snake still dangling from the pin. She told her father what happened.

"This is indeed a miracle," R. Akiva said. "Tell me, daughter, what did you do yesterday? There must have been some special mitzvah that you performed to have been saved from this."

"Well, the only thing that I can remember is this. Last night during the wedding feast, a poor man came in, but nobody seemed to notice him. I saw that the poor man was starving, so I took my portion of the wedding feast and gave it to him."

Moved by his daughter's kindness and overjoyed by her miraculous deliverance, R. Akiva stated the verse, *Tzedakah delivers from death.*

חיים

chaim Life
───────────────────────

RISE IN PEACE

In Jewish thought, the term afterlife is a misnomer. Colloquially, the expression "afterlife" suggests that after life comes to an end, something else follows. In contrast to this, Judaism teaches that life is eternal—it has no end. It is experienced in a physical body for a period of time, and when that time is up, we lay down our body, and the soul returns to a higher dimension of eternal existence.

A contemporary analogy for this can be understood from a television broadcast: a transmitting station broadcasts images and sounds in the form of energy waves, which are received by a physical device that displays them. Imagine that something goes wrong with the device itself, so that its screen and speakers no longer display the images, sounds, ideas, feelings, and actions encoded within the energy waves.

The transmitting station, and the energy waves incorporating the media, exist no less than before; it is only that the receiving device is no longer translating them into physically visible and audible phenomena.

By way of analogy, we can thus envision the soul itself as the transmitting station (i.e., the source of one's personality, character traits, thoughts, emotions, actions, etc.) and the body as the receiving device. The death of the body does not in any way affect the integrity of the soul, nor does it halt the soul's self-expression (analogous to the energy waves that are emanating through space); it is only that we have been deprived of the ability to see and hear it in the phenomenal world.

The comfort in knowing that the soul lives on may be overshadowed by our inability to fully comprehend the concept of life beyond the physical realm. We may have disconcerting questions about the quality of the soul's existence and experience in the next world: What is it like for a soul to be "deprived" of physical existence? What kind of "life" does one have as a soul?

In a letter[252] written to a family who lost a loved one, the Lubavitcher Rebbe described the soul's experience when it departs this world:

"Needless to say, insofar as the soul is concerned, [death] is a release from its 'imprisonment' in the body. For so long as [the soul] is bound up with the body, it suffers from the physical limitations of the body, which necessarily constrain the soul and involve it in physical activities that are essentially alien to its purely spiritual nature.... In other words, the departure of the soul from the body is a great advantage and ascent for the soul."

Accordingly, the Hebrew word for life, *chaim*, is phrased in the plural and literally translates as "lives," indicating multiple phases and expressions of a single, never-ending life.

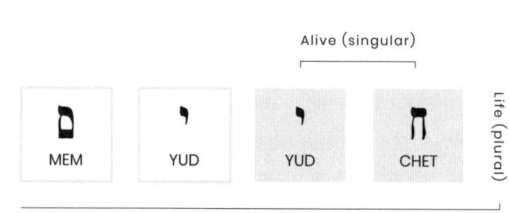

MEM	YUD	YUD	CHET

Alive (singular): YUD CHET
life (plural): MEM YUD YUD CHET

Famously, on the last day of Moses' life, he tells the Jewish people[253]: *See, I set before you this day life and prosperity, death and adversity... choose life.* Obviously, everyone would choose life over death, so what kind of choice is Moses actually offering?

The explanation is that, essentially, Moses is offering sound investment advice. You can spend your life investing in self-centered pursuits that are physically pleasurable but fleeting, or you can invest in that which is eternal—*life*.

The Talmud teaches[254]: "Righteous individuals are considered alive even in their death," whereas "wicked individuals are considered as dead, even during their lifetime."

This is because righteous individuals spend their lives infusing eternal meaning into everything they do.

In stark contrast to the culture of "Eat, drink, and be merry, for tomorrow we die," when Jews have occasion to drink, they say "*l'chaim!*" reminding each other that there is so much more to life than the shallow indulgences of the here and now, and that every meaningful act one does and every mitzvah one performs creates an energetic imprint that outlives our temporary time in a physical body.

In fact, we learn that even after one's body is laid to rest, *mitzvot* performed in the merit of a departed soul help to continue that soul's journey and ascent as it travels through the infinite worlds beyond.

Therefore, instead of saying: "May their soul rest in peace," in Jewish tradition, we say, "May their *neshamah* (soul) continue to have an *aliyah* (ascent)." For the soul does not rest; rather, it rises, continuously, even after death.[255]

Indeed, this perpetual process of ongoing elevation is the very essence of life itself.

The Big Idea

We are not physical beings having a spiritual experience; we are spiritual beings having a physical experience.[256]

It Happened Once

IN 1960, A GROUP of college students came to see the Lubavitcher Rebbe. One of the topics they discussed was the Jewish understanding of death.

The Rebbe explained: "The term used to describe death in Judaism is *histalkut*, which does not mean death in the sense of coming to an end; rather, it refers to an elevation from one level to another. When one completes his or her mission in life, the departed person is elevated to a higher plane.

"Death is not a cessation of life; rather, it describes the process whereby one's spiritual life takes on a new dimension. This notion is consistent with the scientific principle of conservation of matter, which states that nothing physical can be annihilated. This table or a piece of iron can be cut, burned, etc., but in no instance can the matter of the table or the iron be destroyed. It only takes on a different form.

"Likewise, on the spiritual level, our spiritual being—the soul—can never be destroyed. It only changes its form or is elevated to a different plane.

"Accordingly," the Rebbe concluded, "the term 'afterlife' is inappropriate, for what we experience after death is a continuation of life. Until one hundred twenty (the human lifespan mentioned in the Torah), life is experienced on one level, and from one hundred twenty-one, one hundred twenty-two, and one hundred twenty-three onward, it is carried on at another level, and we continue to ascend higher and higher in the realm of the spirit."

Money

kesef   כסף

CHAPTER 21 | MONEY

FOLLOW THE MONEY

MONEY CAN BE A very polarizing subject. Some see it as the root of all evil, while others see it as the key to happiness. Judaism views wealth as neither fundamentally good nor evil; rather, like all neutral and powerful forces, it is ultimately defined by the way we use and relate to it.

Since money can be a force for good—for example, when used to help the less fortunate and support entities that better the world—Judaism does not discourage the accumulation of wealth. Instead, it provides guidelines for how to interact with it in ways that engender integrity, compassion, and righteousness.

There are numerous *mitzvot* in the Torah that demand the highest level of honesty and ethics in one's business practices. Some examples include the prohibition against inaccurate measures and scales, verbal deception, misrepresentation of value or intention, and the fair treatment and prompt payment of one's employees.

Furthermore, there are numerous *mitzvot* that directly address the alleviation of socio-economic imbalance in society. Communal directives such as *pei'ah*, leaving a portion of one's field for the poor; *yovel*, the forgiveness of all debt during the Jubilee year; and *maaser*, committing ten percent of one's annual earnings to *tzedakah*, all serve to instill a sense of social and moral responsibility within one's relationship to property and ownership.[257]

In fact, Judaism considers one's relationship with money and behavior in business so important that it is seen as the proving ground of one's spiritual development and standing.

As we learn in the Talmud,[258] when a person passes on and their soul ascends to heaven for its final reckoning, the first question the heavenly court asks is: "Were you honest in your business dealings?"

From this perspective, it becomes clear why, despite its positive potential, as discussed above, Judaism also contains numerous cautionary insights regarding the possible pitfalls associated with wealth accumulation.

Interestingly, such caveats are encoded within the various words used to refer to money in Biblical Hebrew. *Kesef*, for example, is

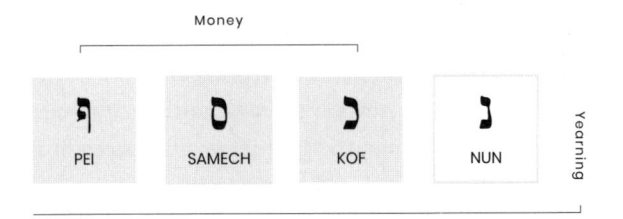

| Money |
| PEI | SAMECH | KOF | NUN | Yearning |

etymologically related to the word *nichsaf*, which means yearning, alluding to the deep-seated and often insatiable drive to acquire and amass wealth.[259] This psychological understanding of money is expressed consistently throughout Jewish literature in memorable quotes such as: "One who has one hundred wants two hundred"[260]; "One who loves money will not be satisfied with money"[261]; and ""No one leaves this world with half his desires fulfilled.'"[262]

Shekel, a word used both in Biblical and modern Hebrew, is etymologically related to the word *mishkal*, which means weight. R. Bachya explains[263] that this alludes to the moral weight we should give to all of our monetary dealings, and that, ideally, we should place equal weight on both our spiritual and material pursuits. Additionally, the word *zuz*, which in modern Hebrew means move, appears as a term for money (literally, coin) in the Talmud. This hints at a crucial lesson: Money does not stay with any one person for very long; rather, it moves from one pocket to the next. The Sages viewed wealth as something that is meant to be circulated and should thus be considered impermanent. All of these Hebrew terms for money reveal its complex inner nature and provide us with guidance as we pursue it.

From a mystical point of view, the very desire to attain wealth, expressed in the word *kesef*, is seen as sacred. For instance, the Baal Shem Tov taught[264] that every material yearning (whether it be for money or food) has an underlying spiritual motivation within it. We are thus drawn towards various physical elements and material possessions by our soul's energetic drive for positive impact. Our attraction and even craving is due to the fact that our soul senses a powerful spiritual force within an object or experience, and it yearns to utilize it for its true spiritual purpose. Thus, when we eat food or earn money and then utilize it to perform *mitzvot*, we transform physicality into a spiritual medium, through which Divine purpose is achieved.

Similarly, in Lurianic Kabbalah, it is taught that there is a holy spark hidden within each physical creation.[265] Our body may desire food, but our soul craves the spark within it in order to elevate it. When we intentionally utilize a mundane object for spiritual purposes, we thereby redeem the sparks of holiness that were trapped within it and activate their latent potential that was waiting to be brought forth. Some mystical texts refer to this process as "redeeming the captives,"[266] a metaphor all too familiar to Jews of the Middle Ages, who were regularly taken captive and held for ransom. In our context, this refers to the sparks of holiness that are concealed and "held captive" within the material realm until they are redeemed through conscious elevation.

In the Talmud,[267] the Sages teach that the Jewish people were exiled and scattered throughout the world in order to "increase converts," which Kabbalah[268] interprets symbolically as referring to the scattered sparks of holiness strewn throughout the world. Read in this manner, the displacement and exile of the Jewish people was Divinely orchestrated in order for us to wander the world redeeming and "converting" fallen aspects of reality and returning them to their original luster in the light of the Divine. This can only be done if our actions are ethical; otherwise, we go from redeeming the fallen to becoming captives ourselves.

This is poignantly illustrated in the Book of Genesis,[269] which tells how Jacob, in mid-flight from his enraged brother, risked his life by crossing back across the Jabbok River. In seeking to explain why Jacob returned to the other side of the Jabbok, R. Eliezer says: "He returned to collect some small jars he left behind."

The obvious question is: Why would Jacob be willing to risk his life by crossing a dangerous river alone at night in order to retrieve a few insignificant belongings? The provocative answer provided by the Talmud[270] is that "the righteous cherish their money more than their own lives!" Without any clarification, this statement might seem to reinforce a host of familiar antisemitic tropes and stereotypes. However, if we replace the word money with positive impact (the potential that money has to do incredible good in the world), we can understand its meaning on a deeper level—the righteous value their ability to positively impact the world above their own lives.

Therefore, in the hands of those committed to positively impacting the world and others beyond themselves, wealth becomes an instrument for redemptive change.

When seen in this light, our craving (*nichsaf*) for money (*kesef*) itself is a soul-prompt to acquire wealth for the express purpose of bringing more light, justice, peace, and G-dliness into the world.

The Big Idea

Spiritually, the human aspiration for wealth stems from the soul's desire to impact our world for the better; heed its call, and you have turned the pursuit of wealth into a noble act.

CHAPTER 21 | MONEY

It Happened Once

EACH YEAR ON SIMCHAT Torah from 1954 until 1964, the Lubavitcher Rebbe taught a new Chasidic song. In addition to teaching the actual melody, the Rebbe would often explain its background and significance.

One year, the Rebbe taught a song called *Anim Zmirot*, based on the devotional words of a liturgical poem attributed to R. Yehudah the Nasi (compiler of the Mishnah), which is recited in some communities following the *Musaf* on Shabbat:

"I shall sing sweet songs, and poems I shall weave, because my soul longs for You.

My soul desires the shadow of your hand, to know every one of Your secrets."

After teaching the song, the Rebbe shared the following story:

Once, on the day after Yom Kippur, the community of a certain *shtetl* arrived at the synagogue for *Shacharit* and were surprised to find one community member dancing around the podium, singing *Anim Zemirot* with great fervor. It turned out that the man had been so engrossed in the melody that he danced the entire night, not even noticing that the fast had ended and that he hadn't eaten for a day and a half!

As the song became popular among the Chasidim, rumors began circulating that the pious individual in the story was actually the Rebbe himself.

When one of the Chasidim visited the Rebbe for a private audience, he decided to clarify the matter once and for all, and he asked the Rebbe if the rumors were true. The Rebbe replied that they weren't and that the story took place before the times of the Baal Shem Tov.

The Rebbe then proceeded to recount the story in full:

"There once lived a rich man who made it his business to travel the region, locating and redeeming Jewish people who had been taken captive. One day, he was passing by the local jail when he heard heartrending cries. He went to the local baron to free the man in captivity, but he was told that the cost of the man's freedom was an exorbitant sum. The rich man was hesitant.

"Returning home, his conscience didn't let him rest. He proceeded to calculate the worth of his entire estate, which turned out to be precisely the amount it would take to free the Jewish man. He liquidated all of his assets and then returned to the baron and handed him the necessary sum.

"With a wicked gleam in his eye, the baron burst out laughing as he opened the cell, calling out: 'Take your Jew, as promised.' To the wealthy man's shock and dismay, the poor man had already passed away.

"Feeling utterly dejected and devastated over selling his possessions to no avail, the now poor man fell into a deep depression. No matter how much his family tried, the man's spirits could not be revived.

"One night, he fell into a deep sleep. As he slept, he had a dream, with a message from Above: 'Your money was not wasted. On the contrary, your altruistic actions are worthy of reward.' The man was given two choices. The first was to return to a life of extraordinary wealth. The second was to experience a taste of Gan Eden, heavenly bliss, while still in this world.

"The man chose the second option, and it was decided in heaven to bless and infuse him with spiritual rapture on Yom Kippur.

"It was then, while singing *Anim Zmirot*, that he experienced this sublime revelation, a taste of the World to Come. So caught up was he in ecstasy, that he danced through the night, oblivious to his bodily needs."

The Rebbe concluded, "The man lived before the times of the Baal Shem Tov. For had he benefited from the teachings of Chasidut, he would have chosen the wealth! Do you know how many more lives he could have saved then?"

Simply put, greater than seeing an angel is becoming an angel for someone else.

maaseh מעשה

Action

CHAPTER 22 | ACTION

JUST DO IT

"Follow your heart" is the prevailing wisdom in today's society; "be true to what you feel" seems to be the mantra of our generation. From this perspective, the main arbiter of our actions should be our emotions.

In Jewish thought, the matter is more complex. Certainly, one's feelings are valued as a source of motivation for our actions and life choices. However, Judaism is also skeptical of leaving everything up to our whims. Some things are simply too important to wait for a surge of inspiration. Sometimes action is required no matter how we may feel in the moment.

Based on this awareness, Judaism posits that "action is paramount"[271]; feelings, and even beliefs, are secondary to how one actually behaves in this world and how one chooses to spend their time and resources. This is the logic underlying *halachah*, the vast system of Jewish law and behavioral requirements for fulfilling the commandments of the Torah.

Halachah literally means walking and is primarily focused on how we navigate the world. It is the Jewish "way" of honoring and actualizing the potential holiness and existential impact of our every step.

The *mitzvot* themselves are almost entirely focused on tangible actions that one must do or not do within the personal, professional, social, and ritual dimensions of life. As commandments, they comprise the bedrock of Jewish religiosity and culture. The *mitzvot* give concrete experiential expression to abstract principles such as justice, self-restraint, love for one's neighbor, righteousness, fairness, etc.

These are the things the Torah considers simply too important to put off until we are graced with the inspiration and motivation to do so.

According to Jewish teaching, it is always the right time to pursue justice, to feed the poor, to take care of the stranger, to pay your employees on time, to act with respect in all manner of relationships, to express gratitude to G-d for the fruits of your labor, and so on. And it is this spiritual investment in obligatory action, rather than fleeting feeling or abstract philosophy, that has led people throughout the ages to characterize Judaism as being a religion defined by "deed over creed."

However, all that is not to say that Judaism disavows or devalues the role and importance of feelings and inspiration in the realm of action. Not at all. But it does suggest that the Torah takes a different approach to ethical action and sustainable practice than to simply "follow your bliss."

Religious, relational, and societal commitments all demand a heightened degree of behavioral consistency and even willful perseverance to maintain and live up to. Truth, faith, love, justice, community, education, success—these values, goals, and ideals all require regular practical action to become realities. It is not enough to just think about or have feelings for them.

This means that anyone who desires to live in accordance with such commitments will inevitably have to show up, support, and contribute to their actualization, even when they don't necessarily *feel* like it.

How then does one ensure that their commitment to sustainable practice does not devolve into a series of mechanistic actions devoid of heart and soul?

Traditional Jewish teaching offers a novel perspective to solve this behavioral conundrum.

Rather than framing the matter as a one-way street from feeling to action, inspiration to initiative, the Sages teach that our feelings can flow and follow from our deeds, not just the other way around. As the thirteenth-century compendium of *mitzvot*, the *Chinuch*,[272] states succinctly: "Hearts are drawn to follow actions."

The recognition that rather than passively waiting for inspiration to strike, one can consciously cultivate feelings of excitement, passion, and even pleasure for their most important commitments *through repeated action* is relevant to all forms of practice, learning, and mastery.

For example, many writers and musicians stress the importance of sitting down to write or practice every single day, whether one is inspired or not. There is something about the rhythm and regularity of the act itself that helps to maintain and even progressively deepen one's abilities and identification with their art form. Sometimes it is just a matter of putting pen to paper, fingers to keys, brush to canvas, or sitting down to meditate that opens the inner channels for inspiration to flow.

Often, the muses are simply hovering and waiting for us to initiate the process. Our proactive instigation is the proverbial lightning rod that can catch and direct the energetic currents of creation. If we never act, our infinite potential remains untapped.

What is true of the creative process is equally true of the spiritual process. For instance, in Judaism, prayer is a thrice-daily obligation whose times are proscribed. Notably, the Sages refer to prayer as the "work" (service) of the heart.[273]

This suggests that the Sages understood that inspired daily prayer does not come easily; it requires actual work. And what is that work? It is the work of preparing,[274] softening, and opening one's heart on a daily basis in order to be fully present and receptive to the Divine Presence in our lives at any given moment. Rather than prayer flowing from a sense of Divine intimacy and inspiration, the inspiration and intimacy follow from the regular act of prayer.

The above psycho-behavioral insight, that our feelings can follow from our actions, has multiple implications. We need not be slaves to our erratic emotional states. We can make our emotions work for us rather than helplessly following their unpredictable and often self-centered lead. If we want to live a certain lifestyle, or according to a certain set of values, then we must actually perform those actions that embody and express those truths, which, in turn, can generate corresponding feelings[275] and inspiration.[276]

All of this, and more, is alluded to in the Hebrew word for deed, *maaseh*, which is related to the word *me'asin*,[277] meaning to compel. This reveals a common thread in Jewish thought—that many of the most fulfilling, impactful, and important things for us to do in this world are not necessarily those that come naturally. To elevate our actions and awareness in light of the Divine, according to Torah, takes effort. Ultimately, we must choose to compel ourselves to act in accord with our highest values and ideals.

Otherwise, if left to their own devices, our emotions and appetites are bound to lead us astray.

Ultimately, inspiration and emotions *are* important, but they are also fleeting. Sometimes we are motivated, but often we are not. When we establish a regular routine, we develop a "second-nature" that enables our chosen actions to endure despite the changing weather patterns of our emotions.

So don't just follow your heart and wait until you feel like doing something important; that may never happen. Instead, follow the timeless Jewish wisdom expressed by Nike's trademark slogan, "Just Do It!"; the feelings will follow like ripples in a pond after a stone has been tossed into its depths.

The Big Idea

Don't wait for inspiration to strike. Just do what's right, and the inspiration will follow.

CHAPTER 22 | ACTION

It Happened Once

A CHASID ONCE TURNED TO his Rebbe, R. Schneur Zalman of Liadi, known as the Alter Rebbe, for a private audience, where he lamented that his religious observance felt mechanical and lacking in passion and inspiration.

The Alter Rebbe responded to his predicament by sharing a novel interpretation of a famous Biblical episode.

In the fourth chapter of the second book of Kings, we read of the miracle of the cruse of oil performed by the prophet Elisha. An impoverished widow sought the help of Elisha, crying that her debtors were about to take her two children as slaves, and all she possessed was a single cruse of oil. The prophet told her to borrow as many empty vessels as possible and fill them with oil from her cruse. Miraculously, the oil kept flowing as long as there were vessels to receive it.

The Alter Rebbe explained the deeper significance of the widow's quandary and Elisha's advice, interpreting the story in a psycho-spiritual manner that spoke to the Chasid directly:

The woman *(ishah)* is analogous to the innate Divine flame of the soul[278] *(eish)*, which constantly yearns to express its love for G-d (represented here by Elisha the prophet).

A woman, the wife of one of the prophets, cried out to Elisha—The soul calls out to G-d: *My husband, your servant, has died*—my service of You is lifeless, devoid of inspiration. I yearn to fill my deeds with passion and meaning. *...And the creditor has come to take my two sons as slaves*—but my base inclinations are monopolizing my emotions. They want me to worship the material and revere the temporal, clouding my vision of Your eternal truth. *Elisha responded: What do you have in your home?*—G-d replies, "What part of your soul can you still access?" *She answered: Your maidservant has nothing in the house,* *save a small cruse of oil*—nothing but its pristine essence, whose inner flame and core remains forever unsullied by the mundanities of life.

Said [Elisha]: Borrow vessels from your neighbors; empty vessels, only that they not be few—Act. Continue to do positive and G-dly deeds, even if they seem "borrowed" and empty to you. Remember, deeds are vessels, ready recipients for Divine light and connection.

...And pour [of your oil] into these vessels—the more vessels you acquire, the more your "oil" will flow from its source and fill your actions with meaning and depth.

Without the vessel of deed, there is nothing to ignite the oil of inspiration. Ultimately, if you persist in doing what you know to be true and right, your Divine essence will fill your every "empty vessel."

The Chasid left with renewed vigor and insight, rededicating himself to the holy vessels his actions would create.

Antisemitism

sinah

שנאה

CHAPTER 23 | ANTISEMITISM

THE MESORAH OF ANTISEMITISM

ANTISEMITISM IS THE GREATEST conundrum at the heart of Jewish existence. Why have we been so hated by the family of nations? Much ink has been spilled trying to explain what antisemitism is, what causes it, and why, whenever it looks like things are getting better, it rears its ugly head again.

But what does Judaism itself have to say about it?

The Talmud[279] says that Mount Sinai, the place where the Torah was given, was named so because it initiated the nations' hatred, *sinah*, of Jews. At Sinai, the Jewish nation was tasked with the sacred duty to be *a kingdom of priests*[280] and to serve as beacons of morality and justice to the world.

As a consequence of accepting this mandate to be *a light unto the nations*,[281] the Jewish people became the subject of the oldest and most persistent hatred in history.

In the Book of Numbers,[282] G-d instructs Moses to confront the Midianites in order to *avenge the vengeance of the Children of Israel*.

The Midrash[283] relates that Moses questioned G-d: "In truth, the vengeance is Yours [not ours]. For if we had been uncircumcised or worshipped the stars or had denied the commandments, they would not have persecuted us. They have done so only because of the Torah and commandments that You have given."

Historically, some enemies of the Jewish people have seen this dynamic of Jewish particularism as a nuisance, others, as an existential threat. In the Book of Esther,[284] Haman tries to bribe King Ahasuerus with ten thousand talents of silver for permission to rid his kingdom of Jews, but Ahasuerus says: *The money is given to you, as is the nation, to do with as you please.*

To explain this interaction, the Talmud[285] describes two types of antisemites. The first is Ahasuerus, the mild antisemite who sees the Jewish people as a mound—an annoying anomaly and eyesore that stands out and refuses to blend in. Sociologists refer to this type of xenophobia as "the dislike for the unlike."

The second is Haman, the ardent antisemite who views the Jew as a ditch—a moral conscience that exposes an existential hole and emptiness in the heart of the antisemite. The owner of the mound tells the owner of the ditch "relieve me of my mound and be rid of your ditch; I ask for no payment in return."

Hitler, one of the most notorious antisemites who ever lived, summed up this sentiment chillingly in a private conversation with his confidant, Hermann Rauschning: "The struggle for world domination is between me and the Jews. All else is meaningless. The Jews have inflicted two wounds on the world: Circumcision for the body and conscience for the soul. I come to free mankind from their shackles."[286]

Elsewhere he elaborated further, "Providence has ordained that I should be the greatest liberator of humanity. I am freeing man from the restraints of an intelligence that has taken charge, from the dirty and degrading self-mortification of a false vision called conscience and morality, and from the demands of a freedom and independence that only a very few can bear."[287]

Historically, there have been two contradictory reactions to the Jewish people, Judeophobia—frustration and hatred directed at the voice of conscience Jews represent—or, on the other extreme, Judeophilia—admiration and the desire to learn from and emulate the Jewish people. This has created an irrational aura of simultaneous fear/suspicion and awe/infatuation around the Jewish people in the eyes of the world.

Ultimately, Judaism is a distinction that Jews cannot hide from.

History has demonstrated that assimilation doesn't help prevent antisemitism, as evidenced in the fate of twentieth-century German Jewry, who had achieved an extraordinary level of integration into the highest echelons of society. In fact, assimilation serves only to advance the cause of the antisemite in ridding the world of its moral torchbearers.

Antisemitism will rear its ugly head whether Jews choose to hide their Judaism or openly embrace it. If we choose the latter—thereby owning up to our role as a light unto the nations—we fulfill our destiny to transform the moral landscape of civilization.

Alluding to the transformative potential of the Jewish mandate, John Adams,[288] second president of the United States, writes: "I will insist the Hebrews have [contributed] more to civilize men than any other nation. If I was an atheist and believed in blind eternal fate, I should still believe that fate had ordained the Jews to be the most essential instrument for civilizing the nations...They have given religion to three-quarters of the globe and have influenced the affairs of mankind more, and more happily, than any other nation, ancient or modern."

Noted Christian historian Paul Johnson[289] put it this way: "All the great conceptual discoveries of the human intellect seem obvious and inescapable once they had been revealed, but it requires a special genius to formulate them for the first time. The Jews had this gift. To them we owe the idea of equality before the law, both Divine and human; of the sanctity of life and the dignity of human person; of the individual conscience and so a personal redemption; of collective conscience and so of social responsibility; of peace as an abstract ideal and love as the foundation of justice, and many other items that constitute the basic moral furniture of the human mind. Without Jews, it [the world] might have been a much emptier place."

Commenting further on the unique role and presence of the Jews in the development of human society, R. Avraham Yitzchak Kook pointed out that all of the great civilizations throughout time, such as Egypt, Greece, Persia, and Rome, appeared on the stage of history, made their contribution, said their piece, and moved on. The Jewish people, however, emerged onto the stage of ancient history and are still standing here, stuttering—for we have yet to clearly articulate the message that we are here to say.

Instead of going underground to hide our Jewish identity, as some tend to do during times of persecution, let us stand up and proudly proclaim to the world the message that we were summoned at Sinai to deliver.

The Big Idea

Antisemitism is fueled not by the hatred of Jews, but by the message and morality of Judaism. Assimilation, then, is part of the problem, not the solution.

CHAPTER 23 | ANTISEMITISM

It Happened Once

ON THE EVENING OF March 4, 1962, the Young Leadership Cabinet of the UJA (United Jewish Appeal) visited the Lubavitcher Rebbe to receive guidance before traveling to Poland.

What follows is an excerpt from their exchange that evening.

Young Jewish leadership: "We are going on a pilgrimage to commemorate the Warsaw Ghetto uprising, going to Warsaw and Auschwitz. As we get deeper and deeper into the [assigned preparatory] readings, we're all having many problems with the questions that the Holocaust and Auschwitz bring.... What did the whole thing mean?"

The Rebbe: "...If history teaches us something that we must not repeat or must emulate, the best lesson can be taken from the destruction of the Second Temple. We witnessed something so terrible, it must bring every Jew to become more identified with his Jewishness...every one of us has an obligation to fight Hitler, [which] can be done by letting that which Hitler had in mind to annihilate, not only continue but grow bigger and on a deeper scale. Hitler was not interested so much in annihilating the body of Jewishness as he was interested in annihilating the spirit. [He decreed that the spiritual and moral ideas that the Jewish people embody] must not infect the German people, the Russian people, or the Polish people...

"If you influence a Jew not to become assimilated but to profess his Jewishness, his pride and inspiration and joy, this is defeating Hitlerism. If someone does his best in his personal life to be Jewish [so that] everyone sees that in the street he is a Jew, that his home is a Jewish home, that he is proud, and that it is not a burden but his pride, his life defeats the idea of Hitlerism.

"When you go to Auschwitz, you must profess there that Auschwitz cannot happen again. You can assure it by becoming a living example of a living Jew."[290]

Humanity *adam*

אדם

CHAPTER 24 | HUMANITY

BETWEEN HEAVEN AND EARTH

As HUMAN BEINGS, WE often find ourselves caught between competing worldviews, inner drives, and value systems. And when we do carve out a moment to reflect on who we are and why we do the things we do, we can be left in a state of doubt and confusion, confronted by gnawing questions like:

Why is it so difficult to align my day-to-day behavior with my higher ideals? How is it that I can so easily identify and relate to both the hedonistic and the holy?

Who am I really? An egocentric animal or an altruistic angel?

Unfortunately, this existential quagmire is all too common and relatable. Some might even call it the human condition. But, in fact, this whole way of thinking is based on a very particular worldview that seeks to one-dimensionalize life, reducing everything into black and white, good vs. bad, etc. If one is spiritual, they may not be self-concerned; if one is driven by physical appetites, they may not be spiritually evolved. This is a hyper-dualistic way of viewing the world and relating to the self that is based on a rigid paradigm of dichotomous mutual exclusivity.

In Jewish thought, however, humans are not seen as monolithic caricatures, but as multifaceted beings, comprised of both self-serving animalistic desires as well as self-transcendent angelic potentials. According to the Torah, this inner tension and conflict is an essential part of the human experience. In fact, we learn at the beginning of

Genesis[291] that man's very creation came about through the fusion of two such opposites: *G-d formed man of dust from the earth*—the earthly, *and He blew into his nostrils a breath of life"*—the heavenly. The human is therefore quite literally a fusion of heaven and earth.[292]

The Hebrew word for man, *adam*, evocatively expresses this dichotomy. For example, the word *adam* is related both to the word *adamah*, earth, and the word *domeh*, likeness, as used in the phrase *adameh la'elyon*, heaven-like,[293] teaching us that the human being can either resemble its earthly origins or reflect its Divine design.

Furthermore, this existential duality can be found in the composition of the word *adam* itself. *Alef*, the first letter of the word *adam*, has a numerical value of one, alluding to the primordial oneness and unity of G-d. The second two letters spell the word *dam*, which means blood, the physical lifeforce and vitality[294] of the human being.[295] Thus, the Torah's conception of the human condition is encoded into the very name given to humanity.

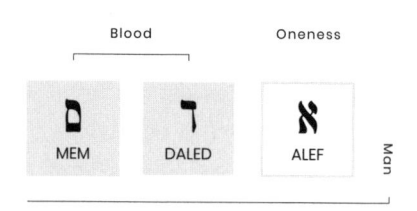

R. Joseph Ber Soloveitchik points out[296] that there are two seemingly contradictory accounts in Genesis for the creation of man. In the first version, Adam is created in the Divine image and summoned to exercise mastery, to *fill the earth and conquer it*. In the second version, Adam is created from the dust of the earth and brought to life by the breath of G-d, and his calling is *to cultivate the garden and keep it*.

This, R. Soloveitchik concludes, is not a glaring contradiction between competing textual traditions, as Biblical critics would assert; rather, it is a meaningful juxtaposition of archetypes that express the inherent contradiction within the nature of humanity. "The first Adam is Majestic Man—aggressive, bold, and victory-minded. His motto is success—to harness and dominate the elemental natural forces and to put them at his disposal. The second Adam is Covenantal Man. His goal is not success but redemption. He seeks not control over his environment but control over himself; not to confront and defeat mute nature, but to allow himself to be confronted and defeated by a Higher and Truer Being. Not to advance to the outer reaches of his universe, but to retreat to its center."

Commenting on R. Soloveitchik's teaching, David Brooks[297] introduces the distinction between resume virtues and eulogy virtues. "Resume virtues consist of the skills you bring to the marketplace. Eulogy virtues are the ones that are mentioned in the eulogy, which are deeper: Who are you in your depth? What is the nature of your relationships? Are you kind, loving, dependable, honest, consistent? Most of us would say that eulogy virtues are the most important. And yet, in many cases, are they the ones that we think about most?

"The tricky thing about these two sides of our nature is that they work by different logics. The external logic is an economic logic: input leads to output, risk leads to reward. The internal side of our nature is a moral logic and often an inverse logic. You have to give to receive. You have to surrender to something outside yourself to gain strength within yourself. You have to conquer desire in order to get what you want. In order to fulfil yourself, you have to forget yourself. In order to find yourself, you have to lose yourself."

In the book of *Tanya*,[298] R. Schneur Zalman of Liadi explains that man's dual impulses come from two different souls. These souls operate by inverse and opposite drives; their gravitational pull could not be more different. For the animal soul, the pull and natural default direction is earth-bound, towards that which is indulgent and self-centered; for the G-dly soul, its drive is heaven-bound, towards the transcendent and other-centered. The animal soul is the seat of the ego and the source of one's base desires, whereas the G-dly soul seeks only to cleave to G-d and occupy itself with selfless and loving acts of goodness.

R. Schneur Zalman compares this psycho-spiritual dynamic to a "battle between two kings, both seeking to dominate the same city."[299] This "city"[300] is understood as referring to a person's inner kingdom, so to speak, which is populated by one's thoughts, words, and deeds. Only one king can rule at a time, but which will it be? Ultimately, we ourselves decide who controls the "keys" to the palace of our mind. By carefully choosing the focus and direction of our thoughts, words, and deeds, we are able to consciously determine which side of ourselves we want to bolster and become.

Margaret Thatcher's father once told her as a child: "Watch your thoughts for they become your words. Watch your words for they become your actions. Watch your actions for they become your habits. Watch your habits for they become your character. And watch your character for it becomes your destiny."

In sum, we are each comprised of both heaven and earth; whom we choose to become is completely in our hands.

The Big Idea

We are not monolithic but multifaceted beings, in constant struggle with conflicting drives and impulses. It is up to us to choose which side of ourselves we will bolster and become at each and every moment.

It Happened Once

A WISE OLD MAN TEACHES his grandson about life:

"A fight is going on inside me," he says to the boy.

"It is a terrible fight, and it is between two wolves. One is evil; he is anger, envy, sorrow, regret, greed, arrogance, self-pity, guilt, resentment, inferiority, lies, false pride, superiority, and ego.

"The other is good; he is joy, peace, love, hope, serenity, humility, kindness, benevolence, empathy, generosity, truth, compassion, and faith. The same fight is going on inside you—and inside every other person, too."

The grandson thinks about it for a minute and then asks: "Which wolf will win?"

The old man replies, "The one that you feed."

דיבור

dibbur   Speech

CHAPTER 25 | SPEECH

FROM THOUGHTS TO THINGS

EVERYONE HAS EXPERIENCED THE power of words in one way or another: A kind word that soothes a broken heart, an authentic compliment that inspires confidence and motivates success, or a disparaging word that crushes the spirit, potentially leaving life-long scars.

Words can harm or heal, but not just because of the thoughts they trigger.

Judaism teaches that a spoken word holds tremendous power. According to the Torah, the world itself was "spoken" into being by G-d,[301] making reality a kind of cosmic prayer or poem, composed of the Divine word.

In Chasidic thought, once a concept has been articulated verbally, it is drawn further down into existence and, thus, can affect other people beyond the speaker, even at the other end of the world.[302] Perhaps this is why Newton and Liebniz are both independently credited with inventing calculus at the same time.

When R. DovBer, the Maggid of Mezritch, would conceive of a new Torah concept, he would make a point of speaking it audibly, even if those present could not understand it. Why? Because speech gives sound to ideas and clothes them in subtle form and matter, which adds a physical dimension to the ethereal fruits of the mind. Thus, through verbalizing the idea, the Maggid would draw it down into the world.[303]

Interestingly, the Hebrew word for speech, *dibbur*, is etymologically

PEOPLE OF THE WORD

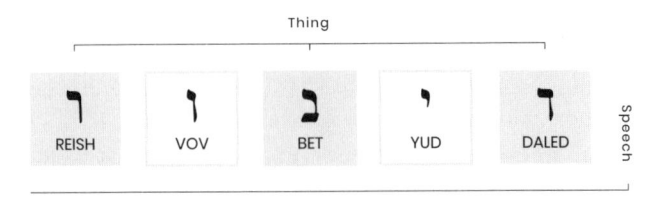

```
              ┌─────────── Thing ───────────┐
            ר        ו        ב        י        ד        ס
                                                         p
          REISH     VOV      BET      YUD    DALED       e
                                                         e
                                                         c
                                                         h
```

linked to the word *davar*, which means thing. That's because, once articulated, a word takes on a life of its own and becomes a tangible reality, a *thing* that exists in dimension, form, and resonance.

The notion that words are the medium through which ideas become things is rooted in centuries of Kabbalistic teaching and based on a metaphysical understanding of the beginning of the Torah in which, as mentioned, G-d speaks the world into being. Based on this understanding, the Sages developed and continuously refined a heightened sensitivity to the power of speech that runs through every facet of Jewish thought and practice, including liturgy, the binding nature of oaths, and the spiritual repercussions of gossip.

For instance, the Talmud[304] teaches: "Gossip slays three. The speaker, the listener, and the person being spoken about." We can easily understand why the ones speaking and listening to gossip are punished, but why is the one about whom gossip was spoken negatively impacted? The answer, according to Chasidic teaching, is that the gossip spoken about them draws forth the negative traits that are within them.[305]

If the gossip would have remained unsaid, the negative trait may have remained dormant within the person and never have been aroused or expressed. Conversely, when we speak positively about a person, we draw forth their positive traits from a state of potential into articulated reality.

Such is the power of the spoken word to affect others on both existential and energetic levels.

Along these lines, the Torah instructs us not to curse a deaf person,[306] even though he cannot hear the curse. This prohibition is not just about exhibiting refined and moral behavior as an end in itself, but, as the following story vividly illustrates, about the actual impact of the spoken word upon its subject even when it goes unheard.[307]

Once, two men had a quarrel while in the Baal Shem Tov's

synagogue, leading one man to shout at the other that he would "tear him to pieces like a fish."

Hearing this, the Baal Shem Tov told his pupils to gather round, hold hands, and stand near him with their eyes closed. Then he placed his holy hands on the shoulders of the two disciples next to him. Suddenly, the disciples began shouting in great terror: They had seen that fellow actually dismembering his disputant, just as he had said.

Every word has an effect—either in physical form or on a spiritual plane that can be perceived only with higher and more refined senses. This presents us with a profound amount of both power and responsibility in respect to the way we use our words. Are we seeking to build or destroy, to uplift or put down, to unify or divide, to bring peace or to sow conflict? For, truly, these are the actual stakes and potentials that exist within each and every word we speak.

In sum, beyond how words make people think or feel on intellectual or emotional levels, there is also an inherent power and potency to them, which, once articulated, endows them with a life of their own. As the famous American poet Emily Dickinson[308] once wrote:

A word is dead when it is said
   Some say—
I say it just begins to live
   That day.

The Big Idea

Words are not just tools of communication; they are instruments of creation.

It Happened Once

On June 10, 1982, Israeli Staff Sergeant Zachary Baumel and his unit were attacked by the Syrian military while on a mission in Lebanon, and a bloody battle ensued, leaving twenty Israeli soldiers dead and more than thirty wounded. Zachary and two of his fellow soldiers were officially declared missing.

Zachary's remains were missing until 2019, when they were finally recovered by the Russian government and returned to Israel for a proper Jewish burial on Mount Herzl.

As recounted by Zachary's sister Osna to Chief Rabbi of Tzfat R. Shmuel Eliyahu,[309] there was more to this story than meets the eye. At the funeral, Osna went over to Prime Minister Benjamin Netanyahu to thank him for retrieving her brother's remains. She told him that for many years, her family was upset with him for not doing enough to recover Zachary's body and would voice their grievances regularly. She continued, "One day, we decided as a family to stop speaking negatively about you and instead try to view you more favorably. We realized that there were things we didn't know; that the situation was complex. And that for a country to request a favor from another country, a lot of political maneuvering is required, and surely there were greater issues on the national agenda than the retrieval of Zachary's body."

Netanyahu was visibly shaken. He told her that Israel had been instrumental in helping Russia avoid a terrorist attack. Knowing that the day would come when the Russians would repay the favor, he sat with his cabinet and made a list of fifty possible things that were important to Israel from a strategic point of view. They then condensed the list to three items. Needless to say, Zachary's remains were not on the list.

When the time came, Netanyahu sat down with Russian President Vladimir Putin. When Netanyahu was asked how Russia could repay

Israel, despite having the list of three things in hand, inexplicably, the cause of Zachary Baumel kept coming to mind.

He told Putin about Zachary, and the surprised president asked why something that happened so long ago mattered so much to Israel.

Netanyahu replied, "To the Jewish people, proper burial is of great importance." Putin replied that if it was that important, he would make sure it was done, and moreover, moved by the depth of care that the Jewish people have for each other, he offered Israel another favor, saying this one was "on him."

This story highlights the power of speech. Just as *lashon hara* draws forth the negative traits within others, even if they are not present to hear them spoken, so too (and even more so), when positive words are spoken, the words themselves, even if unheard by the subject, manifest and reveal their inner good qualities.

Time

rega רגע

CHAPTER 26 | TIME

SEIZE THE MOMENT

SOME VIEW TIME AS a merciless force that forever marches forward, leaving our lives in its wake. Like a conveyor belt that never stops, every moment moves us closer to our end. This understanding of time can be deeply unsettling. In the words of the poet William Carlos Williams: "Time is a storm in which we are all lost."

But is this the only way to view time—as a rapidly dwindling and limited resource that we must hoard or frivolously spend before it's all gone? Or might there be another way to view time—one that doesn't necessarily lead to feelings of scarcity, urgency, and anxiety?

Whereas the English word moment comes from the Latin word *momentum*, implying the relentless march of time, the Hebrew version of the same word, *rega*, stems from the word *ragua*, a state of calm or rest.

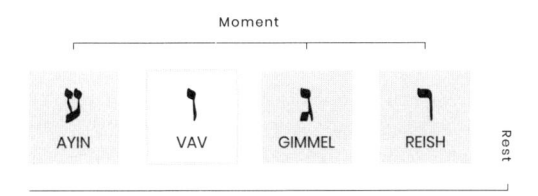

	Moment			
ע	ו	ג	ר	Rest
AYIN	VAV	GIMMEL	REISH	

It's not that in Judaism time stops—time doesn't stop for anyone—instead, time itself consists of a sequence of stops. In other words, you are not on the conveyor belt of time; rather, the conveyor belt is passing before you, delivering new moments in rapid succession for

201

you to enter and inhabit. This is suggested in the Biblical phrase for the process of aging, *ba bayamim*,[310] which literally means entering one's days.

Rashi[311] suggests that the root of the word *r'g'a* (moment) means to be folded like an accordion. Time is thus comprised of a sequence of moments tightly packed together. We can choose to unfold these moments, seeing each one for the unique opportunity it represents; or we can leave time folded up, allowing the unrepeatable moments to pass by unnoticed and unappreciated. This is our choice to make.

The Previous Lubavitcher Rebbe, R. Yosef Yitzchak Schneersohn, writes[312]: "Whether time is long or short is completely up to us. Sometimes many hours can pass in moments, and other times a few hours can seem like a very long time."

This empowering approach to time focuses our attention on the crystalline present rather than on the blur of time's passage, and it is expressed in the many Biblical words that refer to time.

For instance, the word *eit*—the most common Biblical reference to time—is related to the word *atah*, now; not a movement or progression, but a particular point and "stop" in time.

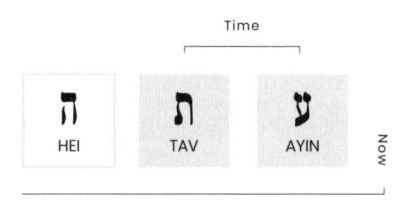

ה	ת	ע
HEI	TAV	AYIN

Time: ה ת | Now: ע

The word *zman*, the Hebrew word for time, is related to the word *hazmanah*—an invitation. Time itself is a kind of invitation,

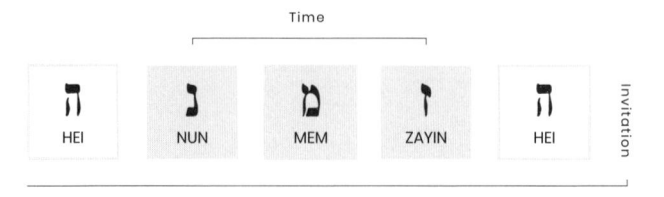

ה	נ	מ	ז	ה
HEI	NUN	MEM	ZAYIN	HEI

Time: ה נ מ ז | Invitation: ה

with each moment calling out to us, inviting us to take advantage of the opportunity it represents. *Zman* is also an acronym for *zeh man*—what is this? At face value, every moment appears the same;

yet this word for time begs us to unfold each moment and seek out its singular significance.

Similarly, the word *shaah*, an hour, also means to turn towards or to pay attention to something, as in *G-d shaah—paid attention to Abel and his gift*.[313]

This view of time as a series of distinct moments rather than an uninterrupted current or passage is based on Judaism's perspective on existence itself.

Judaism does not view creation as a one-off episode that, once put in motion, continues to exist on its own; rather, creation is a miraculous event that requires constant renewal in order to continue to exist. This is alluded to in our daily prayers, where in the blessing preceding the *Shema*, we say: "Who, in His goodness, renews the works of creation every day, *constantly*."

Why does creation require constant renewal? This is because, unlike a craftsman, who merely fashions an item out of existing materials—materials that existed before his interference with them and continue to exist after he finishes reshaping them—the act of creation entails bringing matter into existence *ex nihilo*, generating something from absolutely nothing.

Philosophically speaking, the necessity of a creative force itself indicates that the natural state of existence is a state of nothingness, and like everything that runs contrary to its natural state, creation thus requires a constant and active force to renew it at every moment. For if the creative force would stop creating for even one moment, all of creation would immediately revert to its natural state of nothingness.[314]

From this perspective, as similar as every moment looks to the one that preceded it, it is not part of a continuum at all. Rather, each moment is an entirely new reality that is being created anew. And because, as the Talmud[315] teaches, "G-d doesn't create anything without purpose," every moment has its own unique objective and opportunity that never existed before and will never be available again.

It is therefore our task, as messengers of G-d in this world, to bring that purpose to fruition by utilizing the present moment to fulfill its raison d'être.

This cinematic view of time as a sequence of stills that play out one after the other changes the way we ought to utilize our time.

The *Zohar*[316] interprets the verse,[317] *Abraham was old, coming with days* to mean that "Abraham brought all of his days with him." According to this view of time, days are "collectibles," each with its own distinct calling and value. Abraham's success in distinguishing all of his days derived from his ability to fully enter into the unique potential of every moment.

To quote *Hayom Yom*[318]: "Time must be guarded... Every bit of time, every day that passes, is not just a day but a life's concern..."

Every person is given an allotted number of days to live.[319] Our task is to optimize them by constantly asking ourselves, "What does G-d want from me at this moment?"

The Talmud[320] relates that when R. Yochanan ben Zakai lay on his deathbed, he wept. When his disciples inquired why he was crying, R. Yochanan replied: "I see two paths before me...and I do not know down which path they will lead me. Should I not weep?"

This episode evokes the question,[321] why did R. Yochanan wait until he lay upon his deathbed to question the trajectory of his life? Shouldn't a person always reflect on their life's direction?

One of the explanations[322] is that R. Yochanan was too absorbed in utilizing each moment of his life to think about his personal standing and the sum of his actions—i.e., down which path he was headed. Instead of constantly asking himself, "Where am I headed?" R. Yochanan asked, "What does G-d want from me at this moment?" Only when his time had come did he understand that G-d wanted him to spend those last moments to make a reckoning of his life achievements, which is why it was only then that he looked back upon his life as a whole.

While this may be an unreasonably high bar for the average person to set for themselves, it does provide perspective into how we might choose to live more in the moment and to heed its call.

Ultimately, there are two ways to experience time. One can either be completely preoccupied with the past or the future, without paying attention to the present moment; or he can live completely in the present moment as if nothing else exists. Living in the past or future is often regret- or anxiety-inducing, as the rebuke in Deuteronomy describes,[323] *In the morning you shall say, "If only it were evening!" And in the evening you shall say, "If only it were morning!"* Living in the moment, on the other hand, as the Hebrew word *rega* suggests, is grounding and calming.

However, it is important to point out that the mystical Jewish idea of living in the moment differs radically from the version of this idea put forward by pop psychology. In the Jewish view, living in the moment is not just a way to free ourselves from the regrets of the past or from worries about the future by temporarily disconnecting from reality and choosing not to think about it. It's not a glorified state of mindlessness; instead, *it is the conscientious practice of mindfulness*. To live in the moment is to be eminently aware of and connected to the Divine energy and purpose unique to each moment.

This idea is beautifully expressed by R. Schneur Zalman of Liadi in the *Tanya*[324]: "Every moment brings with it a new and unique lifeforce emanating from the spiritual cosmos, leaving the energy of the previous moment to return to its source and carry up with it all of the good deeds and Torah study that were accomplished in it."

By shifting our mindset from thinking about how quickly time is running out and focusing instead on the sui generis opportunity embedded within each moment, we discover that we are not helpless victims drowning in the raging rapids of a fleeting life; rather, we are sacred musicians playing the song of our soul on the Divine accordion of time.

The Big Idea

In Jewish thought, a life is not measured by jubilees, decades, years, months, or even days, but by how deeply and fully each moment is utilized.

It Happened Once

R. Shlomo ben Avraham ibn Aderet, known as Rashba, was considered the leader of Spanish Jewry during his time. He served as rabbi of the main synagogue of Barcelona for fifty years. Additionally, his reputation as an outstanding rabbinic authority was world renowned, and people from all over the world sent him questions regarding Jewish life, Torah, and Jewish law.

In addition to his extensive halachic knowledge, Rashba was a highly sought-after doctor. Jews and non-Jews alike traveled from all over Spain to see him. He was also the royal physician, which often required him to travel to the palace and remain there for many hours.

As if this wasn't taxing enough, Rashba was the head of a *yeshivah* and gave three Torah lectures to his students every day, which required much study and preparation on his part.

And yet, he managed to take a walk every day for health and relaxation!

How did he do it? How did he manage his time? What was the secret?

During a talk he gave in 1970, the Lubavitcher Rebbe explained, "There is a concept called 'success in time.' We cannot make our days longer, nor can we add additional hours to our nights. But we can maximize our usage of time by regarding each segment of time as a world of its own.

"When we devote a portion of time—whether it is an hour, a day, or a minute—to a certain task, we should be totally invested in what we are doing, as if there exists nothing else in the world.

"You must of course be aware of the differences between things of greater and lesser importance, between means and ends, between journeys and destinations. But whatever it is you are involved in, be fully invested there."[325]

olam עולם

Reality

CHAPTER 27 | REALITY

G-D'S HIDING PLACE

THE WORD WORLD IS an Old English composite of two separate words, *wer old*, meaning "the age of man." The Hebrew word for world, *olam*, on the other hand, means hidden (*helem*),[326] alluding to G-d's concealment in creation.

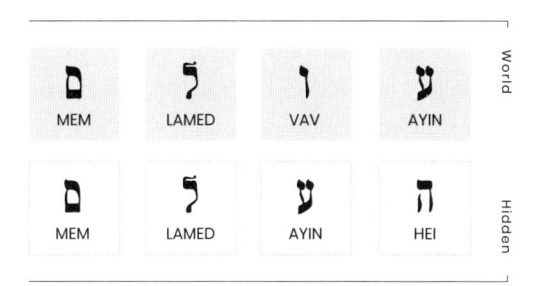

מ	ל	ו	ע	World
MEM	LAMED	VAV	AYIN	
מ	ל	ע	ה	Hidden
MEM	LAMED	AYIN	HEI	

The former expresses an anthropocentric worldview, defining the world by its relationship to humanity; the latter proposes a theocentric worldview, defining the world based on its relationship to G-d.

From the Jewish perspective, the world is not just a mere stage for human history but the theater wherein the Divine mystery unfolds.[327]

According to Jewish mysticism, physical reality as we know it is an illusion.[328] Matter is not mere material; everything is alive and in resonance, connected through a vibrating web of energy. Our normative perception of material reality as inert does not reflect its true nature and origin.

Kabbalah[329] describes the process of creation as a series of curtains

209

that block our view of the unifying infinite light that permeates the universe. Consequently, instead of experiencing the singular G-dly force that animates all of existence, we see billions of disparate parts that lack any revealed cohesion or connection. This appearance of fragmentation was intentionally crafted by Divine design. G-d created the world in just such a way because He wants us to partner with Him by pulling back the curtains of deception and opening the doors of perception in order to discover His Infinite Presence here on earth, revealing the underlying oneness within all.[330]

Abraham was the first[331] to pierce the veil of existence,[332] to question the origins of the universe, and ultimately to discover the one true G-d. In the book of Genesis, before Abraham promoted G-d's presence in the world, G-d is referred to as, *the G-d of the heavens*,[333] because people did not yet recognize the Divine author of creation. Only after Abraham promulgated the idea that the world is, in essence, a manifestation of G-d in disguise is G-d called[334] *the G-d of the heavens and the earth*.[335]

The Talmud[336] teaches that, on Friday evening, whoever recites the verses describing the completion of creation and how G-d "rested" on Shabbat is considered to have partnered with G-d in the creation of the universe. Creation is no small feat! How does one become a collaborating partner in creation by merely reciting a few verses?

From the Jewish point of view, creation is incomplete and has not fulfilled its purpose until mankind recognizes G-d's creative role and continued presence in the world. Our conscious acknowledgment that the world was created by G-d is therefore the realization of its intended purpose. Such intentional acknowledgment on our part turns us into full-fledged partners in creation.[337]

Interestingly, when the *Shema* is written in Torah, *tefillin*, and *mezuzah* scrolls, it includes two enlarged letters, *ayin* and *dalet*. These two letters graphically stand out from the others, forming a seventh word, *eid* (witness).[338] This hidden word, revealed through the hand of the scribe for the eyes of the reader and the ears of the reciter, highlights the testimonial role we play in creation when we recite the *Shema*.

Simply put: Creation is a game of hide and seek, wherein G-d's Presence and Providence are hidden within the world. The obfuscation of His presence was necessary in order to create the prime conditions within which free will could exist and express itself. This deliberate concealment makes sense when one considers the fact that if reality's true G-dly nature was obvious to all, we would be overwhelmed by His presence and lose all sense of agency. Only because G-d's presence is hidden from us can we *choose* to see this world as either mundane or miraculous, secular or sacred.

Accordingly, much of Jewish practice is designed to help us encounter and acknowledge the Divine Presence in this world. For example, Jews are instructed to recite a blessing over food before eating in order to recognize that what they are about to enjoy is from G-d. The blessing recited over a glass of water, for example, is "Blessed are You, L-rd, our G-d, King of the universe, by Whose word everything came into being."[339] If said with mindful intention, the person reciting this blessing recognizes in the simple glass of water that the entire universe is created by G-d. Similar to William Blake's poetic dictum, to "see a world in a grain of sand," our Sages direct us to find G-d in a glass of water.

Judaism teaches that our mission in life is to acknowledge G-d's presence everywhere and in everything, as the verse states,[340] *In all your ways, know Him.*

Like a puzzle composed of seemingly disparate pieces, this world can often seem disjointed and without purpose. Mankind's job is to put the pieces of life's puzzle together, revealing the bigger picture and Divine design at the heart of existence.

This is the deeper meaning behind Judaism's most essential prayer, the *Shema*: *Hear O Israel, the L-rd, our G-d, the L-rd is one.*[341] This doesn't mean that G-d is the one power *above* all; rather, it means that G-d is the singular power *within* all![342]

It is this underlying unity that the multiplicity of the world was designed to conceal. Our G-d-given task is thus to see through the world's veneer of separation and reveal the interconnection and oneness within all of creation.

It Happened Once

ONCE, THE SON OF R. DovBer, the Maggid of Mezritch, came running to him in tears. The Maggid comforted him and asked why he was crying.

The child began to explain that he had been playing a game of hide-and-seek with his friends. He and all his friends were hiding. They remained in their hiding places for a long time, thinking that they had hidden well, and that the person whose turn it was to seek was unable to find them. But soon they grew tired of waiting. They came out of their hiding places and discovered that they had all been wrong. The one whose turn it was to look for them was not even there. He had played a trick on them! After they went into their hiding places, he went home instead of searching for them.

When the Maggid heard this story, he, too, began to cry. When his son asked why he was crying, the Maggid replied that G-d has the same complaint: "It is written,[343] *You are a G-d Who hides*. G-d says, 'I hide Myself from you, but the purpose of My hiding is only so that you should come and search for Me. But sometimes, My children, as a result of your preoccupation with material existence, you stop searching, forgetting the very purpose of creation...'"[344]

The Big Idea

G-d created this world as His hiding place. The purpose of humankind is to "blow His cover," revealing His infinite presence within all.

Still Life
domem

דומם

CHAPTER 28 | STILL LIFE

STILL LIFE WITH G-D

R EALITY IS NOT ALL that it seems.
Put a pebble under a powerful microscope, and you will witness a world alive and buzzing with energy. Scientific observation demonstrates that any substance, when viewed at the atomic level, is comprised of 99.999999999% empty space.[345] This means that everything we see and touch is just projecting an illusion of solidity.

In fact, when we walk upon the ground, for instance, we're really walking on a shifting field of energy that only *feels* solid. Similarly, when we sit on a chair, we are actually sitting on energy, not "matter"—the energy of our body and the energy of the chair propel each other, keeping one from passing through the other. In either case, we don't fall through the ground, because energy keeps us suspended above it.

Hundreds of years before science discovered the anatomy of an atom and understood that matter is mostly comprised of energy, Jewish mystical teachings described the physical substance of reality as an expression of Divine energy.

Commenting on the verse[346]: *G-d, forever Your word stands fixed in the heavens*, the Baal Shem Tov taught: The words and letters that G-d uttered during the Six Days of Creation stand fixed in the heavens, forever keeping them in existence. If these letters were to disappear for even a single moment, the heavens and earth would return to absolute nothingness as if they never existed.[347]

This same life force is present within everything, including so-called inanimate objects.

The word inanimate is derived from Latin and means "without life."

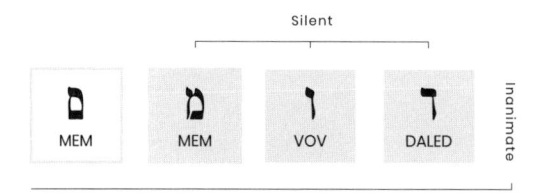

Silent

מ	מַ	ו	ד
MEM	MEM	VOV	DALED

Inanimate

In Hebrew, inanimate objects are referred to as *domem*, which means silent, implying that there is, in fact, life in them, even if that life force is not outwardly expressed or revealed in a perceptible way, such as through self-generated movement or sound.[348]

This philosophy, which considers all aspects of existence to be alive, has real-world ramifications. In fact, Judaism has a long history of promoting sensitivity and respect for all beings, from animal to vegetable to mineral, regardless of their capacity for intelligence or emotive expression.

A moving expression of this idea is found in the Biblical injunction: *You shall not ascend with steps upon My altar [rather build a ramp], so that your nakedness will not be uncovered upon it.*[349]

Rashi[350] explains, "[There was] no actual exposure of nakedness, for it is written, *And make for them linen pants*. Nonetheless, taking wide steps [on stairs] is close to [appears to be] exposing nakedness and therefore treats the stones in a humiliating manner..."

The inconvenience of a *kohen* made to climb a ramp instead of taking the more direct path up steps while fulfilling his sacred duty comes second to the dignity of a slab of "lifeless" stone.

A few more examples of Judaism's sensitivity towards the inorganic world should suffice to demonstrate this point:

On Shabbat, it is customary to cover the challah while saying *Kiddush* over the wine. This is so that the challah does not feel overlooked, because it too would have wanted the honor of *Kiddush* being said over it. In order not to "insult" the challah, we cover it while we bless the wine.[351]

Similarly, when a festival coincides with Shabbat, some people have the practice of singing the traditional Shabbat songs in a lowered voice, so as not to give Shabbat greater attention than the festival.[352]

It is important to point out that the Torah's basis and motive for advocating kindness and compassion towards all of creation is not fueled by simple self-interest or even the fear of our own delicate futures, i.e., "If we don't take care of the planet today, tomorrow it won't be there to take care of us." Or, in the case of human rights efforts, "If we don't campaign for the freedom of all, one day we might lose our own."

Rather, the Torah's concern is rooted in the fact that Judaism, as highlighted in Chasidic philosophy, maintains that there is a point of life, or "a spark of G-d," in every element of creation. That spark is an extension of the Creator and should therefore be treated accordingly.

The respect we give each other, and all of existence, is thus not utilitarian, for the benefit they can give us, but for the sake of the individual "soul" and unique purpose each being possesses, in and of themselves.

Ultimately, Judaism is a religion of spiritual sensitization to the immanence of the Divine within creation, engendering a heightened sense of respect for all lifeforms. This then becomes the basis for how we treat each other as well.

As Rashi[353] so eloquently points out: "Now, if regarding these stones (from the altar as mentioned above), which do not have the intelligence to object to their humiliation, the Torah says, *Do not treat them in a humiliating manner*, in the case of your fellow man, who was created in the image of your Creator and cares about his humiliation, how much more so must you treat him with respect!"

It Happened Once

AN EXCERPT FROM THE diary of the sixth Lubavitcher Rebbe, R. Yosef Yitzchak Schneersohn:

It was the summer of 1896, and Father and I were strolling in the fields of Balivka, a hamlet near Lubavitch. The grain was near to ripening, and the wheat and grass swayed gently in the breeze.

My father to me: "See G-dliness! Every movement of each stalk and grass was included in G-d's Primordial Thought of Creation, in G-d's all-embracing vision of history, and is guided by Divine Providence towards a G-dly purpose."

Walking further, we entered the forest. Engrossed in what I had heard, excited by the softness and seriousness of Father's words, I absentmindedly tore a leaf off a passing tree. Holding it a while in my hands, I continued walking deep in thought, occasionally tearing small pieces of leaf and casting them to the winds.

"The holy Ari," said Father to me, "says that within each and every creation there is a spark of a soul that has descended to earth to find its correction and fulfillment.

"This leaf that you just mindlessly tore and tossed away was created by the Almighty towards a specific purpose and is imbued with a Divine life force. It has a body, and it has its life. In what way is the 'I' of this leaf inferior to yours?"[354]

The Big Idea

All of creation has a soul and song; it's up to us to give it voice.

Nature *teva*
טבע

NATURE'S FACADE

MIRACLES ARE A RETELLING in small letters of the very same story that is written across the whole world in letters too large for some of us to see.[355]

The human propensity to take wonders for granted is truly astonishing. We're constantly trying to find patterns of phenomena, grouping events or people together, and explaining them away to help us simplify and make sense of life. As a result, we tend to overlook the extraordinary reality unfolding before us.

The English word nature is derived from the Latin word *nat*, which means born. This conception of nature is founded on the theory that things are the way they are because they were created that way and can thus never change. This mechanistic mindset shuts down curiosity, wonder, and excitement by downplaying the uniqueness of every single moment and encounter. As the saying goes, "It is what it is."

In contrast, the Hebrew word for nature, *teva*, means to be submerged, as in *tub'u bayam*,[356] submerged in the sea. When you stand on the beach and look out upon the miles of water before you, everything looks the same as far as the eye can see. What you don't see is an entire underwater world teeming with millions of living species expressing an even greater array of biodiversity than exists on land.

From Judaism's perspective, reality itself is like the sea—it is only when one dives in and is fully immersed within it that they can appreciate the wondrous world's rich life concealed beneath its surface.[357] In other words, reality's true nature is hidden, waiting to be discovered, if only we would venture from the safety of the shore to swim in its deeper depths.

To understand the reality of nature, we must first understand the nature of reality. A brief synopsis of the Kabbalistic understanding of creation will prove helpful for this endeavor.

In the beginning, there was only G-d; nothing else existed, and nothing else could exist without compromising G-d's essential singularity. Since G-d is an infinite and unified being, nothing exists outside of G-d.

Therefore, in order to create the world, the Creator contracted and hid His presence to make space for creation to exist. However, this also created a virtual veil of separation between the Creator and creation, allowing the universe to experience itself as possessing its own independent existence. Because of this dynamic, one can observe the universe and not immediately discern its origin, creator, and life-source. This state of affairs leads us to take nature and reality at face value, without looking beyond its facade to ascertain its deeper substance and significance.

Interestingly, in Jewish mysticism, G-d's various names represent different permutations of Divine energy. The force of concealment that hides G-d's presence to make space for the natural order to exist is referred to by the name *Elokim*. This is the particular name of G-d mentioned at the beginning of the Book of Genesis, which describes the creation of the world. The numerical value of the Hebrew letters in the word *Elokim* (eighty-six) [when spelled properly with a *hei*] is the same as the letters that make up the word *hateva* (the nature).[358] The role of *Elokim* in creation is precisely to introduce the element of concealment, simultaneously channeling and camouflaging the miraculous undercurrents that bring reality into existence. *Elokim* paradoxically orchestrates and obfuscates all visible clues to the Divine origin of our universe in the process of its manifestation.[359]

Jewish mysticism therefore views nature as a series of miracles[360] that are perpetually recreated at every moment,[361] yet never exactly the same as before.[362]

This understanding of reality is certainly not the norm, but it is available for those who seek it out. For instance, when a propeller spins slowly, its movement and constituent parts are obvious to the observer, but as it spins faster and faster, its continuous movement ceases to be apparent; it is just a blur.

Judaism's teachings help us slow down the frantic blur of life, sensitizing us to see beneath the veneer of nature and into its miraculous depths. In fact, many Jewish prayers and practices are designed for this very purpose.

For example, when we wake up in the morning, we recite a prayer[363] to express our gratitude to G-d for the gift of a new day, which so often goes unnoticed and underappreciated.

Certainly, if there is one thing we take for granted more than anything else, it is the blessing of life we receive anew each day.

Following this moment of conscious awakening, we most likely need to use the restroom after a long night of sleep, and there is a special blessing for that as well.[364] According to Jewish tradition, the mere act of going to the bathroom is a cause for spiritual celebration and sincere thanksgiving for the wondrous workings of our body.

Where many religious traditions shun the body in favor of the soul, Judaism guides us to become more—not less—aware of the workings of our body, because they are truly expressions of the Creator himself. As the verse says, *From my flesh I will see G-d.*[365]

Additionally, further on in the morning liturgy of daily prayers, there are various blessings to express our thanks to G-d for our renewed vision, vitality, mobility, powers of discernment, and for numerous other physical abilities[366] that we so often take for granted, as well as blessings on the foods we eat and fragrances we enjoy. What's more, Judaism has unique blessings for encountering exquisite beauty, extraordinary wisdom, and various natural phenomena such as thunder, lightning, rainbows, blossoming trees, and the sight of the ocean. In other words: Almost everything that we physically experience or ingest is seen as an opportunity to remember and connect with the source of its, and our, essential being.

What blessings are to nature and embodied experience, the Jewish festivals are to time. As opposed to seeing history as a "trash bag of random coincidences torn open by the wind,"[367] the Jewish calendar reveals the hidden thread of Divine Presence and providence in the tapestry of human affairs. Furthermore, just as the purpose of blessings is to generate an intrapersonal awareness of the Divine within each individual, Jewish festivals serve to cultivate an interpersonal experience of the Divine as we gather to celebrate with our families and communities. Chanukah takes this one step further, as the Sages in the Talmud bid us to engage in acts of *pirsumei nisa*, publicizing the miracle to the wider world.[368] This is but one shining example among many of the essential mission of the Jewish people, which is to illuminate the world with the light of the Divine, revealing for all to see that what we normally perceive as mundane nature is nothing less than miraculous.

The Big Idea

Judaism helps dispel the illusion of an autonomous natural order, revealing the Divine Presence within everyone and everything.

It Happened Once

THE WASHINGTON POST ONCE reported on a creative social experiment performed during rush hour in a busy Washington, DC, subway station: Joshua Bell, one of the world's best concert violinists, played Bach's finest pieces for forty-five minutes on a violin worth three and a half million dollars. Thousands of people passed by, but only seven stopped to listen, and even then, only for a few moments. Two nights earlier, Joshua's show in the Boston Theater was sold out, with tickets averaging a hundred dollars each!

Every day, we find ourselves surrounded by the most beautiful music ever played, by the greatest musician who ever lived, on the finest instruments ever created. To hear the exquisite music within our world, all we need to do is pause and pay attention to the Divine Composer behind it all.

This way of seeing the world is beautifully depicted in a story about the Baal Shem Tov, the founder of the Chasidic movement. One day, as the Baal Shem Tov was walking through the forest with his students, he pointed out a leaf that had just blown off of a tree floating down to rest on the sun-parched dirt road. The Baal Shem Tov told his students that the leaf falling off the tree at this particular time and landing in this specific place was orchestrated by G-d.

He asked his students to lift the leaf off the ground, and there lay a worm dying in the summer heat; the fallen leaf had restored its energy and life, providing comfort and protection from the sun.

G-d's Providence governs every creation, including the most minute. Even this fallen leaf, tossed about by the wind, is an expression and fulfillment of G-d's compassionate orchestration.

שם

shem   Names

CHAPTER 30 | NAMES

MORE THAN JUST A NAME

WE'RE USED TO THINKING of names as labels, contrived for convenience to help us distinguish one person, place, or thing from another.

In Shakespeare's words, "A rose by any other name would smell as sweet."

In Jewish thought, however, a name is much more than mere convention.

The Hebrew word *shem*, name, comprises the central letters of the word *neshamah*, soul.

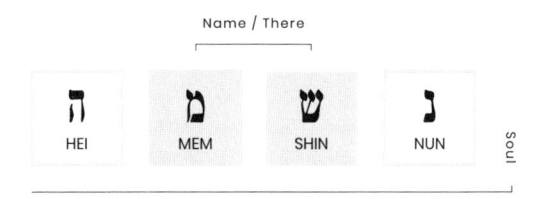

ה	מ	ש	נ
HEI	MEM	SHIN	NUN

Name / There — Soul

This etymological connection teaches us that our names relate to who we are in our essence, providing a window into our soul; or, in the words of the Biblical Abigail, speaking to King David: *As his name, so he is.*[369]

In fact, the Talmud[370] takes this notion of "tell me your name and I'll tell you who you are" quite literally.

It tells of two Sages who were not adept at analyzing names. They debated if they should trust a person named Kidor because his name could be found in the verse: *For they are a generation [ki dor] of upheavals.*

They understood from this that he was possibly an unsavory character. In the end, they decided to trust him with their money anyway, and he ended up betraying their trust.

However, one's given name need not completely define and deterministically confine them to a predestined fate, because a change of name can open new doors of possibility in their life.

Indeed, throughout the Torah, we find that a change in a person's name signals a shift in their fortune and destiny.

For example, in the book of Genesis,[371] G-d changes Abram's name to Abraham to reflect his transformation from a regional leader (*av Aram*, father of Aram[372]) into the progenitor of many nations (*av hamon goyim*).

Indeed, the reverberation of Abraham's change of name is still felt today, as the adherents of Judaism, Christianity, and Islam, which comprise more than half of the world's population at this time, all consider Abraham to be their spiritual father.

Similarly, G-d changes Abraham's wife's name as well, from Sarai to Sarah. Rashi explains that G-d was saying[373]: "Abram indeed may have no son, but *Abraham* will have a son; Sarai may not bear a child, but *Sarah* will bear. I will give you [both] other names, and your destiny will be changed."

Later in Genesis,[374] after Jacob spars with an angel, he is given the name Israel, *for you have struggled (sarita) with beings Divine and human, and you have prevailed.*[375]

Similar to Abraham and Sarah, Jacob's new name signified his inner transformation and new sense of purpose. Previously in his life, whenever Jacob was confronted with conflict, he ran. He fled from his brother Esau, he fled from his uncle Laban, and, in fact, some commentators claim that he was again in mid-flight from Esau and his army when he was accosted by the angel during the night.[376]

Upon prevailing over the angel, he was given his new name Israel, the name of his descendants for all time.

Interestingly, after this transformative night battle, Jacob reunites with his family and confronts Esau peacefully and compassionately,[377] defusing their decades-long enmity and conflict.

In addition to the physical change of destiny experienced by Abraham and Sarah, as well as the psychological shift reflected in the story of Jacob, in the book of Numbers, we find an example of a name that was changed to effect transformation on the spiritual level.

Immediately prior to sending out the twelve spies on an ill-fated reconnaissance mission to Canaan, Moses changed the name of his disciple Hosea to Joshua[378] by adding a *yud*, the first letter of G-d's name, as part of his hope and prayer that: "May G-d save you from the counsel of the spies."[379]

In fact, Kabbalah teaches that so interconnected is a person's name with their essence that it serves as a channel for their fortune.

This is indicated in the word *shmo*, his name, which, according to *gematria*—the Jewish system of linguistically-based numerology—shares the same numerical value as the word *tzinor*, a pipe or channel (both equal three hundred forty-six). Indeed, according to the Arizal,[380] one's name is the channel through which the soul's energy reaches the body.[381]

This is why, according to the Talmud,[382] when a person is critically ill, we give them an additional name such as Chaim or Chayah—which are both variants that mean life—or Refael, which means "G-d heals," in order to change their fortune and avert a negative heavenly decree.

In the words of the prayer recited upon changing someone's name: "If upon so and so (the old name) a harsh verdict was decreed, on so and so (the new name) it was not decreed. Therefore, they are now a different person and not the same person who was called by that original name."

All of the above helps explain why, in the Jewish tradition, the act of naming a child is considered such an awesome responsibility, as it literally affects their destiny.

Accordingly, we are encouraged to name a child after a person who was righteous, and, conversely, we are discouraged from naming them after someone wicked.

In fact, the Kabbalists[383] explain that when naming a child, parents experience a miniature prophecy that guides them to the appropriate name for their child's soul. G-d "plants" a name in their minds that accurately reflects the unique characteristics of each particular child.

Correspondingly, the letters of the word *shem*, given different vowels (in Hebrew, the vowels are separate from the letters), can be read as *sham*, which means there, because a person's name points to their destiny in life.

Similarly, the numerical value of the word *shem* is the same as the word *sefer*, book (both share the numerical value of three hundred forty), because a person's name tells their story.

The mystics[384] teach that so correlated is our name and our destiny that after one hundred twenty years, when our soul ascends to heaven, the first question we will be asked is: "Did you live up to your name?"

Consistent with the theme of this book, which is that words have power and meaning for those who seek it out beneath their purely semantic surface, learning about the deeper dimensions of one's given or chosen name is a significant step along the path of fuller self-realization, and it can serve as a guide to discover their life's purpose.

The Big Idea

Study your name, for it holds the key to your destiny.

It Happened Once

SOME YEARS AGO, A baby girl was born to R. Aryeh and Rachel Trugman three weeks before her due date.

Due to her premature birth, the baby had some health complications and had to stay in the hospital. Her parents waited anxiously in the hospital day after day to see if she would stabilize. The doctors were handling the medical care as best they could, but they informed the parents that they did not know if their daughter would make it.

Seeking spiritual support and guidance, the Trugmans reached out to the Lubavitcher Rebbe's secretariat, asking them to convey the gravity of the situation to the Rebbe.

The Rebbe asked if the couple had given their daughter a name yet. R. Aryeh replied that they had put off naming their daughter until they could do the ceremony properly in a synagogue.

The Rebbe instructed R. Aryeh not to wait but to give his daughter a name immediately. This, the Rebbe explained, would help tether her soul to her body. The Trugmans heeded the Rebbe's advice and named their daughter Chanie at the next possible opportunity. The baby's condition immediately stabilized, and, shortly thereafter, her parents were able to take her home

Soul

neshamah   נשמה

CHAPTER 31 | SOUL

LOOK WITHIN

RESPONDING TO THE TIMELESS question, "Where is G-d?"—the Kotzker Rebbe famously replied, "Wherever you let Him in."[385] Judaism teaches that G-d isn't to be found only in the ether, relegated to the heavens, inaccessibly distant and outside of us; rather, He can be found within each one of us.

Reflecting this spiritual truth, the Hebrew word *neshamah*, soul, shares the same etymological root as the word *neshimah*—breath.[386]

		Soul			
ה	מ	י	שׁ	נ	
HEI	MEM	YUD	SHIN	NUN	Breath

Unlike the rest of creation, which was brought into being through G-d's speech, as in, *G-d said: "Let there be light" and there was light*,[387] the soul of man was not spoken into creation.

Instead, *G-d breathed into his nostrils a living soul, and man thus became a living being.*[388] Our very soul is therefore rooted in G-d's breath, which originates from within His deepest depths.[389]

The difference between speaking and blowing is that in speech, the breath of life within is converted from its essence through the process of verbalization. Whereas the act of blowing merely *transports* the breath of life from within, passing it on unadulterated to its intended recipient.

The human soul is therefore not a *creation of G-d but literally a part of G-d Himself.*[390]

Just as a child is constructed from their parents' DNA, so, too, as children of G-d, each of us is made up of the Divine essence.[391]

Therefore, just as one cannot cease to be their parents' child, even if they choose not to identify or live in accordance with them, similarly, at our core, we always maintain our spiritual essence regardless of the choices we make.

One of the major implications of the human soul's uniqueness is that when we seek to develop a relationship with G-d, we don't need to establish a new connection; we need only access our innate spiritual core and give it expression. As opposed to other traditions, which believe that a person needs an intermediary to connect with G-d, Judaism sees every human being as possessing an intrinsic bond with G-d from birth. In truth, this Divine breath is who we are.

Contrary to the notion that we are "born in sin" and are therefore in need of "redemption," Judaism teaches that we are "born in holiness" and always maintain access to that original state, regardless of our life choices or mistakes. As we say in the morning blessings as a daily reminder, "My G-d, the soul that You have placed within me is pure."[392] We each have a point of indestructible goodness and G-dliness at our core, by virtue of the fact that, at root, our soul is "a part of G-d above."[393]

It follows that this relationship with G-d is not something that we can ever lose. Even when we are not in touch with our soul, our Divine essence lies dormant within us, awaiting expression.

The Big Idea

In order to forge a connection with G-d, one doesn't need to reach upward or outward but inward.

It Happened Once

A YOUNG MUSICIAN ON A spiritual quest once approached the Lubavitcher Rebbe as he was getting out of his car in front of Chabad headquarters.

"I have a question," he exclaimed in the Yiddish of his youth.

"What is it?" the Rebbe asked.

"Where is G-d?" he asked.

"Everywhere," the Rebbe replied.

"I know," the young man continued, "But where?"

"In everything and in every place," said the Rebbe, "In a tree, in a stone…"

The young man persisted, "I know, but *where*?"

"In your heart—if that's how you're asking."[394]

emunah אמונה

Faith

FAITH IS A VERB

IN JUDAISM, FAITH IS not a binary, yes or no proposition.

While according to Jewish law, the minimum requirement of faith is the belief in a singular, omnipresent, omnipotent Being Who is the cause of all existence,[395] to truly live with faith means much more than that.

Interestingly, the Hebrew word for faith, *emunah*, is derived from the same root as *uman*, which means an artisan, craftsman, or practitioner.[396] While becoming an artist often begins with the identification of an inborn talent, that talent, if not exercised, can remain undeveloped.

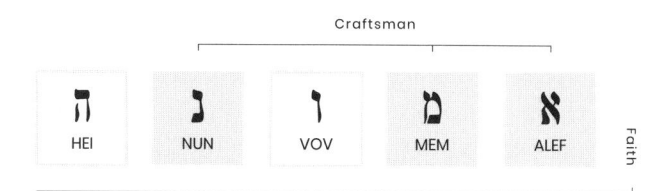

ה	נ	ו	מ	א	
HEI	NUN	VOV	MEM	ALEF	Faith

Craftsman

Real artistry depends on constant cultivation through regular expression and nurturing. To be proficient in a craft, one needs to devote time, effort, and practice to develop their skills. Likewise, faith is an ongoing pursuit, an artistry of sorts that gets better with time and practice.

In fact, in modern Hebrew, *imunim* means exercises. Just as one needs to keep up an exercise routine to maintain a fit body, the soul, too, needs regular nurturing to keep its faith vibrant.

Faith is therefore not a static noun, something one possesses and never loses; rather, it is a dynamic verb, an active pursuit and process that requires constant cultivation.

On the intellectual plane, the journey of faith is one that requires us to understand as much as we can about G-d, Torah, and the soul, and what we cannot grasp or prove we then subscribe to in faith.

Nevertheless, we are bidden by our Sages to constantly deepen and upgrade our understanding.[397] As we do, the ceiling of our faith is raised, so that what once was taken on faith alone is now arrived at through understanding and knowledge. This dialectic dance between faith and intellect is one of the primary expressions of the perpetual journey of faith.

However, despite its common caricature, faith isn't just a stubborn conviction in the absence of reason; faith is a way of knowing that is rooted in experience. We learn by doing, and from within the context of action emerges an insight that could never be accessed through words and thoughts alone. It's like trying to explain the flavor of a strawberry to someone who never ate one before. No amount or manner of words and metaphors could ever do it justice. Such an experience can only be fully appreciated by putting a strawberry into your mouth and biting into it.

Similarly, when it comes to faith, there is a degree of understanding and identification that comes only through the performance of *mitzvot*, the sacred acts and practices prescribed by the Torah.

This is the meaning of the statement of the Israelites at Sinai when they accepted the Torah with the exclamation, *We will do and [and through doing] we will understand.*[398] Herein lies a paradigm shift at the heart of the Jewish understanding of faith. It is not that the more we understand and believe, the more we will do; rather, the more we do, the more we come to understand and believe.[399]

Judaism, therefore, asks of its adherents to take a leap of action, not just a leap of faith. In this light, the *mitzvot* are revealed not only as the fruits of faith, but as its nourishing roots as well.

Ultimately, faith is a lifelong journey that nourishes and is nourished by perpetual intellectual and experiential advancement.

CHAPTER 32 | FAITH

Significantly, in Judaism, a person of faith is not referred to as a "good" Jew but as a "practicing" Jew. To be engaged in the art and act of faith is thus to practice each day and continuously strive to perfect this spiritual craft so that our connection to both Creator and creation expands and deepens with each passing day.

The Big Idea

Faith is not static and fixed but dynamic and fluid. Like the body, the soul needs constant nourishment and exercise in order to flourish.

It Happened Once

IN HIS MEMOIRS, MR. GORDON ZACKS, a prominent Jewish activist, writes about an audience he once had with the Lubavitcher Rebbe:

"Do you believe in revelation, Mr. Zacks?" the Rebbe asked me.

"I believe in G-d, and I believe he inspires... but I don't believe he writes," I answered.

"You mean, Mr. Zacks, that there is this vast structure G-d has created of plants, animals, food chains, stars, and planets. And that the only creature in all of creation that doesn't understand how to fit in and live their life purposefully is the human?"

I told him yes.

"What about the complexity of the human body? What about the jewel of the human cell? How does the body ingest food and renew itself with absolute consistency?"

I could only shrug my shoulders, but my respect for him deepened by the moment.

"And how can you account for the brain and the mind? How do they steer this remarkable system in a purposeful and precise way? And what about how we fit into the earth's ecosystem, where we inhale the oxygen that plants so wonderfully manufacture for us? Could this all be accidental?"

How could I answer him?

"And beyond what happens on earth, what about all the heavenly bodies in the sky that seem to follow such a perfect order and don't collide with each other? Is man the only creature on the planet without guidelines for living its life? Should man ignore the Torah given to us by G-d as a roadmap to guide us? This is the missing link that connects us to the complexity of nature!"

So it went. Comment after comment. More times than not, I could not begin to answer his points.

CHAPTER 32 | FAITH

He quoted Kazantzakis' book *Zorba the Greek* to me during our conversation. "Do you remember the young man talking with Zorba on the beach, when Zorba asks what the purpose of life is? The young fellow admits he doesn't know. And Zorba comments, 'Well, all those books you read—what good are they? Why do you read them?' Zorba's friend says he doesn't know. Zorba can see his friend doesn't have an answer to the most fundamental question. That's the trouble with you. 'A man's head is like a grocer,' Zorba says, 'it keeps accounts.... The head's a careful little shopkeeper; it never risks all it has, always keeps something in reserve. It never breaks the string.' Wise men and grocers weigh everything. They can never cut the cord and be free. Your problem, Mr. Zacks, is that you are trying to find G-d's map through your head. You are unlikely to find it that way. You have to experience before you can truly feel and then be free to learn. Let me send a teacher to live with you for a year and teach you how to be Jewish. You will unleash a whole new dimension to your life. If you really want to change the world, change yourself! It's like dropping a stone into a pool of water and watching the concentric circles radiate to the shore. You will influence all the people around you, and they will influence others in turn. That's how you bring about improvement in the world."

* * *

Kalman Cowl, a music professor at Columbia University, became friendly with some Chasidim and would often visit them at the central Chabad synagogue located at 770 Eastern Parkway in Brooklyn.

Once, he was persuaded by his friends to request a meeting with the Lubavitcher Rebbe.

He was apprehensive about the meeting, though, because, in his own words, "Although I felt fiercely Jewish, I didn't believe in G-d."

At their meeting, after exchanging pleasantries, Kalman told the Rebbe, "I appreciate the privilege of being taught more about my heritage here in 770, but I don't want to be here under false pretenses. I have no faith."

The Rebbe thought for a few moments and said simply, "As long as you are concerned about that, I'm not worried."

Hebrew

ivri

עברי

SURVIVAL OF THE FAITHFUL

THE JEWISH PEOPLE ARE unique among ancient civilizations. Despite the many mighty empires that have come and gone throughout history, the Jews, small and scattered as they have been, have survived with their beliefs, traditions, and practices intact for over three millennia.

One explanation for the fact that so many peoples have vanished over time is that when indigenous populations are conquered or ethnic minorities absorbed by larger societies, they tend to abandon their unique features and cultural differences to blend in with the host civilization. They do this for a number of reasons, most significantly, to escape the persecution that stems from "the dislike of the unlike" and to ensure their physical survival.

Not so the Jewish people. Since the beginning of the Jewish story, starting with Abraham, Jews have stood apart from their neighbors, tenaciously clinging to their beliefs and values, not willing to part from them at any cost.

Indeed, Abraham was known as *Ha'Ivri*, the Hebrew.[400] In context, this meant Abraham from the other side of the Euphrates. However, the Midrash explains that Abraham earned this title not only for his birthplace but also for his faith and culture, which ran against the currents of popular belief. In the evocative words of the Midrash[401]: "The entire world was on one side, and he was willing to be on the other side."

This is one reason Jews were originally called Hebrews, or in Hebrew, *Ivriyim*, because they were willing to take on, and take down, the idols of the day.

To be a Hebrew thus literally means to possess the courage to stand apart, to dare to be different, and Abraham was the first to proudly bear this title of distinction.

In his youth, Abraham uncovered the ultimate reality of Divine unity that exists beneath the veneer of multiplicity in creation—the one G-d Who created and continuously sustains the universe.[402] Even more impressive than his spiritual discovery, however, was his steadfast commitment to his newfound belief despite living in an idolatrous society, which was quick to punish outliers severely.

In the face of such pressure to conform, fueled by his faith, he was not afraid to pay the price for his iconoclasm. According to the Midrash,[403] Abraham was even willing to be cast into a fiery furnace by King Nimrod rather than abandon his monotheistic beliefs.

And what was the result of Abraham's courageous dissent?

T.R. Grover writes in his book, *The Ancient World*[404]: "Mankind, East and West, Christian and Muslim, accepted the Jewish conviction that there is only one G-d. Today it is polytheism that is so difficult to understand, that is so unthinkable."

The former heretic has become the standard bearer.

The seeds of Abraham's revolutionary path, which would transform the landscape of human history, are encapsulated in his first exchange with G-d, in which he was told,[405] *Leave your land, your birthplace, and your father's house, and go to the land I will show you.*

The radical nature and historical context of this journey is eloquently articulated by Thomas Cahill in his bestselling book, *The Gifts of the Jews*: "If we had lived in the second millennium BCE, the millennium of Abraham, and could have canvassed all the nations of the earth, what would they have said of Abraham's journey? In most of Africa and Europe, they would have laughed at Abraham's madness and pointed to the heavens, where the life of earth had been plotted from all eternity… a man cannot escape his fate. The Egyptians would have shaken their heads in disbelief. The early Greeks might have told Abraham the story of Prometheus... Do not overreach, they would advise; come to resignation. In India, he would be told that time is black, irrational and merciless. Do not set yourself the task of accomplishing something in time, which is only the dominion of suffering. On every continent, in every society, Abraham would have been given the same advice that wise men like Herculitas [and others] would give his followers: Do not journey but sit; compose yourself by the river of life, meditate on its ceaseless and meaningless flow."

Against the grain of such fatalistic thinking, Abraham's first journey would set the transformative tone for all of Jewish history. Ancient ideals of static hierarchies, circular time, and strict determinism would give way to Abraham's groundbreaking path of hope, meaning, progress, and redemption.

The Jewish story can, therefore, in some way, be explained by its people's stubborn resistance to conformity. Abraham's heirs have consistently been defined by their willingness to become foreigners, to defy the status quo, and, as poet Robert Frost so eloquently put it, to "take the road less traveled."

In the words of Michael Grant, the renowned historian of Classical Greece[406]: "The Jews proved not only unassimilated, but inassimilable..."

Already in the third century, the famous Greek sophist Philostratus observed[407]: "For the Jews have long been in revolt not only against the Romans but against humanity; and a race that has made its own life apart and irreconcilable, that cannot share with the rest of mankind in the pleasure of the table nor join in their libations or prayers or sacrifices, are separate from ourselves by a greater gulf than divides us from Sura or Bactra of the most distant Indies."

In recent centuries, there have been numerous movements bent on assimilating the Jews into their host cultures, so as to "set them free" from the differential treatment and antisemitic hatred that has forever plagued the Jewish people. What will be the outcome of these attempts? Besides the futility in this argument—antisemitism seldom distinguishes between the devout and assimilated—history can attest to the complete disappearance of Jewish factions that chose to assimilate.

In the words of Cecil Roth's *A History of the Jews*[408]: "Today, the

Jewish people has in it still those elements of strength and endurance that enabled it to surmount all the crises of its past, surviving thus the most powerful empires of antiquity. Throughout our history, there have been weaker elements who have shirked the sacrifices that Judaism entailed. They have been swallowed, long since, in the great majority; only the more stalwart have carried on the traditions of their ancestors and can now look back with pride upon their superb heritage. Are we to be numbered with the weak majority, or with the stalwart minority? It is for ourselves to decide."

Our stubborn commitment to truth, no matter how out of style or step it might be, is why we are still here, while so many others have vanished into the shadows of history. Just as poetry was famously defined in the twentieth century as "news that stays news," Jewish history is defined by *Jews who stay Jews.*

When the entire world stands on one side, and you are on the other, never forget that the very root of Judaism, being an *Ivri*, means having the faith and fortitude to *stand apart* from the crowd and *stand up* for what you most deeply believe.

The Big Idea

The secret behind the singular history, survival, and contribution of the Jewish people is their unique ability to stand alone and stay true to their beliefs no matter the cost.

CHAPTER 33 | HEBREW

It Happened Once

SEVERAL BAR-MITZVAH AGE BOYS had stopped attending their local Hebrew school. Their parents, who were concerned, took the teenagers to visit the Lubavitcher Rebbe, hoping he would convince them to continue seeking a Jewish education.

"Tell me," the Rebbe asked the first boy, "why have you decided to stop attending Hebrew school?"

"All the other boys on my street have stopped going to Hebrew school, so I want to stop as well," he answered.

"And what about you?" the Rebbe asked the second boy.

"Same reason," the boy explained. "The kids on my street don't go, so why should I?"

"Tell me," the Rebbe asked the boys, "who were your favorite Jewish heroes that you learned about?"

One boy responded that he deeply admired Noah, and the other, Abraham.

"Do you know," the Rebbe told the first boy, "that if Noah would have followed all the other kids on his street, we would have no world? And if Abraham would have followed all the kids on his street," the Rebbe told the second boy, "we would have no Jewish people!"[409]

Israel *yisrael*
ישראל

CHAPTER 34 | ISRAEL

NO REST FOR THE HOLY

THE FOUNDATIONAL CREED OF many religions is submission to a higher power. For example, the word Islam literally means submission. Yet, this is not the case for the Children of Israel. The word Israel means to struggle, as the angel conveys to Jacob after struggling with him throughout the night[410]: *Your name shall no longer be Jacob, but Israel, for you have struggled (sarita) with beings Divine and human, and you have prevailed.*

By giving such a name to the Jewish people, G-d was, in effect, teaching them about the importance of thinking critically and not passively accepting authority. This may have contributed to the development of the Jewish proclivity to challenge, an inherited irreverence for dogma, and an instinctive resistance to blind adherence.

When G-d tells Abraham about the impending destruction of Sodom and Gomorra, Abraham challenges G-d[411]: *Will you sweep away the innocent along with the guilty?...Shall the Judge of the entire earth not deal justly?*

Similarly, Moses was not willing to accept G-d's decrees without challenge. He humbly questions G-d about the suffering of his brethren in Egypt[412]: *Why have You brought harm upon this nation? Why did you send me? Ever since I came to Pharaoh to speak in Your name, he has dealt worse with this nation, and You still have not delivered Your people!*

Later, after the sin of the Golden Calf, G-d tells Moses,[413] *Now, leave Me be, that My anger may blaze forth against them and that I may destroy them, and make of you a great nation.* But Moses again speaks up on their behalf: *Turn from Your blazing anger, and renounce this plan to punish Your people.* Moses goes so far as to put his own legacy on the line, boldly declaring: *Now, if You will forgive their sin [then good], but if not, erase me from the book that You have written!*

Indeed, we find that, according to the Talmud,[414] G-d congratulates Moses for having perpetrated a seeming act of sacrilege when he smashed the Tablets in order to protect the people.

In contrast to such holy chutzpah, the *Zohar*[415] criticizes Noah for *not* challenging G-d by praying for the people of his generation as Abraham and Moses did. According to the *Zohar*, G-d said to him: "Where were you for the entire time that I instructed you to build the ark? Why did you not beg for mercy for the inhabitants of the world?" From here we learn that Judaism holds up as its role models and heroes those who stand up against perceived injustice, whether Divine or human.

Incredibly, such principled resistance brings G-d great pleasure. As the verse in Isaiah[416] says: *G-d desires to pronounce him [Israel] victorious.*

Similarly, the Midrash relates[417] how G-d tells the Jewish people: "When I win, I lose, and when I am won over, I win." G-d wants to be challenged and held "accountable" to the values He has given us to uphold.

What's more, Judaism views the existence of evil, suffering, inequality, and injustice not as unavoidable features of society and life but as conditions that exist for us to confront and transform. Indeed, throughout history, this is what the Jewish people have endeavored to do.

To quote historian Paul Johnson:

"Certainly, the world without the Jews would have been a radically different place. To them we owe the idea of equality before the law, both Divine and human; of the sanctity of life and the dignity of the human person; of the individual conscience and so a personal redemption; of collective conscience and so of social responsibility; of peace as an abstract ideal and love as the foundation of justice, and many other items that constitute the basic moral furniture of the human mind. Without Jews, it might have been a much emptier place."[418]

This is what it means to be an Israelite.

In the vivid words of a famous Apple ad: "Here's to the crazy ones, the misfits, the rebels, the troublemakers, the round pegs in the square holes… the ones who see things differently—they're not fond of rules… You can quote them, disagree with them, glorify or vilify them, but the only thing you can't do is ignore them because they change things… They push the human race forward, and while some may see them as the crazy ones, we see genius, because the ones who are crazy enough to think that they can change the world are the ones who do."[419]

The Big Idea

G-d allows pain and injustice to exist in the world in order for us to challenge such suffering and participate in its healing and rectification.

It Happened Once

IN THE AFTERMATH OF the sin of the Golden Calf, the Torah says[420] that, G-d told Moses: "*Now, leave Me be, that My anger may blaze forth against them and that I may destroy them, and make of you a great nation.*"

The Talmudic Sage R. Avahu taught: "Were the verse not written in this manner, it would be impossible to say what I am about to say, in deference to G-d. The phrase: *Leave Me be*, teaches that Moses grabbed the Holy One, blessed be He, as a person who grabs his friend by his garment would, and he said before Him: 'Master of the Universe, I will not leave You be until You forgive and pardon them.'"

The Talmud concludes: "Fortunate is the student whose teacher concedes to him [as the L-rd conceded to Moses]."

R. Yitzchak said: "This teaches that the Holy One, blessed be He, said to Moses: 'Moses, you have given Me life with your words. [I am happy that on account of your arguments, I will forgive the Jewish people.]'"[421]

יהודי

yehudi Jew

CHAPTER 35 | JEW

EVERY DAY IS THANKSGIVING

THE JEWISH PEOPLE ARE not only named after the ancient Kingdom of Judea, the ancestral homeland of today's Jews. The word Jew, or *Yehudi* in Hebrew, comes from the word *hodaah*, which means to acknowledge and express gratitude. The essence of Judaism is thus poignantly expressed in this word.

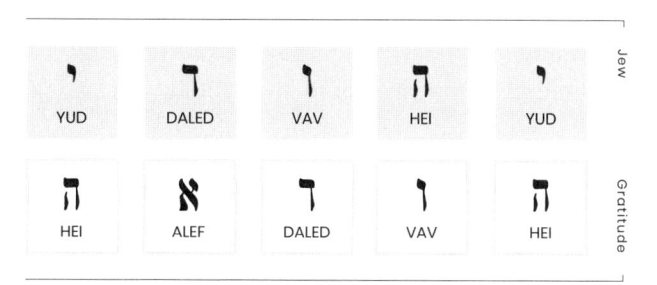

י	ד	ו	ה	י	Jew
YUD	DALED	VAV	HEI	YUD	
ה	א	ד	ו	ה	Gratitude
HEI	ALEF	DALED	VAV	HEI	

In the Torah, Jacob's son Judah (Yehudah in Hebrew) was so named by his mother as an expression of her thanks to G-d for the overwhelming kindness bestowed upon her in the form of the many children with whom she was graced.[422] The Talmud[423] points out that this was the first time G-d was ever thanked verbally in the Torah! The name Yehudah, and by extension *Yehudim* (Jews), is therefore understood to encapsulate this spiritual quality of articulated praise.

Acknowledging the good things we have in our lives is not always easy. We are prone to taking things for granted. In fact, there is a phenomenon psychologists call "hedonic adaptation" that causes us to very quickly assimilate and forget the blessings we receive in life. Scientists explain[424] that the reason for this is that sidelining that which doesn't require our immediate attention helps keep us focused on the challenges we need to overcome in the moment. If we had to continuously pay attention to the myriad of things functioning smoothly in our mind and body at any given moment, we simply wouldn't be alert enough to respond to the urgent necessities and imminent dangers we may encounter.

One of the less helpful side effects of this "adaptation," however, is that it empties our awareness of all of the things for which we ought to be grateful. Hedonic adaptation is therefore what drives us to take our blessings for granted and focus instead on what we are missing rather than feeling grateful for what we have.

Repudiating this tendency of mindless reception is a defining feature of Judaism. Indeed, this attitude of gratitude was a defining characteristic of the first Jew, Abraham, who was determined to renounce what was then the pervading paradigm of his time—to accept the existence of the universe as a matter of course. Instead of taking reality for granted, Abraham searched for and discovered the one Almighty G-d responsible for creating and sustaining the universe, and Whom we are therefore obliged to acknowledge and thank.[425]

So essential was this quality of thankful acknowledgment to Abraham in his approach to spiritual education that, according to the Talmud,[426] he would invite people into his tent for sumptuous meals and lively conversation in order to then pose the question: *From where does such abundance come?* When, through discussion, Abraham revealed that G-d was the source of all life and sustenance, many of those present were moved to recite blessings of gratitude for the food they had just eaten.

Feeling and expressing gratitude for our blessings is a way of actively acknowledging G-d's presence in every area of our lives. Instead of relegating G-d to the realm of the abstract and ceremonial, we encounter Him and experience His kindness with every breath and bite of food we take. This is the essence of Judaism—to actively acknowledge G-d in every dimension and moment of our lives.

In the realm of human relationships, such an attitude of gratitude is expressed in the principle of *hakarat hatov*, which means to show recognition for good. In fact, cultivating such gratitude is so fundamental to Judaism that those who lack it are barred from entering into the Jewish nation.

In Deuteronomy,[427] we are told that *No Ammonite or Moabite shall be admitted into the congregation of the L-rd, none of their descendants, even to the tenth generation....* As a point of contrast, even the Egyptians, who brutally enslaved the Jewish people for hundreds of years, are not sentenced to the same fate of eternal exclusion. Why are Egyptian converts admitted to the faith of Abraham, albeit after a couple of generations, whereas the Ammonites and Moabites are not?

The answer is that the Ammonites and Moabites, descendants of Abraham's orphaned nephew Lot, refused to provide food and water to the Jews in the wilderness even though they knew that Abraham had adopted, raised, and even waged a war on their ancestor's behalf.

Nachmanides[428] explains that after learning about the great lengths Abraham went to care for and save the life of their ancestor, Lot, the Ammonites and Moabites should have shown at least some degree of gratitude to the Jewish people and repaid them in kind. Since they lacked this most basic Jewish trait, they were barred admission to the Jewish nation forever.

It is important to note that in the present day, since we do not know who has descended from the nations of Amon and Moab, no one is excluded from converting to Judaism on account of their hereditary background.[429]

But, on a characterological level, the point is well taken—so essential is this fundamental quality of gratitude that one is incapable of living a truly Jewish life without it.

In fact, *hakarat hatov* is the very rationale behind the Egyptians being granted admittance into the Jewish nation despite having enslaved and oppressed the Israelites for many years! As the Torah teaches: *You shall not despise an Egyptian, for you were a sojourner in his land.*[430]

Incredibly, even those who brutalized us for an extended period of time are still worthy of our gratitude for the good they did for us, no matter how incomplete and deeply flawed. For instance, they took us in during a famine and gave us a section of lush land to live in and to pasture our animals.[431] This contains a profound lesson—namely, that it is incumbent upon us to show gratitude for the good that people have done for us, even if they have also caused us harm.

More than just advocating the importance of gratitude in the abstract, as a beautiful idea and ideal, Judaism offers a rigorous program to help transform the natural human tendency towards entitlement into a cultivated lifestyle of active and articulated appreciation.

Indeed, much of Judaism is a practical system designed to sensitize us to the wondrous workings in our lives and in the world. From our food to our families to our biological processes and physical abilities (including even going to the bathroom) to the intricate workings of nature to our miraculous history and higher cognitive faculties—there is literally no end to the things for which we can be thankful. In fact, the Sages teach[432] that we should each strive to say at least one hundred blessings each day! This is a testament to the high level of sensitivity and gratitude Judaism inspires us to achieve.

For example, one powerful practice instituted by our Sages to inculcate such gratitude is the recital of morning blessings,[433] actively thanking G-d for some of our most basic biological functions, which we so often take for granted.

Additionally, Jewish liturgy in general is full of dozens of prayers and blessings for us to express our acknowledgment and thanks to G-d, the source of all that we have and are.

One particularly poignant blessing that serves as the cornerstone of our consciousness each day is *Modeh Ani*,[434] a twelve-word affirmation of gratitude that we recite immediately upon awakening. While still in bed, before we do anything else, we thank G-d simply for the gift of life itself, and for a new day on this precious earth.

The prayer reads: "I give thanks to You, living and eternal King, for You have compassionately restored my soul within me, abundant is Your faithfulness [in me]!" This humble prayer, said at the opening of every day, is a perfect expression of what it means to be a Jew—alive and awake to G-d's infinite presence and blessings in every moment and facet of our lives.

In our lifetime, we receive so much more than we can ever possibly earn or give. When we make an honest accounting of how much is owed to us compared to how much we owe, this changes our perspective from one of privilege to one of purpose, from hubris to humility.

Such an awareness of our infinite blessings transforms one's entire life into a veritable song of praise and thanksgiving, allowing us to join the symphony of creation in good faith and harmony.

The Big Idea

The opposite of entitlement is not gratitude but cultivating an awareness of our blessings; with awareness of our blessings, gratitude comes automatically.

It Happened Once

THE GREAT *MUSSAR* TEACHER R. Eliyahu Lopian, affectionately known as Reb Elyah, was once talking to a student after prayers while folding his *tallit*. The *tallit* was large and had to be partially placed on a bench in order to be folded properly. After Reb Elyah finished folding it, he noticed that the bench was dusty and went to fetch a towel to wipe it off. The student to whom he was speaking realized what Reb Elyah was doing and ran to get the towel for him. Reb Elyah held up his hand. "No! No! I must clean it myself, because I must show my gratitude to the bench upon which I folded my *tallit.*"[435]

A similar story about *hakarat hatov* is told about the great Chasidic master R. Menachem Mendel of Kotzk. Whenever he would replace a pair of worn-out shoes, he would neatly wrap the old ones in newspaper before placing them in the garbage, declaring, "How can I simply toss away such fine shoes that have served me so well these past years!?"

Torah

torah תורה

CHAPTER 36 | TORAH

A TREE OF LIFE

THE WORD BIBLE IS of Greek origin, possibly a reference to Biblia, a historic port city in modern-day Lebanon that was widely known in ancient times for the superb paper it exported to many parts of the world, including Greece. Bible, then, is a reference to the medium of the book itself, a static form originally designed to function as a record of the past rather than as a living guide for the present.

Torah, the Hebrew word for the Bible, comes from the word *horaah*, to instruct,[436] implying a more dynamic sense of contemporary

ה	ר	ו	ת	Bible
HEI	REISH	VAV	TAV	
ה	א	ר	ו	ה	Instruction
HEI	ALEF	REISH	VAV	HEI	

relevance. Understood as such, the Torah serves not only as a book of ancient history, but, more importantly, as an instruction manual for life.

In fact, the *Zohar*,[437] one of the foundational texts of the Kabbalah, teaches that while the Torah was formally given at Sinai, it predates that revelatory event and even precedes the creation of the world: "The Holy One, blessed be He, looked into the Torah and used it as a blueprint to create the universe." As such, the Torah provides a metaphysical template for understanding the properties and purpose of the world and human existence. By studying it, one is brought into direct contact with the foundational elements of creation itself.

The Torah is thus not a mere piece of literature; rather, it is a guide, and it is meant to be studied accordingly. In the same way that a person would not attempt to operate complex machinery without first consulting the user's manual, the journey of life and human existence in an infinitely complex world requires its own set of instructions for optimal experience.

Following this line of thought, one may rightly ask: If the Torah is an instruction manual for life, why does it include so many stories and accounts of history? Why not just provide a list of commandments, instructing us what to do and what not to do, what to eat and what not to eat, etc.?

The Sages have provided numerous answers to this question, one of which is that these stories are not just tales of bygone characters or events. They, too, are meant to be instructional.[438] In fact, when read accordingly, they offer profound insights and poignant life-wisdom to illuminate our paths and help us navigate our lives. Simply put, the stories of Adam, Eve, Noah, Abraham, Sarah, Rebecca, Leah, Rachel, Moses, etc., represent the stories of our lives. They were included specifically because of their universal and archetypal resonance, and because they so powerfully express and encapsulate the essence of human experience across the ages.

Accordingly, the Torah is not intended to be studied as an academic exercise. As informative as critical scholarship is, to only read Torah in such a way would be to circumvent its primary function, which is to be a guiding force in our lives, not just a fossil of antiquity.

Conventional thinking is that you can analyze, understand, and even teach a particular body of wisdom without having to practice it yourself. You can thus be a respected academic, considered an expert in a particular field, without ever actually being a practitioner. For example, it is told that Aristotle was once caught by his disciples engaging in immoral behavior unbecoming of a person of his stature.

His disciples confronted him: "How is it that you, the founder of a comprehensive approach to ethics, should behave in such a manner?" Aristotle replied, "Don't confuse Aristotle the teacher with Aristotle the person."

Torah is different. Torah is a guidebook, not a purely theoretical treatise meant only for academic study. Its primary wisdom is not in amassing ideas, but in guiding day-to-day behavior, life, and practice.

The Talmud teaches[439]: "One who says, 'I have only Torah' (meaning learning without action)...lacks even Torah. The reason? ...The verse (Deuteronomy 5:1) states: *That you may learn them and perform them*... Therefore, anyone not engaged in performance [of the Torah's instructions] is considered to not have engaged in learning them either."

Without integrating the Torah's wisdom into your life and actions, without, in effect, *taking it personally*, you may have learned something, but you have not learned Torah.

The Mishnah[440] compares one whose Torah study exceeds their good deeds to a tree "whose branches are many but whose roots are few." Such a tree will no doubt be uprooted by the first passing wind, making it both vulnerable and unlikely to sustain itself long enough to bear fruit. The Torah's wisdom is designed to center the person, both body and soul, within a confusing and often contradictory world of moral uncertainty. If taken purely as knowledge and theory, Torah will not have its intended effect, which is to anchor us in a life of spirit while we navigate a material world. After all, it isn't knowledge itself that makes us better people, but how and when we act upon and actualize that knowledge. This is the secret of the Tree of Life.

The Big Idea

The Torah's chief concern is not how and when the world was created, but why, and for what purpose.

It Happened Once

THE LUBAVITCHER REBBE ONCE encouraged a man seeking guidance to use his unique talents to the fullest. At a subsequent meeting, the Rebbe said, "I hope you are fulfilling what we discussed. Don't turn me into a sinner!"

Taken aback, the man asked, "How could I possibly do that?"

The Rebbe replied with a twinkle in his eye, "Our Sages teach that 'whoever engages in excessive talk brings on sin.' If our previous conversation led to no practical outcome, it was merely 'excessive talk.'"

edut עדות

Reminders

A RELIGION OF REMINDERS

JUDAISM SEEMS TO PLACE a disproportionate emphasis on reminders. In fact, there is an entire category of *mitzvot* dedicated to them, which includes several of the most well-known *mitzvot*. One such example is the mitzvah of *mezuzah*, the command to affix a scroll upon the doorpost of one's home.

Regarding this mitzvah, Maimonides[441] writes, "Whenever one enters or leaves a home, he will be confronted with the declaration of G-d's unity; he will remember the love due to G-d and will be aroused from his slumbers and absorption in temporal vanities."

Another example is the mitzvah of *tzitzit*, the command to wear fringes on the corners of four-cornered garments as a constant reminder of one's religious commitments. As the verse states,[442] *And you shall see them [the tzitzit] and remember all of the mitzvot of the L-rd.*

Additionally, in the Talmud, R. Meir expounds[443]: "What is different about sky-blue from all other colors [i.e. why was it specified for the mitzvah of ritual fringes]? Because blue resembles the sea, and the sea resembles the sky, and the sky resembles G-d's seat of glory." The blue thread of *tzitzit* is thus designed to be a reminder of our heavenly connection.

Further examples of such "reminders" include the mitzvah of *tefillin*, the command to don phylacteries on one's head and arm as a daily reminder to bind ourselves to G-d in mind, heart, and deed[444]; reciting the *Shema* as a reminder of G-d's unity, morning and evening;

observing Shabbat as a reminder of Creation[445] and the Exodus[446]; and various Jewish festivals that remind us of different providential events in our nation's history.

The Hebrew word for this particular category of *mitzvot* is *eidot*, or testimonial *mitzvot*.[447] Accordingly, each of these *mitzvot* "testify" and remind us of their underlying ideas and related events. Additionally, by performing the *mitzvot*, we, too, bear witness to G-d's hand in our collective and individual lives.

While not formally part of this same class, there are many other Jewish practices and traditions that are designed with a similar intent.

For example, wearing a headcovering (referred to as a *kippah* in Israel, or by Eastern European Jews as a *yarmulke*, possibly from the Polish word *jarmulka*) as a reminder to fear heaven.

The Talmud[448] relates that astrologers predicted R. Nachman bar Yitzchak would become a thief. His mother would therefore remind him: "Cover your head so that the fear of Heaven will be upon you." Elsewhere,[449] the Talmud relates that "R. Huna ben Yehoshua never walked four cubits bareheaded. He would say: 'The Divine Presence is above my head.'"

Interestingly, many associate the word *yarmulke* with the Aramaic words, *yarei malka*—awe of the King.[450]

Another example of Jewish tradition orchestrating such regular spiritual reminders for us is the practice to read a portion from the Torah scroll every Monday, Thursday, and Shabbat.

This regularly scheduled reading of the Torah was established by Moses to ensure that three days not go by without Torah study,[451] so that our connection to G-d and religious obligations would never be far from our minds.

The entire schedule of the observant Jew seems to revolve around such prompts: prayer, study, ritual, dress—these are all triggers designed to keep the religious practitioner in focus.

Why, one may ask, does Judaism make such a big deal about reminders? Does it view human beings as so forgetful and fickle that they need so many cues, on one's head, arm, clothing, doorpost, and throughout the calendar day, week, and year?

CHAPTER 37 | REMINDERS

Modern-day philosopher Alain De Botton describes the uniqueness of the religious calendar: "In the secular world, we tend to believe that if you tell someone something once, they'll remember it... Religions are cultures of repetition. They circle the great truths again and again and again. The religious calendar is a way of making sure that across the year you will bump into certain very important ideas. In Jewish chronology, Passover reminds us to reflect on the importance of liberty and freedom. Now, you won't typically do that by accident; you will do that because you are guided to do that. In the secular world, we think that 'If an idea is important, I'll bump into it. I'll just come across it.' Nonsense, says the religious worldview. We need calendars, we need to structure time, we need to synchronize encounters."

We need reminders because, while the human brain is wired to calculate and invent many incredible things, one thing our mind is not very good at is remembering. Our brains have a remarkable capacity to compile millions of data points received from our senses to create a single image, and at lightning speeds! Yet, reminding ourselves of simple things is often difficult. In fact, the average person can only retain up to seven objects in their short-term memory!

We are therefore in need of constant reminders, or "synchronized encounters," to ensure that we don't succumb to life's many distractions and instead stay on course to lead a life that is guided by our value system.

Indeed, as the following studies suggest, the key to acting on our values is how regularly we are reminded of them.

For instance, in a study conducted by UCLA Professor Dan Ariely,[452] half the participants were asked to recall the Ten Commandments while the other half were asked to remember ten books they had read in high school before taking a quiz. The results overwhelmingly indicated that the mere fact of being reminded of the Ten Commandments reduced the tendency to cheat.[453]

Another researcher, Deepak Malhotra[454] of Harvard Business School, found that Christians were three hundred percent more likely to give charitable donations if the appeal was made on a Sunday than on any other day of the week. Obviously, the participants did not change their minds about their religious beliefs or about the importance of charitable giving between one day and the next. They were simply more likely to have attended church and thought about G-d on Sunday than on any other day of the week. He referred to this phenomenon as "The Sunday Effect." Similarly, it was found that among Muslims in Morocco, people were more likely to give generously to charity if they lived in a place where they could hear the daily call to prayer from a local minaret.

Interestingly, this finding was not limited to religious individuals—people who reported to be atheists showed equivalent levels of increased benevolence when reminded of religious principles or moral values![455]

Ultimately, it is not what we believe but how regularly we are reminded of our beliefs that transforms our behavior.

This is why, more than any other religion, Judaism inserts choreographed cues into the daily lives of its practitioners so that at every turn we are confronted with signals and symbols to help us recall our most cherished values and to act in accordance with our highest ideals.

The Big Idea

*It is not **what** we believe but how regularly we are reminded of our beliefs that most determines our behavior and the people we become.*

It Happened Once

R. Avraham Mordechai Alter, known as the Imrei Emes, was the third Rebbe of the Gerrer Chasidic dynasty. He once heard that one of his Chasidim would be traveling to Paris on business. In those days, many devoutly religious Jews lived in *shtetls* and more rural areas outside the bustling big cities of Europe, where the secularizing effects of the Enlightenment were most prevalent. Traveling to the big city was therefore considered a spiritual risk, because it was full of distractions and temptations to leave the traditional way of life behind.

"I know that one can purchase excellent cigars in Paris," the Rebbe told the Chasid. "Please purchase some for me when you are there."

Though puzzled by the strange request, the Chasid of course agreed to do so.

After his business was completed, the Chasid boarded a train heading back to Poland. As they passed through Belgium, he suddenly remembered that he had completely forgotten to purchase the cigars for his Rebbe! He got off at the next town and bought the finest cigars he could find.

Boarding the train after this detour, he arrived back in Ger and went to see his Rebbe.

"Rebbe, I must be honest. I did not purchase these cigars in Paris. On the way home, I made a special stop in Belgium and got the best Belgian cigars I could find. They are certainly as good as Parisian cigars, if not better."

"My dear son, do you really think that I needed cigars from Paris?" said the Rebbe with a smile. "I wanted you to remember even in Paris—the epitome of temptation and negative influences—where you come from and the values you stand for."

The Commandments
mitzvah

מצוה

CHAPTER 38 | THE COMMANDMENTS

THE KEYS TO G-D'S HEART

Some find Judaism's fixation on minor details of behavior to be burdensome, even petty. It is indeed puzzling that an infinite G-d would care so much about seemingly trivial aspects of our private lives, such as whether one turns on the lights during Shabbat or enjoys a slice of cheese on a burger. And yet, the Torah, as elucidated by the Talmud, is full of G-d's commandments that impact every moment of our day, from the way we wake up to which shoe we put on first.

Interestingly, the Hebrew word mitzvah, which is commonly translated as commandment, is related to the Aramaic word *tzavta*, to attach.[456] In this light, rather than seeing them simply as rules dictated by a king to his subjects, *mitzvot* take on a more intimate, even romantic, connotation. They are not only acts of law, but also acts of love revealed to us by our Beloved as invitations into a deeper relationship.

Reflecting the notion that *mitzvot* are acts of Divine romance, the blessings we recite before fulfilling *mitzvot* begin with the words, "[Blessed are You, L-rd, our G-d, King of the universe] Who has sanctified us (*kideshanu*) through His *mitzvot*, and has instructed us to… (here the blessing includes the specific mitzvah one is about to perform)."

Remarkably, the *Tanya*[457] points out that the Hebrew word *kideshanu* can mean both sanctified and betrothed.[458] This means that each time we perform a mitzvah, we thank G-d not only for "sanctifying us through His commandments" but also for *betrothing us* through His commandments!

The *Tanya* continues: "...like a man who betroths a wife so that she be united with him in a perfect bond, as it is written,[459] *And he shall cleave to his wife, and they shall be one flesh.* Exactly the same, and even infinitely surpassing it, is the union of the Divine soul that is engaged in Torah and the commandments...with the light of the blessed *Ein Sof*. This is why Solomon, peace be upon him, in the Song of Songs, compared this union [with G-d through the *mitzvot*] to the union of bridegroom and bride..."

Similar to a spouse's request to prepare their favorite dish in a particular way, or to wear a certain piece of jewelry to a special event, the *mitzvot* are expressions of G-d's innermost desires. Our attentive fulfillment of their every detail is thus an expression of our desire to be close with G-d.

From a philosophical point of view, as finite beings we should have no available means to meaningfully engage with an infinite G-d, much less to achieve any degree of intimacy. From a purely rational standpoint, the distance between Creator and creation is unbridgeable.

Nevertheless, G-d chose to invite us into a relationship, which is what makes this connection possible. The cosmic chasm is thus traversed through our inspired acts infused with loving attention, tending to all aspects of our beloved's desire.

In choosing us as the recipients of His love and setting His heart upon our finite gestures of affection, G-d makes Himself vulnerable, so to speak, as He awaits our expressed devotion.

This, however, presents a paradox, for, ultimately, G-d does not *need* us or our *mitzvot*.

By definition, G-d is omnipotent and without any lack or dependency whatsoever, as the verse[460] states, *If you are righteous, what do you give Him; what does He receive from your hand?* G-d did not create humanity because he needs or seeks to gain anything from us, but, to the contrary, in order to bestow goodness upon us.

In any relationship, the ability to express one's love and

meaningfully contribute to the relationship is both gratifying and dignifying. Without any possibility for reciprocity or sense of responsibility, a mature and mutual love is simply not possible.

The *mitzvot* were thus lovingly designed to give us the means to concretely convey our love and to actively participate in our relationship with G-d.

This ought to change our perspective on *mitzvot*.

Mitzvot are not G-d's way of dictating our every action or diminishing our sense of agency and power. Quite the opposite! *Mitzvot* are the G-d-given pathways through which we may enter into a deeper and eternal connection with the Divine. Through their performance, our sense of purpose and impact is enhanced, as our finite actions take on cosmic ramifications and reverberations.

When viewed from this perspective—as active fulfillments of G-d's desires—the seemingly minor technicalities and petty nuances of the *mitzvot* are no longer trivial but are nothing less than the keys to G-d's heart.

The Big Idea

Mitzvot *aren't restrictive commandments that we* have *to do; they are acts of spiritual connection that we get to do.*

It Happened Once[461]

Mr. David Stauber and his wife once went for a private audience with the Lubavitcher Rebbe. He came as an observer without any particular question of his own, but as he was told to write something, he wrote a question that had always bothered him: "If G-d is so great, why does He insist on all these tiny details? It seems to upset G-d if we miss one."

During the meeting, the Rebbe turned to him and said, "I don't understand your question."

Mistakenly thinking that the Rebbe had not understood what he wrote, he proceeded to translate it into Yiddish. The Rebbe raised his hand to stop him, explaining: "It is not for G-d; it is for us. G-d wants us to be close to him, and this is the path He gives us.

"He is essentially saying: 'If you follow this path, you will find me.' It is not 'if you don't follow this path, I will hurt you.' Just the opposite. 'I want you to come close. Here I am giving you a path through which you can find this proximity, this closeness.'"

"It was a very radical thought to me," David recalls. "I had never seen Judaism in that light. To me, Judaism had always seemed focused on what is forbidden, and it seemed to be saying that G-d wants subservience, not love—that I must conform my conduct in order to avoid G-d's wrath and punishment. I had never seen it in a positive way—that G-d loves us and wants us to come close to Him.

"This really intrigued me; I was taken. I felt like I was in a dark room and someone had turned on the light."

Priesthood *kohen*

כהן

CHAPTER 39 | PRIESTHOOD

TO SERVE OR NOT TO SERVE

PEOPLE COMMONLY THINK OF the priesthood as a privileged rank or status symbol, a relic of an antiquated caste or class system in which some were seen as being of higher spiritual standing than others simply by virtue of their birth, and a remnant of an elitist social structure in which those on the bottom served those on the top.

While Judaism's Levitical priesthood may seem to follow this hierarchical template, closer examination reveals that it works in quite the opposite manner. Unlike the English word priest, which is a derivative of the Latin word *prevost*, meaning "one put over others," the Hebrew word *kohen* means servant,[462] or to serve, as in: *...[bring] Aaron your brother and his sons... (l'chahano) to serve Me...*[463]

Therefore, instead of those on the bottom, the masses, serving those on the top, the nobility, in the Jewish model, those on the "top," the priests, are meant to serve on behalf of those on the "bottom," the community.

In other words: The *kohanim* were not meant to lord over the people, but to connect them to the L-rd. Whereas a feudal lord held lands and collected tribute from the commoners who lived in them, the Jewish priestly class were not given any tribal land of their own and had to live on land owned by the people.

The *kohanim* were essentially propertyless, and thus were the sacred property of all Israel.

The reason for this stipulation is explained in Scripture[464]: *"The*

Levites [*the larger tribe of which the* kohanim *were a part*] *have no share among you because the service of G-d is their portion.*

Maimonides explains further[465]:

"Why were the Levites not allotted land in Israel or a share in its spoils along with their brethren? Because they were singled out to serve G-d and minister to Him, to teach His upright ways and just laws to the multitudes, as it is written[466]: *They shall teach Your laws to Jacob, and Your instruction to Israel.* For this reason, they were separated from worldly affairs. They fought no battles like the rest of Israel; they inherited no land…"[467]

Having no land of their own meant that the Levites were not financially self-sufficient or independent; rather, they had to rely entirely on the gifts of the people.

Interestingly, *kohanim* who served in the Holy Temple were required to have a haircut at least once every thirty days,[468] and the high priest once a week. Moreover, when the Levites were first consecrated in the wilderness, they were instructed to shave off all their hair.[469] What is the significance of this requirement? According to Kabbalah,[470] hair represents self-expression. This is reflected in the Hebrew word for hair itself, *saar*, which shares the same letters as the word *shaar*, meaning gate, expressing the idea that one's hair is a gateway into their individual soul and personality. Such self-expression was off-limits for *kohanim*, who were essentially public servants completely committed to devoting their lives to the service of G-d and others. In fact, the more elevated the *kohen*, the more limited was their self-expression, which is why the high priest had to cut his hair weekly rather than monthly!

Similar to the word *kohen*, the name of the priestly tribe Levi also reflects the essence of their role. The word Levi means to join and connect with others, as we find when Leah gave her son Levi his name,[471] *for now my husband will connect (yilaveh) to me.*

Likewise, in the book of Numbers,[472] Aaron was instructed, *Your brothers, the tribe of Levi, will come near alongside you, and they will join (yilavu) with you and serve with you.* Being a Levite of any variety is therefore not an empty symbol of status and prestige; rather, it is a clarion call to selflessly serve G-d and the people.

It is within this context of communal service that we can more deeply understand the strict code of conduct by which the Levites and especially the *kohanim* were expected to live. Above and beyond all the commandments that applied to the Jewish people as a whole, the *kohanim* led even more circumscribed lives. For instance, they could not go to a cemetery or come in contact with the dead.[473] They also could not eat any food that may have come into contact with sources of ritual impurity as defined by the Torah. The purpose of such strictures was so that the *kohanim* would always be pure and available to aid and support the spiritual needs of the Jewish people at a moment's notice.[474]

The uniqueness of the Levites and *kohanim* is therefore not a privilege that sets them above others; instead, it is a responsibility to dedicate their lives to a higher cause beyond themselves.

In a broader sense, this principle can be applied to the oft-misunderstood notion of "Jewish chosenness" in which Jews were chosen by G-d, not to be held above others, but to assume the sacred duty of serving as *a light unto the nations*.[475] In fact, at the revelation of the Torah at Mount Sinai,[476] the Jewish people were referred to collectively as a nation of *kohanim*. Like the *kohanim* in relation to the Jewish people, the Jewish people are meant to live a life of added scrutiny and purity[477] in order to serve the spiritual needs of humanity. Indeed, the Jews were charged by G-d not to pronounce their ontological "aristocracy" to the world, but to lovingly preach and devotedly practice G-d's word, humbly serving as a living example of a morally upright lifestyle based on a sacred value system.

True, *kohanim* and Levites were, and still are, accorded precedence when it comes to religious honors—such as being called to the Torah before others and leading the after-meal blessings.[478] The intention of such practices, however, is not to elevate them as individuals above others; rather, it is meant to honor the value and virtue of selfless public service that they represent. Such an honor therefore should instill within a *kohen* or Levi a sense of humility at the thought of the gravity of their charge and the trust placed in them by G-d and the people.

This is reflected beautifully in a concise teaching from *Ethics of Our Fathers*[479]: "Who is honored? He who honors others." Expressed within this short saying is a complete value system.

As a society, Jews value and publicly celebrate altruism and public service, as exhibited by the deference given to *kohanim* and Levites. In so doing, we seek to inspire and evoke similar aspirations from the wider community to emulate and even outdo such noted acts of caring and righteousness to whatever degree each of us is able to in our own lives.

The Big Idea

In the Jewish tradition, one rises to the top by serving those at the bottom.

CHAPTER 39 | PRIESTHOOD

It Happened Once

WHILE VISITING PARIS AFTER World War II, the Lubavitcher Rebbe attended services at a particular synagogue and was given the honor of addressing the congregation.

The Rebbe accepted the invitation and began his remarks by noting that the Hebrew word for honor, *kavod*, is etymologically linked to the Hebrew word *kaved*, which means heavy.

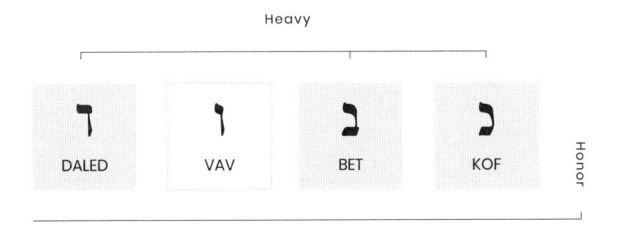

Heavy

ד	ו	ב	כ
DALED	VAV	BET	KOF

Honor

"This teaches that with honor comes the weight of responsibility and service. And the same is true of every promotion and elevation we experience in life, which is G-d's way of saying, 'You have more to give others than you imagined.' Accordingly, when one is honored, it should elicit in them greater humility and dedication to serving the needs of others."

עבודה

avodah　　　Worship
―――――――――――――――――

CHAPTER 40 | WORSHIP

THE POINT OF RELIGION

RELIGIONS THROUGHOUT THE WORLD are comprised of myriad rules, rites, and acts of devotion, leading many to focus primarily on the mediums of religion rather than its message.

The Hebrew word for religious worship, *avodah*, however, has less to do with outward forms of devotion than it does with a person's inner work of character development.

The word *avodah* is etymologically associated with the word *ibud*, to stretch, as in stretching leather.[480] Accordingly, *avodah* refers to

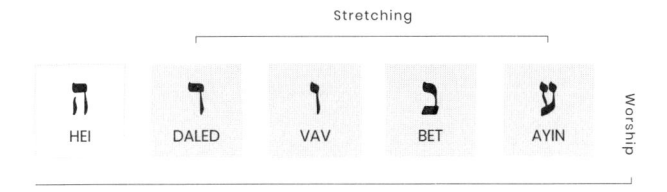

		Stretching			
ה	ד	ו	ב	ע	
HEI	DALED	VAV	BET	AYIN	Worship

the work of "stretching" oneself in order to overcome one's natural self-serving instincts by refining their character and developing their spiritual potential.

In the words of Maimonides[481]: "Most of the Torah's laws are but 'counsel given from He Who is of great counsel' to improve one's character and make one's conduct upright."

In other words, G-d is not only interested in what we do but also, and primarily, in who we are and can become.

The Torah[482] instructs us to *walk in G-d's ways*. The Sages[483] interpret this to mean, "Just as [G-d] is called 'compassionate,' so must you be compassionate; just as the Holy One, blessed be He, is called 'gracious,' so must you be gracious; just as [G-d] is called 'righteous,' so must you be righteous; just as [G-d] is called 'holy,' so must you be holy."

This teaching imparts a radical shift in religious thinking: The way to become more G-dly is not through spiritual detachment and isolation; rather, it is through deep engagement and concern for the well-being of humanity and the world.

To become more G-dly, one must become more humane.

In Judaism, the word *avodah* is used in a general sense to connote our fulfillment of the *mitzvot* as described in the Torah and interpreted by the Sages. In this sense, all of our religious actions and obligations are considered our *avodah*, our "work," or Divine service.

Biblically and liturgically, the term *avodah* primarily refers to the offering of animal sacrifices in the Holy Temple. This central ritual was indeed a fundamental pillar of religious practice during the Temple era, and it is within this context that the tensions between outer behavior and inner transformation come into particularly sharp relief.

The Hebrew word for sacrifice is *korban*, which comes from the word *kiruv*, to draw close,[484] communicating the essential point that the sacrifices were not performed for G-d's sake—as if G-d were in need of our gifts—but for ours.[485]

	To Draw Close			
ן	ב	ר	ק	Sacrifice
NUN	BET	REISH	KUF	

This "drawing close" occurred in two essential ways. First, by taking a valuable asset, in this case one's animal, and donating it to the Temple service, one expressed their devotion to G-d. Additionally, the ritual of animal sacrifice served as a visceral meditation on mortality and life's purpose, because it brought the person into close contact with the fragile and transient nature of physical existence.

From the Chasidic point of view, the *avodah* of animal sacrifices is particularly emblematic of the internal impact that all forms of Jewish religious practice are intended to have on one's personality and character.

Commenting on the verse,[486] *A person who will offer from [among] you a sacrifice to the L-rd...of the domesticated animal, of the cattle, and of the sheep...*" R. Schneur Zalman of Liadi[487] highlights the similarities between certain human and animal characteristics. For example, some people are born with a temperament that is thick-skinned, stubborn, and domineering like an ox. They have a natural propensity to be controlling and are determined to always be right. Others are meek and conformist like sheep, lacking resolve or the ability to think for themselves when it is called for. Yet others are brazen and impudent, as the Hebrew word for goat, *eiz*, connotes. The psycho-spiritual application of Biblical animal sacrifice is thus interpreted as a reference to the inner work of refining whichever animal traits and tendencies one naturally possesses and sublimating them in the service of one's moral and spiritual development.[488]

However, as mentioned, there is always the danger of losing the internally transformative perspective and focusing solely on the ritual's form rather than its substance.

In fact, the prophets would condemn those who offered sacrifices as a kind of bribe or peace offering to G-d in the hope that He would absolve them despite their evil ways. As King David declares[489]: *You do not desire sacrifice [for if You did], I would bring it; You do not want a burnt-offering. The sacrifice to G-d is a broken [repentant] spirit; G-d does not despise a broken and crushed heart.*[490]

R. Jonathan Sacks expounds[491] upon the prophets' numerous rebukes against vain sacrifices:

"They were not criticizing the institution of sacrifices. They were criticizing something as real now as it was in their time. What distressed them to the core of their being was the idea that you could serve G-d and at the same time act disdainfully, cruelly, unjustly, insensitively, or callously towards other people. 'So long as I am in G-d's good graces, that is all that matters.' That is the thought that made the prophets incandescent with indignation. If you think that, they seem to say, then you haven't understood either G-d or Torah.

"...Amos, Hosea, Isaiah, Micah, and Jeremiah all witnessed societies in which people were punctilious in bringing their offerings to the Temple, but in which there was bribery, corruption, perversion of justice, abuse of power, and the exploitation of the powerless by the powerful. The prophets saw in this a profound and dangerous contradiction.

"...G-d cannot be bribed or appeased...any specific wrongs righted by sacrifice do not excuse other wrongs. Intention and mindset were thus absolutely essential in the sacrificial system; they were in fact the rubric of its spiritual success or failure."

Judaism advances the spiritually radical perspective that the aim of religion is not only to worship G-d, but also to refine and elevate the inner character of each worshipper in the process.

Without such inner transformation, the outward motions and mechanisms of any religion—no matter how lofty its stated ideals—can become mere empty shells, and even potential idols that usurp the ultimate goal of their enactment.

From a mystical point of view, the paradigm outlined above sheds light on a theological conundrum that has plagued Kabbalists for centuries: Why would a pure and perfectly righteous soul be uprooted from its spiritual home and thrust into a world of Divine concealment, where it will be forced to face the bodily temptations of greed, lust, desire, anger, jealousy, etc.?

In answer to this question, the mystics teach[492] that the very purpose of the soul's descent into this world is to wrestle[493] with and refine our earthly impulses and egoic character flaws, thereby Divinizing the body and wider world.

From this perspective, a life of true spiritual success is measured not only by the Torah one has learned or the rituals they have performed, but by the inner moral and characterological progress one makes during their time on this earth.[494]

According to Judaism, this is the essence of *avodah*.

CHAPTER 40 | WORSHIP

It Happened Once

R. MORDECHAI OF NESCHIZ HAD longed for a *tallit katan* (a small *tallit*, worn under or over one's clothing) made out of wool from the Holy Land.

When he finally procured the wool, he commissioned one of his students to fashion it into a *tallit*.

Unfortunately, in cutting out the opening, the young man folded the cloth one time too many, resulting in two holes instead of one.

With trepidation, he informed R. Mordechai that he had ruined the *tallit katan* that R. Mordechai had wanted for so long.

R. Mordechai calmly told him not to worry.

"But I ruined your *tallit*," cried the man.

"It isn't ruined," replied R. Mordechai. "One hole is for me to put my head through, and the other is a test to see if I will lose my temper."

The Big Idea

The aim of religion is not only to worship G-d, but to refine and elevate the inner character of the worshipper.

Repentance

teshuvah תשובה

CHAPTER 41 | REPENTANCE

RETURN TO THE LAND OF YOUR SOUL

THE HEBREW WORD *TESHUVAH* is typically translated as repentance, suggesting that its objective is to feel regret, guilt, and shame. In truth, the goal of *teshuvah* is anything but.

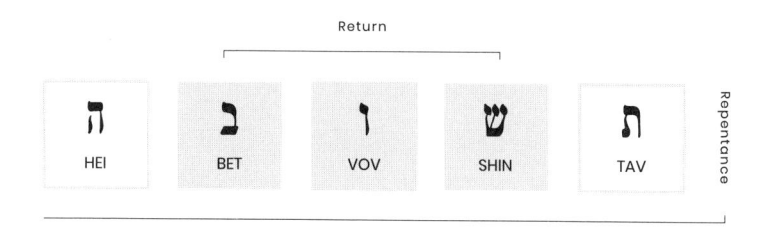

ה	ב	ו	ש	ת
HEI	BET	VOV	SHIN	TAV

Return — Repentance

Teshuvah means to return.[495] But return where? The Sages have taught over the millennia that the essence of each person is his or her soul. According to Chassidic philosophy, the soul is literally "a part of G-d on high"[496] and is therefore incorruptible and can never truly be blemished by sin. Therefore, when we sin, we are merely losing our way and forgetting who we really are—much like being overtaken by "a temporary state of insanity."[497] As Maimonides writes,[498] every Jew, at their deepest level, ultimately "wants to fulfill all of G-d's instructions and distance themselves from any sin, if not for their negative inclination that overcomes them."

According to Jewish thought, then, the journey of *teshuvah* is not about "turning over a new leaf" or being "born again"; rather, it is simply finding our way back to the land of our soul.[499]

What is true of the individual is also true of the Jewish people as a collective; we may distance ourselves, but we are never completely divorced from G-d.

Concerning this, R. Abba bar Zavda teaches in the Talmud[500] that: "Even when the Jewish people sin, they are still called 'Israel.'" In G-d's own words: "It is impossible to replace them with any other nation."[501]

The covenantal bond between G-d and Israel may be tested and strained, but it can never broken; they are always inextricably bound at their core.

This redemptive approach to spiritual rehabilitation stems from Judaism's overwhelmingly positive view of the human being, who is, according to the Torah, created *in the image of G-d*.[502] Every person possesses a core of inherent goodness whose integrity cannot be compromised. While outwardly, one's actions may not always reflect this inner goodness and G-dliness, people always have the ability to shed their superficial facade and do *teshuvah*—returning to their truest, deepest selves.

Certainly, this does not give us license to disown responsibility for any of our past sins and harmful actions. On the contrary, the process of *teshuvah* is a proactive acknowledgment of wrongdoing, but it is one that emerges from a profound realization of who we are at our core, which, in turn, elicits a deeply felt sense of remorse for having acted so out of character.

Teshuvah is therefore a spiritual repudiation of philosopher Will Durant's statement: "We are what we repeatedly do." Judaism teaches us otherwise. We are not our sins or our mistakes. We are all inherently good, holy, righteous souls that sometimes lose our way but can always make the choice to reconnect to our essence.

Teshuvah is this choice.

Rather than focusing our attention exclusively on the specific action or habit that we want to change and obsessing about what it says about us as people,[503] *teshuvah* means reconnecting to our core nature, which is G-dly and good.

Teshuvah, thus, effectively recalibrates our self-image and gives us the strength and confidence to act in alignment with that spiritual essence, which is the cornerstone of our being.

While regret is undoubtedly a necessary component of *teshuvah*, it is only a detail, not its primary focus or goal.

Rather than putting down the person we think we have become and seeing ourselves as defined by the bad choices we've made, *teshuvah* is the process of regaining our senses, remembering who we are at our root, and recasting our behavior to reflect that Divine image.

The Big Idea

Teshuvah *is not about becoming the* new *you, but the real* you.

It Happened Once

THE FAMED MEDIEVAL SPANISH Kabbalist and Biblical commentator, R. Moshe ben Nachman, known as Nachmanides or Ramban, had a disciple named Avner. Following a crisis of faith, Avner rejected his Jewish faith, left the community behind, and became a government official.

One Yom Kippur, Avner sent guards to summon his former teacher to appear before him. Spitefully, he then proceeded to slaughter, roast, and eat a pig in front of Ramban.

Ramban asked him, "What brought you to this point? What caused you to reject the holy ways of your ancestors?!"

"You did, Rabbi!" Avner retorted venomously. "Your teachings were exaggerated and had no basis in reality. You once taught us that in the brief Torah portion of *Haazinu*, a mere fifty-two verses, the Torah encodes the entire history of the Jewish people until the coming of Mashiach.

"That is just ridiculous!" scoffed Avner. "How could three thousand years of history and millions of names be condensed into just six hundred fourteen words?"

"But it's true," replied Ramban, holding his ground.

"Then show me my name and my fate," Avner challenged incredulously.

Ramban fell into a state of meditation and prayed silently to G-d to reveal this secret. After a few minutes, he said, "Your name, Avner, can be found in the third letter of each word in verse 26: *AmaRti (reish) AfEihem (alef) AshBita (bet) Mei'eNosh (nun) ZichRam (reish)*."

The verse reads: *I [G-d] said in my heart that I would scatter them, causing their memory to cease from mankind*, referring to those who had rejected the spiritual and moral way of life.

Avner's face turned pale as heavy tears began to fall.

"Is there any hope for me?" he sobbed. "What can I possibly do to rectify my unthinkable sins?"

"The verse itself has provided the rectification," said Ramban. "It says that G-d will scatter them until their memory is erased. You, too, must scatter those distracting, alien thoughts and impulses that have held you captive for too long, until they are forgotten. Relocate to a new environment, free from your former associations and addictions, and, in this way, you can return to your essence anew and be remembered for good among your people."

At a Chasidic gathering in 1982,[504] the Lubavitcher Rebbe shared that as a child he was taught this story by his teacher. The traditional point stressed by his teacher was the uniqueness of *Parshat Haazinu* and the infinite nature of the Torah. How, indeed, could the Torah contain such esoteric codes and secrets?

"However," the Rebbe added, "there is another layer of depth to the story that has been overlooked. If you notice, the words quoted by Ramban begin not with an *alef*, for Avner, but with a *reish* (*AmaRti*). The letter *reish* is often used as a prefix for Reb, an honorific term. Therefore, his name as quoted in this verse is Reb Avner, revealing how he is actually seen in G-d's eyes through the lens of the Torah—as a spiritual being deserving of respect and reverence."

This self-revelation, like a lightning flash, instantly brought Reb Avner back into alignment with his higher nature. In fact, the moment he was exposed to the error of his ways, a spirit of *teshuvah* was immediately awakened within him. After having left his faith, even going so far as to mock and taunt its devout leaders on its holiest day, the vision of his soul that was reflected back from within the Torah instantly aroused a yearning within him to return to his roots.

beit hakhesset בית הכנסת

Synagogue

CHAPTER 42 | SYNAGOGUE

ALL TOGETHER NOW

WHAT MAKES A PLACE holy? Unlike the words church or temple, which mean "House of the L-rd," the Hebrew term[505] for a synagogue is *beit knesset*, which means "a house of gathering."

Whereas the inauguration of a temple might involve offering sacrifices and anointing oil to introduce holiness into the space, there is no ritual or procedure for inaugurating a synagogue—to formally dedicate it and make it holy, all you need is to gather and pray there.

For, as the Sages teach, when ten individuals pray together in a designated space, their togetherness itself transforms the brick-and-mortar structure into a holy place. No additional rituals or functions are required.

Furthermore, the holiness of a synagogue is not exclusive to the prayer that transpires there.

As the Talmud[506] teaches: "The Divine Presence rests upon *every* gathering of ten," even when those assembled are gathered for reasons other than sacred study or prayer.

Interestingly, the idea that a synagogue is a space whose function is not only to connect people with G-d but with each other, as well, is reflected in the way synagogues were organized historically.

For example, one of the oldest synagogues described in Jewish literature was the great basilica in Alexandria, Egypt. The Talmud[507] describes the socially sensitive setup of this early synagogue in the following way:

"Members of various crafts would sit together. Goldsmiths would sit among themselves, silversmiths among themselves, blacksmiths among themselves, coppersmiths among themselves, and weavers among themselves. When a stranger entered, he would recognize people who plied his craft and would join them. *From there he would secure a livelihood for him and his household, as his colleagues would find him work in that craft.*"

For truly, nothing is more precious and holy to G-d than His children coming together, whether for matters sacred or mundane.[508]

Such togetherness is a foundational element of prayer. Indeed, some communities[509] make a point of opening the morning prayers with the affirmation: "I hereby accept upon myself the positive mitzvah of *You shall love your fellow as yourself.*"

By stating this at the outset of one's prayers, one sensitizes and expands their field of concern and responsibility beyond themselves, connecting their experience, aspirations, and blessings with the larger community of which they are a part.

While many prayers from the liturgy may be recited alone, some of the most important Jewish rituals,[510] such as reading from the Torah, reciting the Mourner's *Kaddish*, or performing a marriage ceremony, cannot be enacted without a *minyan*—a quorum of ten. What's more, even those who aren't present in the synagogue during prayers stand to benefit when the community gathers in prayer, as the Talmud[511] teaches: "When is a time of favor [for one's prayers to be answered]? When the congregation is gathered for prayer."

Why? Because, while G-d is certainly accessible to all on an individual level at any time, He is more readily accessible when we turn to Him as a unified collective,[512] whether in space or time.[513]

When it comes to prayer and community, not only is there strength in numbers, as mentioned above, but also in diversity and inclusivity. Accordingly, we learn that a *minyan* does not have to be made up of only spiritually advanced or learned individuals; rather, it can include people at any level of spiritual development and religious observance. As the saying goes, "Nine great rabbis cannot make a *minyan*, but ten simple shoemakers can."

Notably, the Hebrew word *tzibbur*, another word for a community gathered for prayer, is an acronym for *tzaddik*/righteous person, *beinoni*/intermediate person, and *rasha*/evil person.[514] A real *tzibbur* must include and represent the full spectrum of the community.

Evil Person		Intermediate Person		Righteous Person	
ר REISH	ו VAV	ב BET	י YUD	צ TZADDIK	Community
ש SHIN		י YUD		ד DALED	
ע AYIN		נ NUN		י YUD	
		ו VAV		ק KUF	
		נ NUN			
		י YUD			

The collective setting for Jewish prayer is so important because it models one of the broader functions of prayer in general, which is to move our attention from the particular to the universal, from the subjective to the objective, from the "I" to the "We," shifting our focus from our own self-centered desires to a more selfless concern for the good of the whole that includes and transcends us individually.

This emphasis on communal prayer thus conveys an essential

message about Judaism's approach to our relationship with G-d. When we succeed in overcoming our self-oriented interests by coming together in prayer, that is when and where we are most likely to discover G-d and to find favor in His eyes.

Indeed, the Talmud teaches that G-d is more attentive and available to us when we put the needs of others before our own. As our Sages teach[515]: "Anyone who asks for compassion from Heaven on behalf of another, and he requires compassion from Heaven concerning that same matter, he is answered first."

This dynamic is poignantly expressed in the Book of Job[516]: *And the Lord changed the fortune of Job when he prayed for his friends.*

This powerful idea helps explain the fascinating Jewish custom to cover one's face with a *tallit* during the Priestly Blessings, when the *kohanim* stand before the congregation to bless them on special occasions.

Our Sages teach that just as Moses covered his face when the Divine Presence was revealed to him at the burning bush, we, too, cover our faces at the auspicious moment when these prayers are recited in deference to the unique revelation of G-d's presence elicited by this communal blessing.[517]

But why is G-d's presence more manifest during the Priestly Blessings than at any other time or through any other prayer?

The answer is that this is the one prayer in which members of the congregation bless each other rather than being blessed by G-d directly. Paradoxically, G-d's presence is even more manifest in that moment, despite the role of an intermediary, because there is nothing more precious to G-d than when one of His children blesses another from the depths of their being.[518]

When such love and concern is the foundation of our relationships, G-d's presence is amplified among the community.

This sentiment is echoed in the final words of the *Amidah* prayer, where we say "Bless us, our Father, united all as one, in the radiance of Your countenance." The mystics[519] interpret this to mean: "Bless us, our Father, [*because*] we are united all as one, in the radiance of Your countenance." In other words, it is on account of our togetherness that we merit G-d's blessing.

Accordingly, we find that the greatest milestones and watershed moments in Jewish history took place after, and as a result of, a heightened sense of unity. For instance, Rashi[520] points out that at Mount Sinai, millions of Israelites gathered "like one person, with one heart." Our Sages teach that it was the people's unique display of collective unity that elicited G-d's revelation of the Ten Commandments.[521]

Today, we live in a hyper-individualistic world, where, as time progresses, many tend to burrow deeper and further into themselves, creating micro-universes based on limited, and limiting, personal preferences. This is the age of the self-reinforcing algorithm. Judaism's approach to communal prayer is, in a sense, the antidote to such egoic inertia.

From this perspective, prayer is not only about finding ourselves, but also, and even more importantly, about losing ourselves in the collective pursuit of something beyond us.

The *beit knesset* teaches us that we are all interconnected, that we are incomplete without each other, and that a lack in one is a lack in all.

By gathering together, including and transcending our individuality, we gain access to the Divine Presence and create a fitting receptacle for G-d's blessing. As our Sages teach[522]: "There is no better vessel for Divine blessing than peace." Such sensitized socio-spirituality is the highest form of holiness we can aspire to.

Put simply, we don't gather in a synagogue because it is holy; a synagogue is holy because that's where we gather.

The Big Idea

Where is G-d? Wherever you let others in.

It Happened Once

THE TORAH COMMANDS US to *Love your fellow as yourself*,[523] and to love the L-rd, your G-d.[524] This prompted the disciples of R. Schneur Zalman of Liadi to inquire of their teacher: "Which is a greater virtue—love of G-d or love of one's fellow?"

R. Schneur Zalman replied: "In truth, the two are one and the same. However, since G-d loves His children so dearly, the love of one's fellow is a greater expression of love for G-d than simply loving G-d. Why? Because true love means that you love what your beloved loves."

Another story:

Once, R. Michoel the Elder, who was the spiritual adviser in the *yeshivah* of Lubavitch, was about to recite one of the central parts of the morning prayers, the *Shema*, when he noticed that one of the students had torn shoes. He interrupted his prayers and pointed out the torn shoes to the person who was charged with taking care of the students' material needs.

Later, R. Michoel was asked: "Couldn't the torn shoes have waited until after you completed your prayers?"

"The *Shema* proclaims the Oneness of G-d," replied R. Michoel. "A student wearing torn shoes can, G-d forbid, catch a cold [and become ill]. Being conscious of this is an expression of the Oneness of G-d."[525]

Another story:

On his way to the synagogue one morning, the third Rebbe of Lubavitch, R. Menachem Mendel, known as the Tzemach Tzedek, encountered an individual who asked him for a loan. It being a market day, the man needed the money in order to earn something through buying and selling. The Rebbe asked him to come back after the morning service, and he continued on his way to the synagogue. Once in the synagogue, he realized that the poor fellow needed this loan now. So the Rebbe returned home, got some money, sought out the fellow with great difficulty, gave him the money, and only then went to pray.

In the midst of his prayers, the Tzemach Tzedek had a vision of his late grandfather, R. Schneur Zalman of Liadi, who was beaming and lauding him for his thoughtfulness.

Based on this experience, the Tzemach Tzedek taught that when a person helps another with their livelihood, even with a very modest sum, all the gates to the heavenly chambers are open for them.[526]

Prayer
tefillah

תפילה

CHAPTER 43 | PRAYER

HEART WORK

P RAYER IS ONE OF the most visible expressions of religious life. Prayers are said at public events, around dinner tables, and at all manner of life cycle events. And yet, prayer is also simultaneously one of the least understood spiritual practices. To many, it can feel mechanical, scripted, inauthentic, or unfocused.

Addressing the gap that can emerge between prescribed and habitual prayer, and authentic, experiential prayer is therefore essential.

To do so, one must first ask: What is prayer?

The English word prayer comes from the Old French *preiere*—"obtained by entreaty." Prayer is thus most commonly associated with asking for the fulfillment of our needs.

The Hebrew word for prayer, *tefillah*, however, has a multitude of meanings and associations, each contributing to the rich tapestry of prayer's spiritual significance. Whether we seek to reach out to something greater than ourselves or reclaim our essential self, prayer, as understood and practiced in Judaism, is one of the most potent paths of spiritual development.

On the most essential level, *tefillah* means bonding and connection.[527] For instance, in the Mishnah we find that the etymological root *t-f-l* means to attach or bind together.[528] *Tefillah* is therefore not a transactional exchange but an expression of intimacy.

Whereas asking for what we need is a humbling experience that highlights the great divide between petitioner and provider, *tefillah*

```
           Connect
   ה      ל     י     פ     ת
  HEI   LAMED  YUD   PEI   TAV      Prayer
```

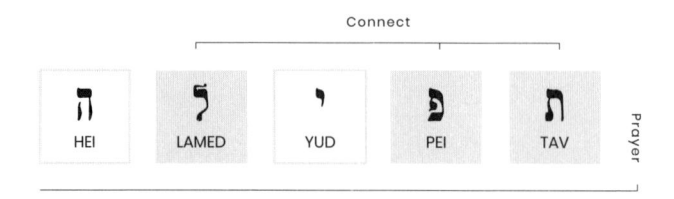

is a declaration of love and an expression of spiritual longing. Its intended outcome is the development of an authentic emotional attachment to G-d. This occurs through the inner cultivation of a sense of nearness during *tefillah* that dissolves the psychic "space" that separates one from G-d.

This inner process of softening and opening the heart pertains to another translation of the word *tefillah*, to struggle. In Genesis, the Torah tells of a rivalry between Rachel and Leah to bear Jacob's children. When Rachel's handmaid gave birth to Jacob's child for the second time, Rachel said:[529] *A fateful struggle* [naftulei] *I waged* [niftalti] *with my sister... So she named him Naphtali.*

The dynamic of "struggle" is an essential—and potentially productive—part of all relationships.

Since we are naturally self-centered beings, in order to engage in a meaningful relationship with another, we each need to work to diminish our natural self-orientation and sense of self-entitlement.

Tefillah is the opportunity to step out of ourselves and our self-absorption and into the awareness and service of our most significant other—G-d. This is the struggle of love.

In any real relationship, a natural dissonance of views and experience exists between the two parties. In the case of the Divine, this perspectival distance is even greater. In G-d's view, we were created to fulfill a Divine mission, whereas, from the human perspective, we are naturally inclined to live life solely for our own benefit and pleasure.

Tefillah is the time we take each day to realign our perspective with that of the Divine—to see the world through G-d's eyes. In that timeless moment of union with the Infinite One, we shift from being profit-minded to prophet-minded. In prayer, we attune ourselves to the *still, small voice*[530] of the Divine, which reminds us that life is so much more than a laundry list of demands and desires, and that we are each here on a sacred mission to better our world.

In addition to all of these essentially relational dynamics, *tefillah* also takes us deep within. This is illustrated in another meaning of the word for prayer, *pelilah*, which means judgment,[531] describing a process of introspection. Prayer, in this sense, is also a time of personal reckoning, a time to evaluate and recalibrate who we really are, what we truly want in life, where we are heading, and how far along that path we have come.

In the words of American theologian Thomas Merton: "People may spend their whole lives climbing the ladder of success only to find, once they reach the top, that the ladder is leaning against the wrong wall."

We are each part body and part soul. And yet, most of the day revolves around feeding our bodily appetites, needs, and drives, strengthening our ego's sense that it is our physical existence that is primary and real. The very act of living itself can relegate our soul to a secondary realm. Left to their own devices, over time our spiritual instincts and impulses can become muted and atrophied.[532]

Against this inertia, prayer is an act of nourishment for the soul. Just as the body needs to be physically fed several times a day, and the psyche needs to be emotionally nourished regularly, so does the soul need constant spiritual sustenance.[533] Prayer gives voice and expression to the soul and its aims, allowing it to sing and soar, revealing and reveling in its natural desire to serve and connect with G-d.

Following this idea even further, R. David Aaron writes[534]: "*L'hitpallel* [lit. to pray] has nothing to do with begging G-d to change His mind. *L'hitpallel* is a reflexive verb that means to do something to yourself. When praying, your question shouldn't be, 'Is G-d listening to my prayers?' Rather, 'Am I listening to my prayers?' 'Does what I say impact me? Have I changed?'

"If one is under the impression that praying is communicating to G-d information that He does not already know, then the whole prayer experience becomes ridiculous. G-d knows that your business is falling apart. G-d knows that you desperately want your soulmate.

G-d knows exactly what is going on in your life. *L'hitpallel* is not about G-d hearing your prayer, although He surely does. It is about you hearing your prayers. You need to say these things to G-d because you need to hear yourself saying them.

"*L'hitpallel*, then, means to do something to yourself. But what exactly is that?"

In the Torah's account of Jacob and his son Joseph, we encounter another permutation of the word *Tefillah—filalti*.

When Joseph learns that Jacob's passing is imminent, he goes to his father to receive a blessing for his two children. Jacob says,[535] *I never filalti that I would ever see your face again...* In this context, the word *filalti* could mean variously: to hope, to imagine, to dream, to envision, to anticipate. In the words of Rashi, *filalti* in this context implies "filling [one's] heart with hopeful thoughts."

Therefore, when we pray mindfully, we are filling our hearts with thoughts and dreams of what it is that we want to see and do in this world. Upon internalization, such prayerful visualizations help effectuate the shifts within ourselves necessary to bring about those desired changes in our lives and in the world.

To connect, to reflect, to project is what the Talmud refers to as *avodah shebalev*, the service of the heart—this is the essence of *tefillah*.

The Big Idea

The point of prayer is not to remind G-d of what we need from Him; rather, it is to remind ourselves of what He "needs" from us.

It Happened Once

A FORMERLY WEALTHY CHASID WHO had lost his entire fortune came to see his Rebbe, R. Schneur Zalman of Liadi. "If G-d has chosen to afflict me with poverty," he wept, "I accept the Divine judgment. But how can I be reconciled with the fact that I cannot repay my debts? That I am unable to meet the dowry I promised for my daughter's upcoming marriage? Never have I reneged on my commitments. Why is the Almighty doing this to me? Why is He causing me such terrible humiliation?

"Rebbe!" cried the Chasid. "I must repay my debts! I must give what I have promised for my daughter!"

R. Schneur Zalman sat with his head in his arms in a state of *dveikut* (meditative attachment to G-d). In this manner he listened to the Chasid's tearful pleas. After a long pause, R. Schneur Zalman lifted his head and said with great feeling: "You speak of all that you need. But you say nothing of what you are needed for."

The Rebbe's words pierced the innermost point of the Chasid's heart, and he fell in a dead faint. The Rebbe's attendant, who stood in the doorway, called to two Chasidim who were in the Rebbe's anteroom. Together they carried the Chasid out of the Rebbe's room, poured water over him, and finally managed to revive him.

When the Chasid opened his eyes, he didn't say anything to anyone. He simply applied himself to the study of Torah and the service of prayer with renewed life and with such devotion and diligence that he forgot all else. Although he spoke to no one and fasted every day, he was in a perpetual state of joy.

Several weeks later, R. Schneur Zalman summoned this Chasid, blessed him with success, and told him to return to his home and business. In time, the Chasid regained his wealth, made good on his debts and promises, married off his daughters, and resumed his philanthropy on an even more generous level than before.

Sabbath

shabbat

שבת

CHAPTER 44 | SABBATH

MORE THAN ENOUGH

It is estimated that in 2019 alone, advertising spending worldwide surpassed five hundred ninety billion dollars. So ubiquitous is the reach of advertising that the average person is exposed to nearly ten thousand marketing images every day.[536]

The main objective of the marketing industry is to make potential consumers feel a sense of lack, and specifically one that can only be filled through their product and the accompanying purchaser's high. According to this view, we must constantly strive to have the newest, the best, and the most in order to achieve happiness.

In contrast to this never-ending pursuit of "more," Ben Zoma taught in the Talmud: "Who is wealthy? He who is happy with his lot."[537] Similarly, the philosopher Seneca said: "It's not the man who has too little but the man who craves more who is poor."

This way of thinking is poignantly captured in the following story. Kurt Vonnegut once met the novelist Joseph Heller at a party hosted by a wealthy hedge-fund manager. Vonnegut pointed out that their wealthy host made more money in one day than Heller would ever make from his best-selling novel, *Catch-22*.

Heller replied, "Yes, but I have something he will never have: Enough."

On the most basic level, Shabbat is a day of *enough*. On Shabbat, we are invited to embrace the fact that whatever we did or did not get done in the preceding six days, whatever we acquired or did not acquire, was exactly enough. This day of enough welcomes us into an oasis in time and spirit, where we can drink deeply from an infinite wellspring, suspending, at least temporarily, our weekday anxieties around scarcity or success.

Shabbat, then, is a twenty-four-hour period that enables us to step off the manic treadmill of physical existence and progress so that we might experience the power and blessing of *enough*. For six days of the week, we strive to produce and perfect, but on Shabbat we stop to appreciate the intrinsic perfection that is already present within creation. We cease all of our efforts to acquire and amass, and instead we celebrate the world around and within us.

Shabbat is our weekly reminder that a joyous life comes not from *having the things we want,* but from *wanting the things we have.*

This shift in perspectival priority is represented by the two loaves of challah traditionally placed on every Shabbat table. The presence of these two loaves is meant to remind us of the two portions of manna that fell each Friday in the wilderness, so that on Shabbat our ancestors could enjoy what they already had rather than seek out what they lacked.[538] It is this very ability to stop our search for *more* that allows us to recognize the blessings present in what we already have.

On a deeper level, Shabbat reminds us not only that we *have* enough, but that we *are* enough!

One of the most toxic phrases in the English language is: How much is he or she worth?

Such a statement reveals a perverse metric, vulgarly confusing and equating one's net worth with their self-worth.

In contrast to most of our lives, which we spend perpetually doing and "becoming," Shabbat is a day of just "being." By slowing us down and focusing our attention on matters of the spirit and family, Shabbat reminds us that our value isn't determined by volatile markets or fluctuating bank accounts. Rather, it derives from the infinite G-d, Who chose to be in a relationship with each of us personally, and Whose love for us is unlimited and unconditional.

In his book, *The Sabbath*, Abraham Joshua Heschel eloquently expresses this vital shift in consciousness: "There is a realm of time where the goal is not to have but to be, not to own but to give, not to control but to share, not to subdue but to be in accord. Life goes wrong when the control of space, the acquisition of things, of space, becomes our sole concern."

Shabbat is that realm of time in which we allow ourselves to just be, without fixating on what we might become.

This illuminates the deeper meaning behind the verse: *Six days you may work, and on the seventh day you shall rest.*[539]

For six days of the week, we seek to "work on" and perfect ourselves, others, and the universe. However, on Shabbat, we recognize and celebrate the inherent point of perfection within all of creation.

Interestingly, the specific activities prohibited on Shabbat are derived from the different forms of work that went into constructing the Tabernacle.[540] The common denominator of these forbidden activities is not that they are energy consuming, per se, but that they are creative and constructive in nature.[541] Some examples include planting, cooking, sewing, building, transforming material, and bringing things into being, such as lighting a fire. On Shabbat, we cease from such creative activity in order to be reminded that the source of our creativity is the Creator of all, and that our existence and value does not come from productivity alone. While creating is something we do, it does not define who we are. Life has its own independent, infinite value that far surpasses any utility we could possibly offer.

Heschel puts it this way: "Six days a week we wrestle with the world, wringing profit from the earth; on the Sabbath we especially care for the seed of eternity planted in the soul. The world has our hands, but our soul belongs to Someone Else."

These days, it is popular to say that Shabbat is particularly relevant to our age of increasingly pervasive and invasive technology, as more and more people feel the need for a day of unplugging.

Interestingly, this was a revolutionary idea when first introduced/practiced by the Jews, as Thomas Cahill illustrates in his book, *The Gifts of the Jews*: "No ancient society before the Jews had a day of rest...the Sabbath is surely one of the simplest and sanest recommendations any god has ever made; and those who live without such septimanal punctuation are emptier and less resourceful."

While this is certainly true, and Shabbat is particularly helpful towards this end, what Shabbat *offers* should not be confused with what Shabbat *is*! Unplugging is a form of "rest from" or even "freedom from." While such "detoxing" is absolutely necessary, Shabbat is much more than that. Its specialness is most fully expressed not in *what we don't do* on this day, but in *what we do* to create the sacred mind and soul space in which we can simply be. Therefore, Shabbat is not just a means to an end, it is an endless end in itself.

The Hebrew word for rest is *nach*. Shabbat, however, means to pause or to settle, from the word *shev*, meaning to sit—to simply stop. There is "rest from," and there is "rest for." Shabbat is not just a weekend—a day to rest from the previous week's work—nor is it just a day to recharge in anticipation of a busy week ahead; it is a proactive pause for its own sake, meant to reconnect us to our souls.

In the words of American author Dan Seidman:[542] "When you press the pause button on a machine, it stops. But when you press the pause button on human beings, they start. You start to reflect, you start to rethink your assumptions, you start to reimagine what is possible, and, most importantly, you start to reconnect with your most deeply held beliefs. Once you've done that, you can begin to reimagine a better path."

Shabbat is thus a day of spiritual recalibration, storytelling, and appreciating family and community; it is a day of higher vision, when we take the time to remember not only what we want, but, most importantly, why we're here.

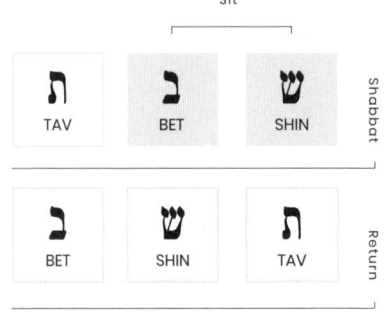

All of this is included in the letters that spell Shabbat, which, when rearranged, spell *tashev*,[543] to return. On Shabbat, we return to the land of our souls. Furthermore, the Talmud[544] teaches that on Shabbat, a person receives an additional soul, or expanded level of spiritual consciousness. Thus, for one day each week, we set aside our material ambitions in order to more actively explore our spiritual origins, essence, and purpose.

This illuminates the fact that Shabbat is infinitely more than simply a day of rest. As the verse states, *And G-d blessed the seventh day and declared it holy...* As evocative and powerful as this statement is, the question remains: What exactly makes Shabbat holy and what does that mean?

Before *Kiddush* on Shabbat day, we recite *V'shamru*, a passage from the Torah describing the six days of creation. The passage ends with the word *vayinafash,* typically translated as [*and on the seventh day*] *He rested.*

However, there is a deeper interpretation of this passage, based on an etymological understanding of the word *vayinafash,* which shares the same root letters as the word *nefesh,* the vivified soul.

Significantly, the word *nefesh* can also refer to the act of breathing, particularly in the context of catching one's breath. Read in this way, we can surmise that the world itself is being infused with spirit on Shabbat from a concentrated influx of Divine breath.

This connection between rest, spirit, and revivification through breath, alluded to in the word *vayinafash,* suggests that the entirety of creation was and is *ensouled* on Shabbat, the seventh day, a phenomenon referred to by the Kabbalists as *aliyat haolamot,* the elevation of the worlds. This spiritualization through Divine breath that the world experiences on Shabbat is congruent with the ensoulment of the human being through the medium of G-d's breath on the sixth day of creation.

When we harmonize with that cosmic energy and rhythm, we enter into complete alignment with our soul, with the Creator, and with all of creation. Such is the gift of Shabbat. "It is a day on which we are called upon to share in what is eternal in time, to turn from the results of creation to the mystery of creation, from the world of creation to the creation of the world."[545]

It Happened Once

In *This Is My G-d,* Pulitzer Prize winning author Herman Wouk describes his own experience with Shabbat observance:

The Shabbat has cut most sharply athwart my own life when one of my plays has been in rehearsal or in tryout.

The crisis atmosphere of an attempt at Broadway is a legend of our time, and a true one; I have felt under less pressure going into battle at sea.

Friday afternoon, during these rehearsals, inevitably seems to come when the project is tottering on the edge of ruin. I have sometimes felt guilty of treason, holding to the Shabbat in such a desperate situation. But then, experience has taught me that a theater enterprise almost always is in such a case. Sometimes it does totter to ruin, and sometimes it totters to great prosperity, but tottering is its normal gait, and cries of anguish are its normal tone of voice.

So I have reluctantly taken leave of my colleagues on Friday afternoon and rejoined them on Saturday night. The play has never collapsed in the meantime. When I return, I find it tottering as before, and the anguished cries as normally despairing as ever. My plays have encountered in the end both success and failure, but I cannot honestly ascribe either result to my observing the Shabbat.

Leaving the gloomy theater, the littered coffee cups, the jumbled scarred-up scripts, the haggard actors, the knuckle-gnawing producer, the clattering typewriter, and the dense tobacco smoke has been a startling change, very like a brief return from the wars.

My wife and my boys, whose existence I have almost forgotten in the anxious shoring up of the tottering ruin, are waiting for me, dressed in holiday clothes, and looking to me marvelously attractive.

We have sat down to a splendid dinner, at a table graced with flowers and the old Shabbat symbols: the burning candles, the twisted challah loaves, the stuffed fish, and my grandfather's silver goblet brimming with wine. I have blessed my boys with the ancient blessings; we have sung the pleasantly syncopated Shabbat table hymns.

The talk has little to do with tottering ruins. My wife and I have caught up with our week's conversation.

The boys, knowing that Shabbat is the occasion for asking questions, have asked them. We talk of Judaism. For me, it is a retreat into restorative magic.

Shabbat has passed much in the same manner. The boys are at home in the synagogue, and they like it.

They like even more the assured presence of their parents.

In the weekday press of schooling, household chores, and work—and especially in play producing time—it often happens that they see little of us. On Shabbat, we are always there, and they know it. They know too that I am not working and that my wife is at her ease. It is their day.

It is my day, too. The telephone is silent. I can think, read, study, walk, or do nothing. It is an oasis of quiet.

One Saturday night, my producer said to me, "I don't envy you your religion, but I envy you your Shabbat."

The Big Idea

Shabbat is not just a day to rest from the previous week's work, nor simply a day to recharge in anticipation of a busy week ahead; it is a proactive pause for its own sake, meant to reconnect us to our souls and the Soul within all.

מועד

moed Festivals

CHAPTER 45 | FESTIVALS

APPOINTMENTS WITH G-D

MORE THAN THE COMMEMORATION of bygone events that transpired in ancient history, Jewish festivals are contemporary celebrations of ideas and energies present in the here and now. This is why they are called *moadim*—appointments.[546]

Just as the Tabernacle in the wilderness was referred to as the *ohel moed*,[547]—a tent of meeting—implying an appointed *place* to encounter G-d,[548] the Jewish festival, the *moed*, is an appointed *time* to connect with G-d and contemplate essential Jewish themes.

Put simply: *What the tabernacle was in space, Jewish festivals are in time.*

We can value certain ideals in theory, but if we don't set aside specific times to engage and reflect upon their importance and to experientially incorporate them into our lives, they are as good as lost to us. Festivals are thus sacred appointments entered into our calendars, ensuring that we regularly encounter and internalize Judaism's core principles and values. In this way, the Jewish calendar is like a spiritual curriculum that we review and renew on an annual basis.

From a mystical perspective, the synchronization of specific themes and times is not arbitrary. Each festival is a portal for the emergence of a unique spiritual energy that is manifest and available exclusively during that window of time. This energy is the seed out of which each festival grows. It is not the historical events we commemorate on each festival that give rise to that day's unique energy; rather, it is the unique energy inherent in that day that gave rise to those events.

For example: The fifteenth of Nisan (the first day of Pesach) is special not because the Jews were liberated from Egypt on that day; rather, the Jews were liberated from Egypt on that day *because the day itself is special.*[549] Meaning, the fifteenth of Nisan is *intrinsically liberatory* and already possessed the unique Divine energy of freedom; the exodus was but an expression of that eternal energy embedded in time.

Accordingly, Pesach is called "the time of our freedom,"[550] because it is a time when the energy and spiritual inspiration needed to overcome our individual and collective limitations is more available to us. This is why we are told that Abraham "baked matzot and celebrated Pesach"[551] centuries before the exodus from Egypt. Abraham wasn't celebrating an event in the future; he was tapping into a spiritual energy of freedom that was, and always is, present at that time of year.[552] The energy of liberation is encoded into the composition of the annual cycle.

Therefore, Pesach is more than just a celebration of freedom granted to our ancestors; it is an appointed time for each of us to gain our own personal freedom by transcending the limitations, real or imagined, that hold us back from achieving our life's mission. This is why we are instructed in the *Haggadah* to "see ourselves as having [personally] left Egypt." It was not only our distant relatives in a faraway land who achieved such liberation; we must also leave our inner Egypt, each and every day.

The same is true for every festival; each one is a personal encounter with the Divine through which we gain special access to that day's resident spiritual energy.

In fact, like a transistor radio, the *mitzvot* of each particular festival are finely tuned instruments that allow us to receive and transmit the special frequency of the day. R. Shalom DovBer, the fifth Lubavitcher Rebbe, known as the Rebbe Rashab, while assembling his Seder plate, once put it this way: "[We have] prepared the wagon," meaning that the Seder plate has the power to transport us on a spiritual journey to our desired destination. He then went on to explain the mystical significance of seemingly mundane objects in the material world (in this case, the food items on the Seder plate), which, when harnessed with the proper intention, have the ability to become "vehicles" that carry us to spiritual destinations far greater than the disembodied soul could reach on its own.

Blowing the *shofar* on Rosh Hashanah, eating matzah on Pesach, waving the Four Species on Sukkot—each of these are like spiritual antennas that help receive and broadcast the Divine energies available during that particular time.

What's more, it is also understood that our experiences and efforts during each particular festival serve to irrigate the rest of our year with that very energy. Each festival is thus the wellspring of a particular quality of G-d's blessing that will flow throughout the next calendrical cycle.

However, this process is not just cyclical. Every year, during each festival, our world is graced with an influx of a *new, never before revealed* dimension of that day's particular energy. Thus, Chasidut teaches that the Divine energy we can tap into this Pesach, Rosh Hashanah, and Shavuot never existed before and will never be available again.[553] Far from being merely theoretical, this Chasidic approach to the Jewish festivals has the power to completely transform one's perception and experience of these sacred times.

From this perspective, Jewish festivals are no longer seen simply as reenactments of ancient events; rather, they become dynamic encounters with an ever-evolving energy and Divine Presence in the universe and our lives. Therefore, when we tap into each festival's particular energy, we are not just commemorating history, *we are making it!*

By keeping these appointments with the Divine, by fully inhabiting each of these moments and opportunities, and by observing the various *mitzvot* and customs associated with each festival, we have the opportunity to channel unimaginable blessings into our lives. As the Rebbe Rashab once stated: "The forty-eight hours of Shemini Atzeret and Simchat Torah should be highly treasured. Every moment is an opportunity to draw down bucketfuls of material and spiritual treasures. And this is accomplished through dancing" (the primary mitzvah of the festival).

The Previous Lubavitcher Rebbe, R. Yosef Yitzchak, put it this way[554]: The Jewish calendar year is like a train ride through time. Each festival is another stop where we alight and head to the local market to acquire the unique wares available only at that juncture. We then get back on the train and head to the next station to obtain its unique offerings. The main point after making the journey and acquiring such precious merchandise is to remember to unpack our wares when we return home from our trip; meaning, after each festival, we must make the effort to internalize and integrate these unique spiritual gifts and energies into our daily lives. In this way, we, too, become vehicles for those Divine energies and blessings, and we help carry them further into the world of the future.

The Big Idea

Jewish festivals are in the realm of time what the Tent of Meeting was in the realm of space—an encounter with the Divine, and a singular opportunity to access spiritual offerings never before or afterwards available for the taking.

It Happened Once

THE LUBAVITCHER REBBE ONCE visited a communal Pesach Seder being held at an educational institution in Crown Heights. He turned to the youngest child present and asked, "Do you know the Four Questions by heart?" The boy nodded his head in the affirmative. With a smile, the Rebbe turned to the boy's father and asked, "But do you know the answers?"

The next day, the Rebbe explained to the father: "When I questioned your son, I used the expression 'by heart' intentionally, rather than the Hebrew *b'al peh*, by rote, because children don't connect with ceremonies that are merely memorized.

"On Pesach, the child asks: 'We did this whole ritual last year, why are we doing it again?' And he's asking it with all his heart! That's why I asked your son if he knows the Four Questions *by heart*.

"And my question to you was whether you know the answers to his questions. Do you know how to answer your child in such a way that he experiences Pesach in a new way this year than he did last year?"

Sin

chet — חטא

CHAPTER 46 | SIN

MISSING THE MARK

THE JEWISH CONCEPT OF sin differs radically from the common understanding of this fraught term. The English word sin comes from the Latin word *sons*, which means guilty or criminal. Whereas the Hebrew word for sin, *chet*, means something akin to a missed opportunity, like an arrow missing its mark.[555]

Many people believe that sin leaves an indelible blemish on a person's soul—as if a person's actions can affect their essential state of being.

Inevitably, this approach to the consequences of immoral behavior will induce not only feelings of guilt for the action itself but feelings of shame as well, which conflate the sinner with their sin.

According to Jewish thought, sin doesn't mean that one's soul has become tainted or corroded, it merely means one acted in conflict with their essence, which is eternally pure and incorruptible.

In Talmudic thought, to sin is to be overcome by a moment of temporary insanity, as the Sage Reish Lakish teaches[556]: "A person doesn't commit a transgression unless a spirit of madness enters them."

Like an amygdala hijacking,[557] a transgression similarly blocks out the spiritual voice of reason and logic emanating from our G-dly soul. It harnesses our faculties in pursuit of a deed or experience that does not reflect our true essence and well-being.

Sin is, therefore, a foolish investment in an empty and worthless behavior; it does not, however, ultimately define us.

For the innermost core of our soul is always pure[558] and holy; it is just a matter of whether we respect and reflect that innate state of being, or whether we devalue and desecrate it.

We find this idea expressed poignantly in the following story in the Talmud[559]: "There was a group of hooligans in R. Meir's neighborhood who caused him a great deal of pain. R. Meir prayed that they should die. R. Meir's wife, Berurya, said to him, 'What is your thinking?' He replied, 'It is written: *Let sins cease from the land.*' Said Berurya, 'Is it written, "let sinners cease?"... Moreover, look to the end of the verse, *and the wicked will be no more...* [implying that] transgressions will cease [not the sinners], and [as a result] the wicked will be no more. Instead, pray that they should repent.' Indeed, he prayed for them, and they repented."

If wickedness was an essential aspect of our inner being, it would make sense to pray for the eradication of the wicked themselves, but Judaism doesn't see humanity that way. All people have a Divine spark at their core that is indestructible.[560] True, people are also capable of doing bad things, but once they stop engaging in those negative behaviors, their essential goodness can radiate once more. From this perspective, sinful behavior merely covers up one's inner Divine light; it does not extinguish or even alter it. In other words, a sin is what one does, not who they are.

This is not to say that Judaism does not hold individuals responsible for the choices they make; it does. As G-d tells Cain[561]: *Sin crouches at your door and desires that you let it in, but you can control yourself.* According to Judaism, it is our responsibility to guard ourselves from the "spirit of folly" that constantly lurks, waiting for us to drop our defenses, so it can infiltrate our lives and wreak havoc.

We alone are responsible for the influences we allow to enter our psyches and senses. In the words of a Talmudic proverb[562]: "It is not the mouse that is [to blame], but the hole [it came through]."

For this reason, rather than using the feelings of guilt and shame that often follow one's regrettable actions as motivators for behavioral change after the fact, Judaism encourages us to invest our efforts in proactive and preventative measures to ward off sins before they happen.

In fact, according to Chasidic teaching,[563] the negative feelings one entertains following a transgression can themselves be considered a sin of sorts, a kind of emotional indulgence that only serves to bring one down even further.[564] Such feelings can be a ploy of the negative inclination to make us feel even worse about our previous behavior in order to plunge us even deeper into the quagmire of depression, despair, and lethargy.[565]

But what is the appropriate response for one who has "missed their mark" according to Judaism?

Ultimately, everything that transpires in our lives, even sin, has a purpose and is a necessary part of our life's journey. Indeed, once a person has already sinned, they now have an opportunity to attain greater spiritual sensitivity and growth than they could have achieved without it.[566]

For this reason, the Sages teach: A *baal teshuvah* or penitent is considered to be of even greater spiritual standing than a *tzaddik*—a saintly individual who has never known sin.[567]

This is because, having experienced the intense feeling of distance from G-d brought on by sin, the penitent experiences a uniquely intense yearning and thirst for closeness to G-d, triggered by their prior feelings of separation and disconnection.[568]

The *tzaddik*, however, can never experience such fervor, because he has never strayed from the path of G-d and does not know the pain and suffering caused by sin and the consequential burning desire for connection.

In sum: Sin is not an expression of a corrupted nature, nor does it fundamentally mar one's essence. The soul is eternally pure and good, and nothing can ever change that spiritual reality. Sin is simply what happens when a person is distracted from their soul-mission and veers off course. But, with effort and support, we can always redirect our energies, realign our priorities, and reclaim our essential goodness. It would surely be a sin to not make the most out of such an opportunity.

The Big Idea

In Judaism, a sin is understood as a moment of temporary "insanity" rather than a permanent stain on our soul, which always remains irrevocably good and G-dly.

It Happened Once

NOTED PSYCHOLOGIST R. DR. Abraham Twersky once shared a valuable lesson from his childhood:

"One of the few memories I have of being disciplined by my father for something of which he disapproved was his telling me in a quiet, firm, and no-nonsense tone three Yiddish words, '*Es past nisht*,' which means 'this does not become you.' The message was clear. I knew what I was not to do, but it was not until many years later that I appreciated the full content of my father's rebuke. He had told me that I was not to do something [not because *it* was bad, but because *I* was good, therefore] that particular behavior was beneath me. *Es past nisht* meant simply that I was too good for that. This is the diametric opposite of a put down. I was told I was a person of excellence. [Essentially, my father was telling me]: This [behavior] is incompatible and out of character for someone like you."

מותר אסור
mutar
asur

Prohibitions

CHAPTER 47 | PROHIBITIONS

GPS: G-D'S POSITIONING SYSTEM

THIS WORLD CAN BE a confusing place. At times it can be difficult to know what's truly worth pursuing, and what is just a superficial distraction—or worse, destructive.

Jewish wisdom describes our universe as a simulated reality in which G-d imbues us with free choice in order to give us the opportunity to choose between the path of life and growth and that of death and decay. As the verse[569] states, G-d says: *I have placed before you life and death, blessing and curse. Choose life—so that you and your offspring will live.*

To truly live, it is not enough to just exist. The Talmud[570] teaches: "The wicked are considered dead even during their lifetime," whereas, "the righteous are considered alive even in death." To *live* means to lead a meaningful life in which we utilize every opportunity to learn, grow, and refine ourselves and the world around us.

As part of the game of life, G-d planted decoys and obstacles along the way. Some of these are intensely personal to each of us, while others are applicable to the larger communities, species, or phylums of which we are a part.

The "game" was intentionally designed this way in order to challenge our resolve and test our ability to resist fleeting temptation and create a life of eternal value.

Alongside the game, G-d also provided a map to help us identify where blessings can be found and alert us to the shadowlands and liminal spaces where danger often lurks.

This map is the Torah, the blueprint of creation,[571] which illuminates the various routes through the labyrinth, revealing which pursuits are meaningful and nourishing and which are ultimately empty and vain.

Accordingly, the Torah functions like a spiritual GPS device, indicating where to turn and which roadblocks to avoid. These "directions" are communicated to us in a series of prohibited actions and permitted behaviors. The Hebrew terms for prohibited and permitted are *asur* and *mutar*, which literally mean tied and untied. But what does this dialectical image imply?

This is best explained by Lurianic Kabbalah,[572] which views everything in this world as being composed of a mixture of good and evil—or, more accurately—of holy sparks that transparently reflect their Divine origin, and of *klipot*, or shells, which conceal and confine the holy sparks in this world.[573]

Our purpose on this earth is to purify and elevate the world by extracting the good from the bad, the blessing from the curse, the sparks from the shells, through mindfulness, sensitivity, and intentionality, and, in so doing, to return the sparks to their former luster in the light of the Divine. Kabbalistically speaking, this gathering of the sparks is our contribution to the culmination of creation; it is how we collaborate with G-d in the art of redemption.

However, left to our own devices, we are not reliably capable of discerning the subtle contours and boundaries of such spiritual energies and properties. Furthermore, it is not always clear if and when we have the capability to successfully execute such a spiritually sensitive extraction of spark from shell. Such miscalculation can result in our soul's entrapment in trivial distractions or spiritually dangerous situations, leading us, like the sparks, to lose some of our own soul's transparent luminescence.

How then do we identify the presence of such redeemable sparks in order to know where true holiness might be found and elevated?

Additionally, how do we determine when something might simply be irredeemable in general, or at least in relation to us?

This, according to the Kabbalists,[574] is the function of Jewish law: By delineating for us between what is forbidden and permitted, the Torah reveals which sparks are "tied-up" and irredeemable, and which opportunities are "untied" and energetically available for us to engage and integrate into holiness. Indeed, the Hebrew word for transgression, *aveirah*, literally means to cross over (a line).

Like a treasure map, Jewish law helps us traverse the complex landscape of life by identifying where spiritual bounty is to be found.

It does this in three fundamental ways: 1) It tells us what is a mitzvah to do, providing us with clear paths to connect with G-d through positive action (what to do); 2) it alerts us to which pursuits or behaviors will prove harmful to our soul and should therefore be avoided (what not to do); and 3) it demarcates the "neutral" or "permissible mundane" areas of life that have the potential to be incorporated into the realm of the holy through Divine consciousness and intentionality.

It is in this third realm, the realm of the permissible mundane, that we can do our most creative, challenging, and important work.

Creative, because that is where we have the freedom to proactively determine the spiritual context of our actions through the application of our clarified intention.

Challenging, because when something is either clearly forbidden or obligated, we know exactly what we need to abstain from or engage with, and its status is thus clearly delineated. When something is in the neutral zone, however, we need to employ our own powers of discernment to determine how it might best be elevated and transformed into something sacred.

And important, because these areas of the permissible mundane are precisely the neutral realms in which we might deepen and expand the spiritual presence within the world, beyond even what is explicitly outlined in the Torah. This is the Jewish alchemy of gradually Divinizing the world, revealing and releasing the fallen sparks hidden within every nook and cranny of creation.[575]

Ultimately, in the Divine scheme,[576] there are only three possible responses to any given situation. Either it is a mitzvah to do, a prohibition to avoid, or an opportunity to take initiative and create meaning from within the realm of the permissible mundane by transforming something ordinary or even hedonistic into something extraordinary and holy.

The halachic lifestyle, filled as it is with permissions and prohibitions, is not meant to be experienced as one of purely technical rigidity and mechanistic behavior, as unfortunately some see it. Instead, it is a vital way of life in which every moment of every day is an exciting opportunity to utilize our temporal lives to discover and unlock treasures of eternal value. The Torah—our guide, our map, our blueprint, our compass—points the way for us to reach the Promised Land of perfected, redeemed reality. It is up to us to take the necessary steps to achieve that goal.

The Big Idea

The Torah is not merely a legal code but a cosmic map whose instructions help attune us to the spiritual frequency of the universe.

It Happened Once

THE BAAL SHEM TOV once sent one of his young disciples, R. Moshe Meshel, with a letter to his disciple, the great scholar R. Chaim Rapaport.

The letter instructed R. Rapaport to travel to a designated place in the forest outside the city and study Torah there in depth, recite *Minchah*, then return home. Despite not knowing the purpose of this mission, R. Rapaport implicitly followed his teacher's instructions.

After traveling to the designated location and studying there for a few hours, R. Rapaport became very thirsty. While he continued studying, his companions went to search for some water. In the midst of the thick forest undergrowth, they discovered a fountain and brought back fresh water for him to drink. He also used the water to wash his hands before praying *Minchah*, after which they returned home.

Soon after, R. Rapaport visited the Baal Shem Tov and told him that ever since going on the mission, his eyes and heart were opened in Torah study and the service of G-d, and he had made more spiritual progress in that brief period than ever before. He thanked the Baal Shem Tov for sending him there.

The Baal Shem Tov replied: "Without even knowing it, you accomplished a great task there. It is written in the holy *Zohar* that ever since G-d separated the lower waters from the upper waters on the second day of creation, the lower waters have been weeping and begging to appear before the Holy King, that they be used for holy purposes, such as hand washing before prayer, Torah study, and eating bread, and immersion in a *mikveh*.

"Near the place where I sent you, there was a fountain that had been weeping for five thousand, five hundred nineteen years—since the creation of the world: Why should it be less than all the other fountains in the world? Why should its waters be denied their elevation? Since the Holy One, blessed be He, had created it, no one had ever made a blessing over its waters, and they had never been used for holy purposes. That day, when you drank its water and used it to wash your hands for prayer, you elevated that fountain. This was all the working of Divine Providence. Every creature and creation has a time for its elevation, and it is preordained when it will occur and by whom. And that is true for each and every soul; it too has its time for elevation."[577]

Pork
chazir

חזיר

CHAPTER 48 | PORK

WHEN PIGS FLY

J UDAISM HAS A VERY strange relationship with the pig. Technically, it is no less unkosher than any other non-kosher food. Yet, in Rabbinic literature and in the popular Jewish imagination, it has come to epitomize everything non-kosher. Even mentioning the pig by name was considered so repugnant to our Sages that it was simply referred to as *"davar acher*—the other thing."[578]

Even more strange is the fact that encoded within the letters that make up its name is a prophetically kosher future. According to its etymological root, *chazir*, the name for pig, means "to return"—"For our Sages teach us that it will return to become permitted in the future."[579]

That's right—the time will come when pork will become kosher. The pig is, therefore, named not after its past or present status, but after its future state of being.

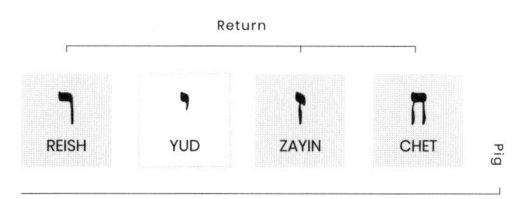

REISH	YUD	ZAYIN	CHET
ר	י	ז	ח

Return

Pig

This begs the obvious question: How will the quintessential nemesis of everything kosher eventually become kosher itself? To answer this question, we first need to understand what makes an animal kosher in the first place.

The Torah distinguishes kosher mammals from others through two specifications: a kosher mammal must chew its cud and have split hooves.[580] This disqualifies all mammals that possess neither, or even only one of these characteristics.

The pig is explicitly mentioned in the Torah as the only mammal that has split hooves but does not chew its cud.[581] It therefore appears kosher externally, but its internal reality renders it unkosher.

The Sages see in the pig's biology a symbolic form of deceptive posturing.[582] The pig tricks others into thinking that it is kosher by displaying its visibly kosher feature, its split hooves, without possessing the requisite inner feature, chewing its cud, to back it up.

The pig, at present, thus represents a two-faced character—what you see is *not* what you get.

The Midrash[583] describes Esau as having embodied this piggish nature. He would present himself to his father, Isaac, as pious and G-d fearing, despite the fact that he was actively engaged in immoral behavior and idolatrous practices. He was, in effect, merely playing a role to satisfy what he thought Isaac wanted to see from him.

Transparency is a central value in Judaism. Maimonidies[584] lists misrepresenting oneself to others as a Torah prohibition, a form of theft—"stealing people's minds"—even when it causes no monetary loss. In R. Gamliel's *yeshivah* in the city of Yavneh, any student whose internal character and external conduct did not match was not permitted to enter the study hall.[585] Even more strongly, the Talmud[586] declares that any Torah scholar whose outward expression of righteousness is insincere "should not be considered a Torah scholar."

However, all hope is not lost for the pig. Reflecting the purpose of creation, which is to reveal the currently concealed presence of G-d within all, the future messianic age will be an age of transparency, when whatever is concealed on the inside will be exposed, and truth will become ubiquitous. No longer will it be possible to harbor insincere or hypocritical thoughts or behaviors.

Indeed, we are already seeing considerable advances in this area. Thanks in part to the explosion of public information, transparency has become a baseline value that we now expect from financial firms, companies, and elected officials. It is becoming increasingly harder to pretend that you are something other than what you truly are.

Adapting to this change in the world, rabbinical sources teach that the anatomy of the pig will evolve accordingly so that its inner and outer features are aligned, and, as a result, it will become kosher.

In the final analysis, the very animal that is the archetypal antithesis of all things kosher serves as the ultimate reminder that being kosher, rather than merely eating kosher, is a matter of character, not just consumption.

The Big Idea

In Jewish thought, it is not enough to eat *kosher, one must also strive to* be *kosher in all that one does.*

It Happened Once

ONE DAY, THE BAAL Shem Tov instructed several of his disciples to embark on a journey. The Baal Shem Tov did not tell them where to go, nor did they ask; they allowed Divine Providence to direct their wagon where it may, confident that the destination and purpose of their trip would be revealed in due time.

After traveling for several hours, they stopped at a wayside inn to eat and rest. The Baal Shem Tov's disciples were pious Jews who insisted on the highest standards of *kashrut*. When they learned that their host planned to serve them meat in their meal, they asked to see the *shochet* of the house, interrogated him as to his knowledge and piety, and examined his knife for any possible blemishes.

Their discussion of the *kashrut* standard of the food continued throughout the meal, as they inquired after the source of every ingredient in each dish set before them.

As they spoke and ate, a voice emerged from behind the oven, where an old beggar was resting amidst his bundles. "Dear Jews," he called out, "are you as careful with what comes out of your mouth as you are with what enters into it?"

The party of Chasidim concluded their meal in silence, climbed onto their wagon, and turned it back towards Mezhibuzh. They now understood the purpose for which their master had dispatched them on their journey that morning.[587]

Satan
satan

שטן

CHAPTER 49 | SATAN

A TEST, NOT A TRAP

THE COMMON PERCEPTION OF Satan is largely derived from the Christian idea of the devil, an independent evil force in the world. In such a paradigm, G-d is dualistically pitted against the devil, or Satan.

Unlike Christianity, Judaism doesn't believe in the devil or that evil has any independent power whatsoever. Instead, the Hebrew word *satan* means one who turns people astray.

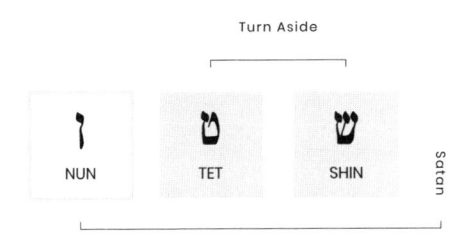

This understanding is based on the etymological root of *satan*, *sat*, which means to turn aside. Accordingly, the role of the *satan* is to lure people to act out of spiritual character, or in a manner of *shtut*, foolishness, because "a person does not commit a sin unless they are overcome by foolishness."[588]

We see this reflected throughout the Torah. For example, some Biblical commentators[589] claim that the snake that tricked Adam and Eve to commit mankind's first sin was the *satan*. According to a fascinating Midrash, the *satan*, disguised as an old man along the road, repeatedly tried to deter Abraham from following through with G-d's instructions to sacrifice his son, Isaac, as an offering, all to no avail.

Additionally, the Talmud suggests that King David would never have sinned with Bathsheba were it not for the meddling of the *satan*.[590]

In all of these examples, among many more, the *satan* appears to those in the midst of existential or spiritual struggles and tries to lead them astray.

However, it is essential to note that, according to Judaism, the *satan* is not an independent entity with its own agenda; rather, it is a G-dly force that is deployed to seduce people to sin.

The obvious question is: Why? Why does the *satan* exist? Why would G-d create and employ a force in the fabric of creation to lead us astray?

To address this quintessential question, the Talmud[591] comments on the actions of two infamous Biblical characters, Penina and the *satan*, asserting that, rather than being inherently "evil," they were in fact both motivated to act for the sake of heaven.

Penina, who repeatedly drove her co-wife Hannah to tears over being childless, did so to drive Hannah to pray to G-d from the depths of her heart and be granted a son. The *satan*, which notoriously afflicted Job, did so in an attempt to weaken his faith so G-d would not forget His love for Abraham amidst His affection for Job.

In both cases, we see characters acting in ways that compromise and impinge upon others. On the surface, therefore, it would be easy to denigrate them and their intentions.

Yet, the Talmud teaches us something deeper.

G-d is never absent from our affairs, and even people or circumstances that seem "bad" or "evil" issue forth from G-d for a purpose—namely, the fulfillment of our ultimate potential. From this perspective, the *satan* does not lay traps for us to fall into; rather, it administers tests for us to overcome and learn from.

Another way the Talmud describes the *satan* is as one's *yetzer hara*, the negative inclination—an internal counterbalance to one's good inclination, both of which are under a person's control. Rather than someone or something external to us, the *satan*, when understood this way, is part and parcel of our psycho-spiritual makeup. Similar to the stories and ideas explored above, our negative inclination is not an aberration but a necessary element of who we are. Without it, humanity would lose its free will, and, according to one teaching in the Midrash, even the desire to be creative and productive.

In the words of our Sages,[592] "Were it not for the negative inclination, no one would build a house, have children, or engage in commerce."

Indeed, this is why, according to the Midrash, the Torah says[593]: *And G-d saw everything that he had made and, behold, it was very good. Good* refers to the good inclination, while *very good* refers to the negative inclination.[594]

Illustrating both the deceptive as well as the productive roles that the *satan* plays in our spiritual lives, the *Zohar*[595] relates a parable about a wise king who, seeking to test the limits of his son's morality, hires a harlot to seduce the prince. Although the harlot does her best to lure the young prince, the ultimate aim of the king in hiring her is not for her to succeed in her seductions but for the prince to withstand her advances.

In a similar vein, the Baal Shem Tov relates a parable[596] about a senior nobleman and close adviser to a king who traveled the countryside calling to raise an army to revolt against the king. His charm and charisma captured the hearts of the people, and many joined his ranks.

One day, he came upon a village of wise men. After hearing his rant against the king, the wise villagers turned to him in disbelief, saying, "Our king is so great that it cannot be true that someone who knows him as well as you do should oppose him or seek to rebel against him. This must be a trick of the king himself to test our loyalty!"

Similarly, a truly wise person recognizes that G-d is everywhere, is responsible for everything that happens, and is always acting solely in their best interests. With this in mind, one can see past the *satan*'s seductions and recognize the devious designs as the tests they truly are, aimed at revealing the depth of our commitment to our Father in Heaven.

The *satan* is G-d's undercover agent. When we recognize that its ploys are actually a farce and do not even reflect the *satan's* own true desire, this helps us take them less seriously and see them for what they are—an opportunity for us to rise above our current station and prove ourselves in the face of such generative adversity.

The Big Idea

The satan *is an* agent *rather than an* adversary *of G-d, deployed to test our spiritual integrity rather than to trap or trip us up in sin.*

It Happened Once

A KING HAD AN ONLY son whom he loved dearly. He therefore warned him not to go near any promiscuous women, lest he be deemed unworthy of entering his father's palace. Hearing this and knowing how much his father loved him, the prince declared his allegiance to his father and promised that he would never act contrary to his wishes.

Days passed, and the king wished to give the kingdom to his son. In order to do so, however, the king had to first test his son's loyalty.

He hired a beautiful courtesan to attempt to seduce his son and thus test him. If the prince is able to overcome the lure of her charms and pushes her away, thus maintaining his allegiance to the king, his father then rejoices doubly in his son and brings him into the inner chambers of his palace. He showers him with precious gifts. Who occasioned all the honor for the king's son? Was it not the courtesan? Should she not be praised for her efforts?[597]

גאולה

geulah   Messianic Era
___

CHAPTER 50 | MESSIANIC ERA

THE LINE BETWEEN EXILE AND REDEMPTION

In the ancient world, time was understood as circular, with set cycles repeating themselves over and over without progress or destination. This is commonly referred to as "the law of eternal return."

In Judaism, time has a clear trajectory and goal that was defined from its very inception. According to Jewish thought, the desired destination of all time and history is a perfected world of peace and prosperity, distinguished by a pervading awareness of G-d's presence.[598]

Before creation reaches its crescendo, however, humanity in general, and the Jewish people in particular, are in a state of exile. Whether as a result of our collective eviction from the Garden of Eden, the loss of our ancient homeland and sovereignty, or an acute sense of existential alienation, it often feels like the human race is adrift through the choppy seas of history.

And what is the shore that we are all aiming to reach? Redemption, return, reconnection, renewal.

This dynamic dialectic of exile and redemption runs throughout human history, but it will one day resolve in an era of ultimate redemption, described by the Sages as *yom shekulo Shabbat*, a [never-ending] day of Shabbat.[599]

In Hebrew, the difference between the words exile, *golah*, and redemption, *geulah*, is but a single letter, *alef*. *Alef*, a silent letter,

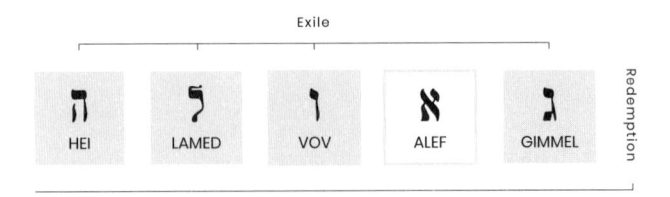

Exile					Redemption
ה	ל	ו	א	ג	
HEI	LAMED	VOV	ALEF	GIMMEL	

numerically equals one, representing the underlying presence and unity of G-d that pervades all of existence.[600] The transition from *golah* to *geulah* is thus marked by the discovery of G-d's infinite oneness hiding within the fragmentation of the finite world.

According to Kabbalah, G-d created a world in which His presence is not overt; we must seek Him out.[601]

But why? Doesn't this Divine occlusion introduce the very experience of exile we strive to overcome? The answer is that in order for the Infinite One to create a finite world teeming with multiplicity, He had to constrict His own omnipresence, thus creating the space within which creation itself could arise and exist.

In the language of the mystics, this is referred to as G-d's *tzimtzum*, or self-contraction.[602] Such concealment allowed for the emergence of a purely materialistic worldview, in which the so-called "natural order" is perceived to be completely independent from its Divine origins.

Furthermore, G-d's *tzimtzum* created the conditions necessary for the phenomenon of human free will to emerge, which is an integral component of G-d's plan for creation. Accordingly, it is the task of humanity to "bring G-d home" from His self-imposed "exile," thus fulfilling the original intention of creation, which is to reveal G-d's Presence and Providence within the world.

This meta-historical process will culminate with an awareness that nature itself is supernatural—that there is truly nothing other than G-d. As the prophet Habakuk[603] says: *For the earth shall be filled with the knowledge of the glory of G-d as the waters cover the sea.*

This shift from exile to redemption, from fragmentation to unity, is therefore quite literally radical, because it is simultaneously a decisive break with what has been (dualistic consciousness based on artificial binaries), as well as having been present and available at the root of our experience all along. G-d's unity, like the silent *alef*, is always present, just waiting to be acknowledged and aligned with, thereby transforming *golah*, exile, into *geulah*, redemption.

This dawning of Divine consciousness will disclose the seamless fusion of the natural and supernatural orders revealing that the perceived dichotomy between nature and Divinity was never truly accurate; the Divine hand was guiding the natural order all along. As Isaiah[604] prophesies: *Your Teacher will no longer hide from you, for your eyes will behold your Teacher*. The invisible G-d will be seen from within His handiwork. The earth, our bodies, nature will all be appreciated for what they truly are—expressions of Divinity. As the verse[605] says: *G-d's unity will be perceived within one's own flesh*!

Such revelation of Divinity from within the natural order itself is part of the messianic unveiling. For if it were to occur otherwise, through miraculous intervention or purely spiritual means, the current dichotomies and binaries that fragment us and our world would only become more entrenched, taking us further afield from time's ultimate destination—which is the revelation of G-d's hand in creation.

Fittingly, as the arc of history bends ever forward, the fulfillment of Judaism's utopian vision for the future as articulated by the Hebrew prophets is already materializing all around us, not through miraculous means, but through natural progress and scientific discovery.

For example, according to Swedish economic historian Johan Norberg:

"If someone had told you in 1990 that over the next twenty-five years world hunger would decline by 40%, child mortality would halve, and extreme poverty would fall by three quarters, you'd have told them they were a naive fool. But the fools were right. This is truly what has happened."

Additionally, through too many medical advances to count, miracles are all around us. Today the "lame are dancing" with the aid of prosthetics, the "blind can see," as eighty percent of visual impairment has already been cured, and through stem cell research scientists are well on their way to curing deafness, bringing to life the messianic prophecies of Isaiah: *Then will the eyes of the blind be opened and the ears of the deaf unstopped. Then will the lame leap like a deer....*

Incredibly, after so many millennia of aggression between nations of the world, there is now a move towards nuclear disarmament. Echoing Isaiah's famous prophecy,[606] *They shall beat their swords into plowshares, and their spears into pruning hooks; nation shall not lift up sword against nation, neither shall they learn war anymore*, technologies once developed for weapons of mass destruction are now being harnessed for medical and agricultural purposes—to improve, rather than destroy, people's lives.

War, hunger, and disease—the three greatest struggles in humanity's long history—are becoming increasingly more manageable and could potentially be eradicated if humanity were to undergo a messianic shift of consciousness. If we were to adopt a mindset of abundance and redemptive cooperation rather than the current exilic paradigm of scarcity and competition, many of the artificial boundaries and superficial obstacles to universal peace and prosperity would dissipate and disappear.

Only when humanity begins to see the world through G-d's eyes will our world achieve its full messianic potential. Such Divine consciousness is the lens through which the essential oneness of everyone and everything in existence becomes apparent.

It is this singular change in our perception that precipitates and embodies the messianic era. Everything else in the Biblical prophecies is merely an external expression of this internal shift. By consciously illuminating and creatively articulating the integral presence of the silent *alef* hidden within all creation, we are able to bring the world a quantum leap closer to crossing over that thinnest of lines between *golah* and *geulah*, bringing humanity across the finish line of history once and for all.

CHAPTER 50 | MESSIANIC ERA

It Happened Once

After the passing of R. DovBer of Mezritch in 1772, R. Menachem Mendel of Horodok led a group of Chasidim to settle in the Holy Land.

One day, an individual climbed the Mount of Olives in Jerusalem and sounded a *shofar*. Soon the rumor spread that Mashiach had arrived, setting off a great commotion in the street.

R. Menachem Mendel went to his window and sniffed the air. "No," he said, "unfortunately, the redeemer has not yet arrived. On that day, *The earth shall be filled with the knowledge of G-d as the waters cover the sea*, and *all flesh will perceive the reality of the Creator*. I do not sense the Divine truth that will permeate the world in the era of Mashiach."

R. Gronem Estherman, a renowned spiritual teacher, explained, "Why did R. Menachem Mendel need to go to the window to sniff for the presence of Mashiach? Because the immanent presence of G-d was already a tangible reality within the walls of his room."

The Big Idea

A universal shift in Divine consciousness is what will result in global change and redemption, not the other way around.

387

Jubilee

yovel   יובל

APPENDIX | JUBILEE

RETURN AGAIN

TURNING FIFTY* CAN BE sobering. Our prime is behind us. From here on out, the mind and body will only degenerate further. Fifty can seem like the beginning of the end. In Jewish thought, however, turning fifty is not the beginning of the end; rather, it is the end of the beginning.

The English word jubilee (fifty-year commemoration) comes from the word *yovel*, referring to the fiftieth year in the sabbatical cycle, when fields and properties in Israel were returned to their original owners and indentured servants were granted freedom.[607]

Yovel expresses the idea that, at fifty, things return to their original state. Fifty is thus a comprehensive reset button, rebooting the system for a fresh start.

In fact, the word *yovel* means freedom or sending off, referring specifically to this quality of renewal and self-determination, as exemplified by the release of servants and the return of land to its original owners.[608]

Interestingly, *yovel* can also refer to a stream, as understood from the verse,[609] *He shall be like a tree planted by water, sending forth its roots by a stream [yuval]: It does not sense the coming of heat, and its*

---

* This book is dedicated in honor of David (Vadim) Aminov's fiftieth birthday. The following entry explains the significance of the Hebrew word for Jubilee and the significance of the number fifty.

391

leaves are ever fresh. It has no care in a year of drought, and it does not cease to yield fruit.[610]

In this evocative verse, man is compared to a tree. Like a tree with roots firmly set in a brook of water, when we are anchored and in tune with ourselves, we are able to flourish even when subject to adverse conditions. *Yovel* represents just such a returning to the roots of our truest self, reconnecting with what is most essential in our lives.

Earlier in life, we tend to focus on developing our resume with the aim of building a successful career. To do so, we branch out, trying our hand at different opportunities to find the path to success. In doing so, we invariably encounter all kinds of successes and failures along the way, and we end up learning valuable life lessons.

At fifty, we turn the page and start a new phase of our lives. As we become more firmly rooted in life experience and increasingly in touch with our core values, fifty is the age of return.

It is thus a time to direct our focus inward, to actively address our more spiritual aspirations, and rededicate ourselves to what is most personally meaningful. This recalibration of consciousness inspires us to develop the types of virtues we would want to have recounted in a eulogy rather than the skills we would want written in our resume.[611]

Such a redirection of our energies towards a more holistic sense of health and happiness invariably results in a surge of spiritual regeneration.[612]

Fifty is when we begin to realize that we are in fact aging. However, in Judaism, this is precisely when we truly begin saging. "Fifty is the age for dispensing advice," says the Mishnah.[613]

Advice is personal and situation-specific, necessarily drawing from an accumulated reservoir of life experiences that have developed our sense of judgment and deepened our ability to be attuned to the needs of others as well as ourselves.

A wise man once said, "To know where you're going and how to get there, you must first have a good sense of where you're coming from." Fifty is that time of reflection and rejuvenation, a personal *yovel*, giving us the opportunity to reconnect to our roots, to reclaim our inheritance, and to cultivate the nourishing wisdom that lies within.

The Big Idea

Mindful introspection throughout the course of one's life transforms the natural process of aging into a spiritual journey of saging.

It Happened Once

ON THE OCCASION OF his seventieth birthday, the Lubavitcher Rebbe received thousands of letters from well-wishers around the globe. Among these were several that suggested that perhaps it was time he considered "slowing down" and "taking it easy" after his many fruitful decades as a leader and activist.

During a public gathering celebrating his birthday, the Rebbe shared, "I have been asked: 'Now that you have attained the age of seventy, what are your plans? It would seem that this is an appropriate time to rest a bit....'

"My response to that is that we must begin to accomplish even more.

"On the occasion of entering the seventies, this year we should establish at least seventy new institutions!

"And don't be disturbed if during this year we'll start not seventy but eighty, and maybe even one hundred. On the contrary! May blessings be bestowed upon all those involved—there will surely be no impediments as far as the ten percent is concerned..."

A decade later, when the Rebbe celebrated his eightieth birthday, he again called for a massive expansion of Chabad's activities during a gathering held in honor of the occasion.

Upon the conclusion of the final segment of the six-hour address—which began at 9:30 p.m. following a full day's work—the Rebbe personally distributed a gift to each of the ten thousand men, women, and children present: a special edition of the *Tanya*. The last participant received his copy at 6:15 a.m.

The way the Rebbe celebrated his eightieth birthday relates to a moving exchange he had with a Canadian Jewish senator named Jerry Grafstein, who served in the Canadian Senate for over twenty-five years.

Grafstein related: "It's been many years now that on my birthday, especially those that mark a full decade, a feeling of sadness and depression accompanies the celebration. We all want to be young, and our birthdays mark the aging process."

The years passed, and each new decade in his life was accompanied by a period of severe depression.

When celebrating his fiftieth, he experienced a severe crisis.

In his own words: "My mental state was terrible, and I could not recover, even after I received help from professionals.

"My wife suggested I meet the Lubavitcher Rebbe and receive his advice to heal my pain.

"When I arrived, I was welcomed and brought to the Rebbe, who gave me a dollar and blessed me with the traditional 'blessing and success.'

"Then, unexpectedly, the Rebbe gave me another dollar. When I asked him why the extra one, the Rebbe asked me: 'What's bothering you?'

"I felt ashamed to talk to the Rebbe in such a public setting, but the Rebbe handed me a third dollar and gestured at his ears, as if to say: No one's listening to us.

"Again he asked: 'What's bothering you?'

"I told him briefly about my age and sense of lack of fulfilment with each passing decade. The Rebbe asked me, 'Who was the greatest leader in Jewish history?'

"I knew the answer: 'Moses.'

"'And how old was Moses when he took "the first step in his career" and became the leader of the Jewish people?'

"I did not know, so the Rebbe replied: 'Eighty.

"'How is it possible that at the age of eighty, Moses began to lead such a complex people like the Jews?' wondered the Rebbe. He continued to explain: 'Because Moses never looked back at what he had already done. Instead, he looked ahead—at what else needed to be done.

"'Anyone who looks at what needs to be done is young! Whoever looks back at what he did prior will always be old,' concluded the Rebbe, and he again wished me 'blessing and success.'"

Endnotes

Introduction

1. The Midrash (*Avot D'Rabbi Natan* 34:10) counts ten: *sason, simchah, gilah, rinah, ditzah, tzahalah, alizah, chedvah, tiferet,* and *alitzah*.
2. https://www.wsj.com/articles/SB10001424052748703467304575383131592767868#:~:text=One%20of%20the%20key%20advances,of%20looking%20at%20the%20world.
3. The examples included below are based on numerous sources, including https://journals.sagepub.com/doi/abs/10.1177/0956797610386621, https://www.wsj.com/articles/SB10001424052748703467304575383131592767868, https://www.psychologytoday.com/us/blog/the-biolinguistic-turn/201702/how-the-language-we-speak-affects-the-way-we-think#:~:text=Likewise%2C%20the%20way%20people%20think,recent%20events%20to%20remote%20past, https://www.theatlantic.com/national/archive/2010/07/yes-language-does-shape-culture/340451/
4. In studies conducted by Caitlin Fausey at Stanford, speakers of English, Spanish, and Japanese watched videos of two people popping balloons, breaking eggs, and spilling drinks either intentionally or accidentally. Later, everyone got a surprise memory test: For each event, can you remember who did it? She discovered a striking cross-linguistic difference in eyewitness memory. Spanish and Japanese speakers did not remember the agents of accidental events as well as English speakers.
5. For example, Chinese-speaking children learn to count earlier than English-speaking children because Chinese numbers are more regular and transparent than English numbers (in Chinese, "eleven" is "ten one"). https://www.psychologytoday.com/us/blog/the-biolinguistic-turn/201702/how-the-language-we-speak-affects-the-way-we-think#:~:text=Likewise%2C%20the%20way%20people%20think,recent%20events%20to%20remote%20past.
6. https://www.psychologytoday.com/us/blog/the-biolinguistic-turn/201702/how-the-language-we-speak-affects-the-way-we-think#:~:text=Likewise%2C%20the%20way%20people%20think,recent%20events%20to%20remote%20past.
7. As referenced in the following links/articles: https://economix.blogs.nytimes.com/2011/01/07/american-jews-lead-the-happiest-lives/, http://www.huffingtonpost.com/2011/01/08/gallup-jews-score-highest_n_806247.html, http://newsfeed.time.com/2011/01/16/jubilant-jews-study-finds-jewish-people-are-the-happiest-religious-group/, http://news.gallup.com/poll/152723/religious-americans-enjoy-higher-wellbeing.aspx, https://www.nytimes.com/2011/03/06/weekinreview/06happy.html?_r=1.
8. https://en.wikipedia.org/wiki/List_of_Jewish_Nobel_laureates.

9 https://www.thejc.com/culture/features/tzedakah-a-concept-that-changed-the-world-1.506918.
10 See the following article to gain a better understanding of the giving habits of American Jews: https://theconversation.com/american-jews-and-charitable-giving-an-enduring-tradition-87993.
11 https://www.jpost.com/jewish-world/jewish-news/jews-take-5-of-top-6-spots-in-annual-list-of-top-us-givers.
12 See *Pardes Rimonim* 22:1 and 27:2; *Kuzari* 4:25.
13 *Shem MiShmuel*, Purim 5673.
14 2:20.
15 *Bamidbar Rabbah* 19:3; see also *Bereishit Rabbah* 17.
16 See *Likkutei Sichot*, Vol. 15, pp. 13-19.

People of the Word

1 *Tikkunei Zohar* 22.
2 See *Kohelet Rabbah* 1:13, 3:10; Ramban and R. Bachya *Chayei Sarah*; *Shaarei Teshuvah, Shaar* 2, 27; *Menorat Hamaor* by R. Yisrael Alnaqua, Vol. 4, Ch. 14, p. 250.
3 *Avot* 4:1.
4 See *Keter Shem Tov* Appendix 48.
5 https://www.chabad.org/library/article_cdo/aid/2262/jewish/Perspective.htm.
6 See R. Samson Raphael Hirsch, *Chorev, Bereishit* 22:2; *Michtav Mei'Eliyahu* Vol. 1 *Kuntres Hachesed*; *Lev Eliyahu* Vol. 1, p. 110.
7 Leviticus 19:18.
8 *Mishneh Torah*, Laws of Temperaments 6:3
9 *Shabbat* 31a.
10 Jewish wedding canopy.
11 See *Chinuch* 16.
12 Genesis 22:1.
13 See *Pirkei d'Rabbi Eliezer* 26, *Avot d'Rabbi Natan* 33, and *Avot* 5:3.
14 According to the listing of R. Ovadiah of Bartenura. Other sages offer different lists; see, for example, *Pirkei d'Rabbi Eliezer* and *Avot d'Rabbi Natan* ibid., Maimonides' commentary to the Mishnah ad loc., and *Midrash Tehillim* (where two lists are cited, one on chapter 18 and another on chapter 95.)
15 *Zohar* I:139a.
16 *Avodah Zarah* 3a.
17 Proverbs 3:12.
18 *Sukkah* 52a.
19 See *Petach Einayim* ad loc.
20 See *Maamarim Melukatim* Vol. 4, p. 69.
21 *Likkutei Moharan, Torah* 114:1.
22 As told by R. Shabtai Slavaticki. https://www.chabad.org/therebbe/article_cdo/aid/4405219/jewish/Chapter-19-Moral-Struggles-Vice-or-Virtue.htm.

23 *Sefer Ha'ikarim* 2:30.
24 *Brachot* 54a.
25 *Brachot* 9:2.
26 Fascinatingly, the Talmud (*Pesachim* 50a) relates that in our current, unredeemed reality, the blessing we say for the good in our lives is different from the one we say over the bad. However, in the World to Come, when G-d's presence and plan will be fully revealed, we will say the same blessing for every experience—"Blessed is He Who is good and does good."
27 *Man's Search for Meaning*, Part II: Logotherapy in a Nutshell, The Meaning of Suffering.
28 *Noam Elimelech Noach* 3d; *Heichal Habrachah Bereishit* 30d; ibid. *Bamidbar* 1:1.
29 *Tanchuma, Vayigash* 9.
30 *Menachot* 53b.
31 *Brachot* 60b.
32 Deuteronomy 16:3. See *Brachot* 21a, Rashi ad loc. *Shulchan Aruch Admur Hazaken Orach Chaim* 67:1.
33 *Pesachim* 10:5. See *Tanya, Likkutei Amarim*, Ch. 47.
34 See *Torah Or, Va'era* 57b; *Beshalach* 64a-b; *Yitro* 71c, et al.
35 Job, V; Dweck, CS; Walton, GM: Ego Depletion—Is It All in Your Head?: Implicit Theories About Willpower Affect Self-Regulation. *Psychological Science* Vol. 21, Number 11, pp. 1686-1693.
36 *Mindset: The New Psychology of Success* by Carol S. Dweck.
37 *Likkutei Torah* and *Shaar Hapesukim* (*Arizal*) *Vayeishev* 40a. *Likkutei Torah* (*Arizal*), opening of *Shemot*, et al.
38 Exodus 7:14; 8:11; 8:28; 9:7; 9:34; 10:1, et al.
39 Exodus 2:10.
40 Ibid. Ch. 14.
41 *Bereishit Rabbah* 42:3.
42 *Shir Hashirim Rabbah* 1:3, 1.
43 As quoted by R. Simon Jacobson in his book, *Towards a Meaningful Life*; also accessible online: https://www.chabad.org/therebbe/article_cdo/aid/60699/jewish/Teenagers.htm.
44 *Sotah* 11b.
45 *Shabbat* 119b.
46 Bava Batra 12b.
47 Psalms 8:2.
48 *Esther Rabbah*, towards the end of sec. 7:17. An abbreviated version is to be found in *Yalkut Shimoni* on Esther, sec. 1057. See also *Aggadat Esther* 3:9, *Midrash Abba Gurion* 4:1, and *Midrash Lekach Tov* 4:10.
49 Proverbs 3:25.
50 Isaiah 8:10.
51 Isaiah 46:4.
52 These three verses are recited at the conclusion of each of the three daily prayers.
53 Exodus 33:11.

54 Ibn Ezra to Exodus 33:11.
55 See *Midrash Lekach Tov* ad loc.; see also *Midrash Agadah* to Exodus 24:5.
56 See *Shu"t Harivash* 157.
57 https://www.chabad.org/library/article_cdo/aid/4473/jewish/-The-Boy-Who-Crowed-Like-a-Rooster-and-Saved-a-City.htm.
58 *Avot* 4:12; *Mishneh Torah*, Laws of Torah Study 5:1; *Shulchan Aruch Yoreh De'ah* 242.
59 *Brachot* 53a.
60 Ibid. 62a.
61 *Makkot* 22b.
62 Of course, this is not a carte blanche for a student to treat a teacher dismissively or disrespectfully. In fact, there are specific laws for how to respectfully challenge and even correct a teacher.
63 *Kiddushin* 30b.
64 *Sanhedrin* 42a; ibid. 93b; *Megillah* 15b; *Chagigah* 14a, et al.
65 Ecclesiastes 9:17.
66 *Avot* 2:5.
67 1:3.
68 *Taanit* 7a.
69 *Brachot* 5b, *Nedarim* 7b, and *Sanhedrin* 95a.
70 *Brachot* 63b.
71 *Bava Metzia* 59a-b.
72 Deuteronomy 30:12.
73 Exodus 23:2.
74 22:6.
75 *Moed Katan* 1:6.
76 20:5.
77 Ad loc.
78 One of the Hebrew words for teacher, *moreh*, which means an archer or marksman (I Chronicles 10:3) reflects this idea. Put simply, just as an expert marksman knows how to aim his arrow from the bow to hit the precise target, the *moreh* is a master teacher who knows the mind of the child and can expertly guide them towards their own personal intellectual abilities and targets.
79 See the commentary of *Metzudat David* Proverbs 23:24.
80 Genesis 6:8.
81 Kohelet 9:17.
82 *Avot* 2:5: "A short-tempered person cannot teach."
83 Genesis 14:14.
84 See *Yalkut Shimoni* Genesis 3:34; *Tana D'vei Eliyahu* 1.
85 *Hayom Yom*, 23 Elul.
86 *Principles of Education and Guidance*.
87 *Sefer Hasichot* 5747 Vol. 1, p. 74.
88 11:12.
89 Accordingly, another word for teacher is *moreh*, which refers to a guide who leads the way by example. If modeling integrity is essential in all

areas of life and leadership, nowhere is this more critical than when trying to inspire others, especially children, to advance in their character development.

90 See *Hashkafa in Chinuch: How Lashon Hakodesh & Chazal Define Teaching Al Pi Darko*, p. 11.
91 27:19.
92 *Shabbat* 30b (see Rashi ad loc.); *Pesachim* 117a.
93 *Avodah Zarah* 19a (see Rashi ad loc.).
94 *Bava Batra* 8b.
95 *Albert Einstein.*
96 *Kiddushin* 29a.
97 18:19.
98 Deuteronomy 6:7.
99 https://www.waterford.org/education/how-parent-involvment-leads-to-student-success/
100 The importance of parental participation in their child's education and development is highlighted in the following entry in *Hayom Yom* (Tevet 22): "My father proclaimed at a *farbrengen*: Just as wearing *tefillin* every day is a mitzvah commanded by the Torah to every individual regardless of his standing in Torah, whether deeply learned or simple, so too is it an absolute duty for every person to spend a half hour every day thinking about the education of their children, and to do everything in his power—and beyond his power—to inspire children to follow the path along which they are being guided."
101 Genesis 21:8.
102 *Pesachim* 112a.
103 Interestingly, the Hebrew word for camel, *gamal*, is a derivative of the word *ligmol*. A camel can be self-sufficient for many days without needing food or water due to the surplus fat it stores in its hump, making it the perfect animal for desert travel. This etymological association underscores the quality of independence that is the goal of all good parenting.
104 *Mishneh Torah*, Laws of Tzedakah 10:7-14.
105 *Shabbat* 21a.
106 See *Likkutei Torah, B'haalotecha*; *Torat Menachem* 5711 Vol. 2, p.161.
107 *Baal Haturim* Exodus 30:12.
108 Elizabeth W. Dunn, Lara B. Aknin, and Michael I. Norton, "Spending Money on Others Promotes Happiness," *Science*, 319:5870 (March 21, 2008), pp. 1687–1688.
109 See "The Paradox of Generosity," by sociologists Christian Smith and Hilary Davidson.
110 "Forty-one percent say they rarely or never experience depression, versus thirty-two percent for everyone else." See ibid. You can read more about these findings here: https://newrepublic.com/article/119477/science-generosity-why-giving-makes-you-happy.
111 Social Capital Community Benchmark Survey (Harvard, 2000); William T. Harbaugh, Ulrich Mayr, and Daniel R. Burghart, "Neural Responses to

Taxation and Voluntary Giving Reveal Motives for Charitable Donations," *Science*, 316:5831 (June 15, 2007), pp. 1622-1625.
112 Lara Aknin (Simon Fraser University), Christopher Barrister-Leigh (McGill University), and John Heliwell (University of British Columbia, as documented in their study titled: "Prosocial Spending and Well-Being: Cross-Cultural Evidence for a Psychological Universal."
113 Deuteronomy 12:22.
114 *Taanit* 9a.
115 *Tur, Yoreh De'ah* 247.
116 *Bava Kama* 92a.
117 Amos 5:6.
118 II Samuel 19:18.
119 Daniel 3:30.
120 *Biur Hamilot* to Amos ad loc.
121 From this point of view, success is not just the inheritance of a lucky few who can make/fight their way to the top of the pile. Rather, success is attainable and within reach of every single one of us, each in our own way.
122 *Seeds of Wisdom*, p. 31.
123 II Samuel ibid.
124 Genesis 39:2.
125 Ibid. 23.
126 Interestingly, the word *tzalachat* in Hebrew, another variation of this root-letter structure, means a plate or a container (See II Kings 21:13 and II Chronicles 35:13), implying that at the root of success is the ability to "handle" or "carry" oneself with dignity and integrity in the midst of a difficult situation.
127 This is true in the spiritual and moral realm, as well. For example, the *baal teshuvah*, the person who slips or veers from the path of religious devotion but then gets back up or corrects their course, is viewed in Jewish sources to be of even greater spiritual standing than a *tzaddik*—a righteous person who never failed.
128 24:16.
129 The Chinese philosopher Confucius put it this way: "Our greatest glory is not in never falling, but in rising every time we fall."
130 *Bat Ayin, Tazria* 10, et al.
131 *Likkutei Sichot* Vol. 2, p. 410.
132 "...In the Graeco-Roman world, philanthropy was about education and the arts. It was about developing the good character of the donor. But it was also about honor, prestige, status, and reputation, and maintaining the social order. There was one key thing it was not about. It was not about the recipients. It was not about kindness or a duty of common humanity. It was about the rich rather than the poor." To access the full article: https://www.thejc.com/culture/features/tzedakah-a-concept-that-changed-the-world-1.506918.
133 There is a separate mitzvah called *maaser*, better known as tithing, which is more defined in terms of its details and requirements. For instance,

there is a mitzvah to give ten percent of one's annual income to a Levite of their choosing. *Tzedakah*, however, is a more broadly defined category of individual giving aimed at redressing economic disparity in society. The two concepts are related but distinct.

134 *Bava Batra* 10a.
135 *Yoreh De'ah* 247.
136 In the words of R. Elazar of Bartota in the Mishnah (*Avot* 3:7): "Give Him what is His, for you, and whatever is yours, are His. As David says: *For everything comes from You, and from Your own hand we give to You* (I Chronicles 29:14).
137 *Rut Rabbah* 5:9.
138 See *Pardes Yosef Parshat Terumah* 25.
139 *Avot* 4:1.
140 Numbers 12:3.
141 *Tikkunei Zohar* 111a.
142 Deuteronomy 6:20.
143 *The Essential Talmud*, Chapter 1.
144 This perspective is referred to in modern psychology (Carol S. Dweck, PhD, *Mindset: The New Psychology of Success*) as a "growth mindset." A growth mindset, as opposed to a "fixed mindset," is defined by one's positive and productive relationship to failure or mistakes, seeing them as potential catalysts for deeper learning rather than as defining judgments of one's intelligence. A fixed mindset, on the other hand, views intelligence and success as something that one either already has and can demonstrate, or they don't and can't. For someone with a fixed mindset, failure is irredeemable and should be avoided at all costs, while for someone with a growth mindset, it is learning itself that is considered a success. Similarly, in Judaism the ability and decision to assume a receptive and open posture towards a particular problem or question is specifically what is deemed wise rather than the resolution or answer at which one arrives. This defines wisdom as a process orientation, as opposed to an arrived-at destination.
145 P. 27.
146 *Eruvin* 13b.
147 See Jerusalem Talmud *Shabbat* 1:4, Babylonian Talmud *Shabbat* 17a, and *Tosefta Shabbat* 1:8.
148 Ibid.
149 5:7.
150 *Brachot* 40a.
151 *Bava Metzia* 85a.
152 *Avot* 6:1.
153 Joshua 1:8.
154 *Avot* 5:22.
155 Indeed, mystical sources describe how "sanctifying oneself at the time of intimacy" through noble intention-infused actions has the potential to channel a holy and pure soul into the world (See *Tanya*, Ch. 2 citing

156 *Zohar* I: 112a and III: 41b, and *Zohar Chadash* 11a. See also R. Bachya to Leviticus 19:2 and Rekanati to *Vayeitzei* 31).
156 *Yoma* 1:1.
157 26:8.
158 Rashi from *Bereishit Rabbah* 64.
159 *Chagigah* 5b; see also *Shitah Mekubetzet* to *Nedarim* 20b.
160 Genesis 2:24.
161 See Exodus 21:10.
162 *Ketubot* 48a.
163 4:1.
164 *Shulchan Aruch Orach Chaim* 240.
165 *Sefer Chasidim.*
166 *Mishneh Torah,* Laws of Shabbat 30:14.
167 3:80a-b.
168 *Guide to the Perplexed* III:8.
169 *Yoma* 54a.
170 Ibid. 54b
171 *Kedushat Shabbat, Ma'amar* 6.
172 Ramban, *Igeret Hakodesh* 2.
173 *Yadayim* 3:5.
174 *Avot* 3:17.
175 See *Ma'amarei Admur Hazaken* 5566 Vol. 2, p. 490.
176 III:272a.
177 Ibid. 188b.
178 Indeed, the Talmud (*Brachot* 62a) relates that R. Kahana once entered and lay beneath the bed of his teacher, Rav. He heard Rav chatting and laughing with his wife during intercourse. R. Kahana said to Rav, "The mouth of Rav is like one who has never eaten a cooked dish," i.e., his behavior was lustful. Rav said to him, "Kahana, you are here?! Leave, as this is an undesirable mode of behavior! R. Kahana replied, "This, too, is Torah, and I must learn."
179 See Genesis 39:6.
180 See *Nazir* 19a.
181 *Nedarim* 9:1.
182 *Eruvin* 65b.
183 *Shabbat* 31a.
184 R. DovBer, known as the Magid of Mezritch, had many holy and scholarly students. One of them, known as R. Leib Sarah's, used to say: "My colleagues all come to our master to hear his profound Torah ideas. I come to see how he ties his shoes."
185 *Mishneh Torah,* Laws of Temperaments 5:1.
186 *Menachot* 97a.
187 Deuteronomy 8:3.
188 Cited in *Pri Tzadik Toldot* 8, et al.
189 Indeed, according to the Sages (*Brachot* 35b), eating without saying a blessing is akin to stealing the food from G-d. It is our acknowledgment

of the Divine within the terrestrial that gives us permission to partake of it.

190 See *Tanya, Iggeret Hakodesh,* Ch. 26 regarding utilizing the energy for prayer and Torah study.

191 In the words of the *Tanya* (Ch. 7): "One [may] eat fat beef and drink spiced wine [not out of physical desire but] in order to broaden his mind for the service of G-d and for His Torah, as Rava said (*Yoma* 76b), 'Wine and fragrance [make my mind more receptive].'"

192 *Pesachim* 49b.

193 See *Menachot* 97a.

194 See Rashi to II Kings 11:2. Interestingly, our Sages teach (*Yoma* 54a) that in the Holy of Holies in the Temple, perched atop the Ark of the Covenant, were two cherubs intertwined in an intimate embrace, and it was through them that the word of G-d would emerge (see, for example, Numbers 7:89).

195 See Ramban, *Igeret Hakodesh.*

196 *Yoma* 1:1.

197 Indeed, during the Enlightenment period, for example, many secularizing Jews lived by the slogan: "A Jew in your home and a citizen on the street."

198 3:6.

199 *Tanya,* Ch. 38; see also ibid. Ch. 7.

200 See Nehemiah 7:3; *Keilim* 9:1; *Chulin* 107a; *Parah* 6:1; *Ohalot* 13:4.

201 14:4.

202 *Likkutei Torah Shemini,* et al.

203 *Bava Batra* 21b.

204 Deuteronomy 4:15.

205 *Chulin* 10a.

206 There are three exceptions to this principle: the cardinal sins of murder, idolatry, and adultery.

207 Cited in *Igrot Kodesh* Vol. 4, p. 341 from a letter printed in *Hatamim.*

208 See *Torat Shmuel* 5637, p. 91-92.

209 *Zohar* I: 122b.

210 Genesis 21:12.

211 See *Likkutei Sichot* Vol. 1, p. 31 *ff.*, for further explanation.

212 Interestingly, our understanding of the profound level of intelligence and potential healing the body possesses is only slowly beginning to be discovered. One example of this is the popular book titled: *The Body Keeps the Score: Brain, Mind, and Body in the Healing of Trauma*, by Bessel van der Kolk.

213 In fact, Chasidic teaching (see *Tanya, Igeret Hakodesh* 15) sees the verse (Job 19:26) *From my flesh I perceive G-d* as a reference to the idea that the body has its own innate, internal, spiritual intelligence, and that, moreover, by analyzing the bodily design and construct that mirrors its Creator, one can learn about the Divine design and construct of the universe, the cosmos, and even certain aspects and attributes of G-d Himself.

214 Laws of Teshuvah 8:8.

215 See *Likkutei Torah, Behar* 42a, et. al.
216 End of *Shaar Hagemul*.
217 In the words of Isaiah (40:5), *And the glory of the L-rd shall be revealed, and all flesh together shall see that the mouth of the L-rd spoke.*
218 *Avot* 4:17.
219 In this Mishnah, "the World to Come" is a reference to the state of existence experienced by souls after their physical passing. The term World to Come is used elsewhere in Jewish literature to describe a phase of the messianic era in which, according to Nachmanides, as mentioned, the soul will become embodied in the physical world again.
220 *Midrash Tanchuma, Naso* 15.
221 https://www.chabad.org/library/article_cdo/aid/2734/jewish/The-Physical-World-According-to-Rabbi-Schneur-Zalman-of-Liadi.htm.
222 For more on this topic, see the chapter on *hatzlachah*.
223 *Sanhedrin* 37a.
224 *Genesis* 18:27.
225 *Sotah* 49b.
226 *Sefer Hama'amarim* 5710, p. 237.
227 *Numbers* 12:3.
228 Judaism does have a different word for lowliness, which is *shiflut* or *shefal ruach*, from the root word *shafel*, low. However, the Hebrew word for humility means something altogether different.
229 ABC Religion and Ethics, June 14, 2018; Covenant and Conversation, *B'haalotecha* 5768.
230 C.S. Lewis.
231 https://rabbisacks.org/covenant-conversation-5768-behaalotcha-humility/
232 https://rabbisacks.org/shoftim-5776/
233 Interestingly, the word *massel* also means luck in German and Dutch, indicating that it possibly crept into these languages from the popular Jewish usage.
234 *Breishit Rabbah* 10:6.
235 *Shabbat* 156a.
236 *Shabbat* 156b.
237 *Brachot* 64a.
238 *Moed Katan* 28a.
239 *Rosh Hashanah* 3:8.
240 Indeed, the Talmud (*Megillah* 3a) utilizes the word *mazal* to describe "a person's guardian angel above (see Rashi ad loc.)." More than simply there to protect us, this guardian force and energy, or "higher self," communicates with our spiritual subconscious at times, whispering words of premonition and intuition into our soul. As Ravina teaches in the Talmud: "If one becomes frightened for no apparent reason, although he does not see anything to be frightened about, his *mazal* sees it," and as a remedy "he should recite the *Shema*." The same is true in the positive sense: There are times when we feel suddenly and unexpectedly inspired, guided towards spiritual growth for no obvious reason and without a conscious cause.

This, too, according to the mystics, is the work of our "higher self" in an effort to motivate us for the better. Mystical sources (see *Sefer Hama'amarim* 5672 Vol. 1, p. 114; ibid. Vol. 2, p. 1182) teach that this *mazal* is the source of a person's innate faith in G-d. For although we don't see G-d with our own eyes, our "*mazal*," our transcendent soul, witnesses Divinity in a sublime and suprarational sense, which in turn influences our faith in G-d.

241 *Rosh Hashanah* 17b.
242 *Torah Or, Miketz* 37c.
243 *Kilayim* 7:1.
244 *Sefer Taamei Hamitzvot, Peirush Barchu*; *Kad Hakemach, Brachah*; *Chinuch*, Mitzvah 430; responsa of Rashba 1:423.
245 Originally, the expression *mazal tov* was likely only used before or during an auspicious event, as it suggested an attempt to positively influence an event in process. The earliest mention of this expression in Jewish literature is in *Sefer Hachasidim*, a thirteenth-century book of *Ashkenazi* customs, suggesting to those who are present in a home where a woman is in labor that they should "beseech mercy on her behalf and for the child to be born with *mazal tov*." It was also common for medieval *ketubot* (marriage documents) that were written in advance of a wedding to contain a decorative header that reads: "*B'simana tava uv'mazala maalya*," which means "with a good sign and auspicious *mazal*."
246 *Shabbat* 156a.
247 Laws of Idolatry 11:8-9.
248 Ad loc.
249 Ibid.
250 Ibid.
251 This story is recounted in the Talmud (*Shabbat* 156b), a version of which can be accessed here: https://www.chabad.org/library/article_cdo/aid/4022098/jewish/The-Daughter-of-Rabbi-Akiba.htm.
252 To the Zippel Family of Milan, Italy; dated September 27, 1978.
253 Deuteronomy 30:15.
254 *Brachot* 18b.
255 Based on Mishnah, *Eduyot* 2:10: "The judgement of the wicked in Gehinom continues for twelve months."
256 This statement is attributed to Pierre Teilhard de Chardin.
257 This ideal and perspective on wealth is alluded to in the etymological connection between the Hebrew words *ashir*, meaning wealthy, and *eser*, meaning ten. Built into the Jewish concept of wealth is the mitzvah of *maaser*, setting aside ten percent of our income for charity.
258 *Shabbat* 31a. *Kohelet Rabbah* 1:13.
259 *Tanya*, Ch. 50.
260 *Kohelet Rabbah* 1:34
261 Ecclesiastes 5:9
262 *Kohelet Rabbah* 1:13
263 Exodus 30:13.

264 In a verse describing wanderers lost in the wilderness, the verse says: *Being both hungry and thirsty, their soul languished within them* (Psalms 107:5). The Baal Shem Tov interprets the verse mystically and teaches that when a person experiences hunger or thirst, it is only an external and physical reflection of a subliminal spiritual hunger and thirst within. Though one may be conscious of nothing more than the demands of his stomach, it is his soul that is "languishing within," yearning to refine and elevate the sparks of G-dliness that are embedded within the food and drink before him (*Keter Shem Tov*, p. 25b [p. 110 of 2004 edition]).
265 *Etz Chaim*.
266 *Keter Shem Tov, Miketz* 1:2.
267 *Pesachim* 87b.
268 *Torah Or, Bereishit* 6a.
269 32:23-33.
270 *Chulin* 91a.
271 *Avot* 1:17; see also *Kiddushin* 40b.
272 Mitzvah 16.
273 *Taanit* 2a.
274 See *Brachot* 5:1.
275 This is true of intentions as well. The Talmud (*Sanhedrin* 105b) teaches that a person should always study Torah, even for all the wrong reasons, such as for fame or power. Because "Acting with improper intention [eventually] leads to acting with proper intention." When we perform holy or righteous deeds, even if they are forced or transactional to begin with, their inherent positivity will eventually emerge, and the requisite intentions and feelings will follow.
276 The reverse is also true. Our patterns of behavior are a method of training that we enact upon ourselves, whether we are conscious of it or not. If there are specific actions or appetites we do not want to indulge or even entertain, then the best defense against them taking hold of us is simply to not do them. This may sound trite, but it is ultimately unavoidable. As the Sages teach (*Kiddushin* 20a; ibid. 40a; see also *Yoma* 86b, *Moed Katan* 27b, *Sotah* 22a, *Arachin* 30b): "If one transgressed one time and then again, that act will [begin to] appear to him as permissible." The body records and remembers everything, much more deeply and reliably than the mind. The more we indulge our unwanted urges, the more attached and identified to them we will become, making it that much harder to fully live a life of integral authenticity rather than helpless hypocrisy. To paraphrase the oft-quoted English writer Dr. Samuel Johnson: "The chains of habit are too light to be felt until they are too heavy to be broken."
277 *Torat Shmuel* 5629, p. 381; ibid. 5638, p. 349; et. al. See also *Gittin* 88b.
278 As in, *The soul of humankind is the flame of G-d* (Proverbs 20:27).
279 *Shabbat* 89a.
280 Exodus 19:6.
281 Isaiah 49:6.
282 31:2.

283 *Midrash Tanchuma, Matot* 3.
284 3:8-11.
285 *Megillah* 13b-14a.
286 *Hitler Speaks*, p. 220.
287 Ibid., p. 222.
288 In a letter to François Adriaan Van der Kemp, 16 February 1809, Historical Society of Pennsylvania, *Adams Papers*.
289 Epilogue, *A History of The Jews*.
290 The Rebbe continued: "It has nothing to do with chauvinism. You are not trying to convert anyone to be a Jew, but you are fighting, you are struggling for survival not only as a human being but as a Jew. In our time, it is a very acute problem, because every one of us must do something not only to perform his task but to replace all those Jews who were murdered and annihilated. Their [lives and] tasks are our direct duty."
291 2:7.
292 See *Bereishit Rabbah* 8:11 and 12:8. See Rashi to Genesis ibid.
293 Isaiah 14:14. See *Shnei Luchot Habrit, Torah Shebichtav, Vayeishev* 301b.
294 *For the soul of the flesh is in the blood*, Leviticus 17:11
295 *Shnei Luchot Habrit*, Introduction to *Beit Yisrael Beit David* (21a); *Likkutei Torah, Tazria* 24a.
296 *The Lonely Man of Faith*.
297 Introduction to *The Road to Character*.
298 Ch. 1; citing the interpretation of *Eitz Chaim* (Gate 50, Ch. 2) of the verse in Isaiah (57:16) *and I have made souls*.
299 *Tanya*, Ch. 9.
300 Ecclesiastes 9:14.
301 See Genesis 1:3.
302 *Ma'amarei Admur Hazaken Haketzarim*, p. 464.
303 Ibid.
304 *Arachin* 15b.
305 See *Likkutei Sichot* Vol. 27, p. 163-165.
306 Leviticus 19:14.
307 Proof of this is the fact that there is no prohibition against cursing someone who is deceased. If cursing another was prohibited on moral grounds, there would be no distinction between cursing the living or the dead. Since the dead are not existentially or energetically impacted by the speech of the living, there is no prohibition against cursing them. See *Kli Yakar* to Leviticus ibid.
308 F278 (1862) 1212.
309 https://www.hidabroot.org/article/1124317.
310 Genesis 18:11.
311 Jeremiah 31:34.
312 *Sefer Hasichot 5680-5687*, p. 227.
313 Genesis 4:4.
314 See *Tanya, Shaar Hayichud V'ha'emunah*, Ch. 2.
315 *Shabbat* 77b.

316 I:224a.
317 Genesis 24:1.
318 Entry for 17 Cheshvan, accessible online at https://www.chabad.org/therebbe/article_cdo/aid/5977/jewish/Hayom-Yom-Cheshvan-17.htm.
319 See *Likkutei Torah, Shelach* 52a, *Shir Hashirim* 22b et al.
320 *Brachot* 28b.
321 See *Likkutei Torah, Vayikra* 50d.
322 See *Likkutei Sichot* Vol. 16, pp. 271-273.
323 28:67.
324 Ch. 41.
325 *Torat Menachem—Hitvaaduyot* Vol. 59, p. 187.
326 *Pesachim* 50a.
327 *Likkutei Torah, Bamidbar* 5c.
328 *Sefer Hama'amarim* 5743, p. 95.
329 *Etz Chaim* Gate 47, Ch. 1 et al.
330 See *Torat Shmuel* 5632 Vol. 2, p. 559.
331 See *Mishneh Torah*, Laws of Idol Worship 1:2.
332 See *Bereishit Rabbah* 39:1.
333 Genesis 24:7.
334 Ibid. 3.
335 *Bereishit Rabbah* 59.
336 *Shabbat* 119b.
337 See *Likkutei Sichot* Vol. 6, p. 23, fn. 73.
338 *Baal Haturim* Deuteronomy 6:4.
339 *Brachot* 6:3.
340 Proverbs 3:6.
341 Deuteronomy 6:4.
342 See *Bet Yosef* to *Tur, Orach Chaim* 1.
343 Isaiah 45:15.
344 *Likkutei Sippurim*, p. 30. See https://www.chabad.org/therebbe/article_cdo/aid/2980182/jewish/Game-of-Hide-and-Seek.htm.
345 Longair, M. S. (2003). *Theoretical Concepts in Physics: An Alternative View of Theoretical Reasoning in Physics,* pp. 377–378.
346 Psalms 119:89.
347 See *Tanya, Sha'ar Hayichud V'ha'emunah,* Ch. 1.
348 An interesting story to illustrate this point was shared by R. Nissan Mangel, an author of note, who was commissioned by the Lubavitcher Rebbe to translate the *Tanya* into English. When it came to translating the word *domem*, he used the standard translation of inanimate.

One of the major themes of *Tanya*, however, is that there is no such thing as an inanimate being, because everything contains a Divine spark.

The Rebbe edited his translation and replaced inanimate with silent, meaning that while there is life even in *domem*, an object in this realm is "silent" about it, concealing the inherent Divine spark it possesses. R. Mangel, still wanting to maintain an elegant style, kept the word inanimate and placed the word silent nearby in brackets. When the Rebbe

edited the translation for the final time, he removed the brackets around silent and placed them around inanimate.
349   Exodus 20:23.
350   Ad loc., from *Mechilta d'Rabbi Yishmael* 20:23.
351   *Tur Orach Chaim* 271:1.
352   *Hayom Yom,* 17 Tishrei.
353   Ibid.
354   Based on https://www.chabad.org/library/article_cdo/aid/66990/jewish/The-Leaf.htm.
355   C.S. Lewis.
356   Exodus 15:4.
357   See *Sefer Hama'amarim* 5678, p. 89.
358   *Shnei Luchot Habrit, Torah Ohr, Terumah* 325a.
359   See *Likkutei Torah, Shelach* 37d and *Chukat* 65a. See also *Pesachim* 50a, *Kohelet Rabbah* 3:11, *Tikkunei Zohar* 442 (82a), *Sefer Habahir* 10, and *Siddur Arizal* to *Musaf Rosh Hashanah* (*Hayom Harat Olam*).
360   *Chacham Tzvi* 18.
361   See the blessings before the *Shema* in the morning prayer: "Who, in His goodness, renews the works of creation every day, constantly."
362   See *Igeret Hakodesh*, Epistle 14.
363   *Seder Hayom* (16th century) and cited by *Ateret Zahav* to the opening of *Shulchan Aruch, Orach Chaim.*
364   *Brachot* 60b.
365   Job 19:26.
366   *Brachot* 60b.
367   Joseph Heller, *Good as Gold*, p.72.
368   *Shabbat* 23b.
369   I Samuel 25:25.
370   *Yoma* 83b.
371   Genesis 17:5.
372   See Rashi ad loc.
373   See commentary to Genesis 15:5, citing the Midrashic interpretation.
374   32:29.
375   Interestingly, another source for the link between one's name and one's life mission comes from this episode itself. In his commentary to the verse: *And Jacob asked and said, "Now tell me your name,"* and he said, *"Why is it that you ask for my name?"* Rashi quotes the Midrash (*Bereishit Rabbah* 78:4), which explains the angel's response to Jacob this way: "We have no permanent name. Our names change, (all) according to the service we are commanded [to do] in the mission upon which we are sent."
376   See Rashbam, Chizkuni, and Netziv ad loc.
377   In Ch. 33.
378   Numbers 13:16; see Rashi ad loc.
379   Indeed, the Midrash (*Tanchuma, Haazinu* 7) demonstrates how each of the names of the spies who slandered the Land of Israel had a name that would indicate a predisposition to the sin of slander. It's important to

note, however, that although the Midrash and Talmud speak of tendencies that originate with a person's name, they hardly suggest that one is incapable of overcoming them. Indeed, the Midrash tells us (*Bamidbar Rabbah* 16:10) that there were people who led righteous lives despite having been given names with negative connotations. This demonstrates that it is possible for one to rise above the negative disposition that a name might otherwise have given him.

380 *Sefer Hagilgulim*, Introduction 23, quoted in *Taamei Haminhagim* 929; see also commentary of *Ohr Hachaim* on Deuteronomy 29:17.
381 Indeed, according to the *Tanya* (*Shaar Hayichud Vehaemunah*, Ch. 2.) the Hebrew name of every object is considered to be the conduit for its Divine, animating energy.
382 See *Rosh Hashanah* 16b.
383 See *Shaar Hagilgulim* 23:8.
384 Ibid. See also *Your Name Is Your Blessing*, p. 5.
385 Cited by R. Aryeh Kaplan, *Innerspace: Introduction to Kabbalah, Meditation and Prophecy*, p. 160; *Pitgamei Chasidim*, p. 41.
386 See *Bereishit Rabbah* 14:9.
387 Genesis 1:3.
388 Ibid. 2:7.
389 See *Tanya*, Ch. 2, citing *Zohar*.
390 See introduction to *Shefa Tal*.
391 In the words of Kabbalist R. Chaim Vital: "The soul's light arises and flows from the light of the ten *sefirot* (Divine powers) themselves, without any intermediary, which is why the verse states: *You are children of G-d* (Deuteronomy 14:1). For (the soul) is like a child who is completely attached to his father, from whom his being flows." *Shaarei Hakedushah* 3:2. See also *Practical Tanya* (Miller), p. 44.
392 *Brachot* 60b.
393 Job, 31:2. See also *Pardes Rimonim* 31:3, *Reishis Chochmah* 2:1, and *Tanya*, Ch. 2.
394 https://www.facebook.com/jewishmedia/posts/a-young-musician-on-a-spiritual-quest-once-approached-the-rebbe-as-he-was-gettin/10158894295610410/
395 See *Mishneh Torah*, Foundations of the Torah, Ch. 1.
396 See *Tanya*, Ch. 42.
397 *Rosh Amanah* Ch. 17; *Metzudat David* by Radbaz, Mitzvah 1; *Or Ne'erav* Vol. 2 Ch. 1; *Maaseh Rokeach* on *Mishneh Torah* ibid.
398 Exodus 24:7.
399 *Or Gedalyahu, Shavuot*, p. 164.
400 Genesis 14:13.
401 *Bereishit Rabbah* 42:8.
402 Ibid. 30:8.
403 Ibid. 38:13; 44:1; Rashi Genesis 11:28; *Esther Rabbah* 6:2; *Yalkut Shimoni* Genesis 15:7; *Eruvin* 53a, et al.
404 p. 186.

405 Genesis 12:1.
406 *From Alexander to Cleopatra*, p. 75.
407 *Life of Apollonius* 5:33.
408 P. 423.
409 https://www.chabad.org/library/article_cdo/aid/113207/jewish/Conformity.htm.
410 Genesis 32:29.
411 Ibid. 18:23, 25.
412 Exodus 5:22-23.
413 Ibid. 32:12, 32.
414 *Shabbat* 87a, *Bava Batra* 14b, *Menachot* 99b, *Yevamot* 62a, et al.
415 *Zohar* I:67b.
416 42:21.
417 *Pesikta Rabbati* 40.
418 *A History of the Jews*.
419 Think Different, 1997.
420 Exodus 32:10.
421 *Brachot* 32a.
422 Genesis 29:35. See Rashi ad loc.
423 *Brachot* 7b.
424 See Baumeister et al., 2001.
425 Maimonides, *Mishneh Torah*, Laws of Idolatry 1:2-3.
426 *Sotah* 10b.
427 23:4-7.
428 Ad loc.
429 *Brachot* 28a; *Tosefta Kiddushin* 5:4; *Mishneh Torah*, Laws of Forbidden Relationships 12:25; *Tur* and *Shulchan Aruch Even Ha'ezer* 4:10.
430 Deuteronomy 23:8-9.
431 Rashi ad loc.
432 *Menachot* 43b; *Shulchan Aruch, Orach Chaim* 46:3.
433 *Brachot* 60b.
434 This prayer first appears in *Seder Hayom*, by R. Moshe ben Machir.
435 From *Reb Elyah: The Life and Accomplishments of Rabbi Elyah Lopian* by David Schlossberg, p.121.
436 *Zohar* III:53b; *Gur Aryeh* to the opening of Genesis citing *Radak*.
437 III:178a; see also *Bereishit Rabbah* 1:2.
438 See *Zohar* III:152a.
439 *Yevamot* 109b.
440 *Avot* 3:17.
441 Laws of Mezuzah 6:13.
442 Numbers 15:39.
443 *Sotah* 17a.
444 See *Tefillin and Its Significance* (Kehot Publication Society 1981).
445 Exodus 20:9-11.
446 Deuteronomy 5:15.
447 The two other classes of *mitzvot* are called *chukim*—laws that we do on

faith without a rational explanation, such as the laws of *kashrut*; and *mishpatim*, rational precepts, such as the prohibitions against murder and theft (See *Mishneh Torah*, Laws of Me'ilah 8:8.)

448 *Shabbat* 156b.
449 *Kiddushin* 31a.
450 *Ohel Yehoshua*, cited in *Vayishma Moshe, Toldot*, p. 49.
451 *Bava Kama* 82a; see also *Mishneh Torah*, Laws of Prayer 12:1.
452 *Predictably Irrational*, p. 206.
453 In another study, conducted by Brandon Randolph-Seng and Michael Nielsen, participants were exposed to words flashed for less than one hundred milliseconds, that is, long enough to be detected by the brain but not long enough for conscious awareness. They were then given a test in which they had the opportunity to cheat. Those who had been shown words relating to G-d were significantly less likely to do so than people who had been shown neutral words.
454 Malhotra, Deepak. "(When) Are Religious People Nicer? Religious Salience and the 'Sunday Effect' on Pro-social Behavior." *Judgment and Decision Making* 5, no. 2 (April 2010), p. 138–143.
455 Interestingly, Ludwig Wittgenstein once said that "the work of the philosopher consists in assembling reminders." *Philosophical Investigations*, §127.
456 See *Likkutei Torah, Bechukotai* 45c.
457 *Likkutei Amarim*, Ch. 46. See also *Akeidah* Gate 88; *Likkutei Torah, Bamidbar* 16:3; ibid. *Derushei Shemini Atzeret* 91a.
458 From the Hebrew word *kiddushin*.
459 Genesis 2:24.
460 Job 35:7.
461 https://www.chabad.org/therebbe/article_cdo/aid/2737970/jewish/Why-Does-G-d-Care-So-Much-About-Little-Details.htm.
462 See Targum to Jeremiah 48:7.
463 Exodus 28:1.
464 Joshua 18:7.
465 Laws of Shemitah 13:12.
466 Deuteronomy 33:10.
467 In fact, the Levites were given residence in a specific set of forty-eight cities allocated for them by the various tribes of Israel. And even these cities were not for their use exclusively, as they also served as cities of refuge for those who had to be exiled after inadvertently killing someone. These forty-eight cities scattered throughout Israel were in effect a kind of no-man's-land for those in need of protection and purification.
468 *Mishneh Torah*, Laws of Entering the Temple 1:11.
469 Numbers 8:7.
470 Based on *Upsherin: Exploring the Laws, Customs & Meanings of a Boy's First Haircut*.
471 Genesis 29:34.
472 18:2.
473 Leviticus 21:1; *Tur, Yoreh De'ah* 369.

474 See *Chinuch* 263.
475 Isaiah 49:6.
476 Exodus 19:6.
477 Indeed, whereas there are seven universal *mitzvot* incumbent upon the people of the world, known as the Seven Noahide Laws (see *Avodah Zarah* 64b), the Jewish people were commanded to observe six hundred thirteen *mitzvot*, which define, limit, and sanctify their daily lives on every imaginable level.
478 *Gittin* 59b, citing Leviticus 21:8.
479 4:1.
480 See *Likkutei Torah*, Balak 72c, et. al.
481 Laws of *Temurah* 4:13.
482 Deuteronomy 28:9.
483 *Sifrei, Eikev* 11:22.
484 *Sefer Habahir* 109; Bechaye Leviticus 1:9, et. al.
485 See R. Saadya Gaon, *Emunot V'deot* 3.
486 Leviticus 1:2.
487 *Likkutei Torah, Vayikra* 2b; *Ma'amarei Admur Hazaken* 5572, p. 215.
488 Indeed, Psalms (90:10) states, *The span of our lives* bahem *is seventy years, or, given the strength, eighty years*. The word *bahem* is literally translated as "with them" and seems somewhat superfluous in this context. Mystical commentaries explain that the letters of this word are the same as the word *beheimah*, an animal. As the verse (Job 11:12) states: *Man is born a wild donkey*. Accordingly, the verse in Psalms is teaching us that the span of our lives ought to be utilized to refine the inner animal.
489 Psalms 51:18-19.
490 Another example is in Samuel's rebuke of King Saul when he spared the cattle of Amalek to sacrifice them to G-d, Who had commanded Saul to kill them in battle. Samuel says (I Samuel 15:22): *Does the L-rd delight in burnt offerings and sacrifices as much as in obedience to the L-rd's command?*
491 Covenant and Conversation, Vayikra 5780.
492 *Etz Chaim, Shaar* 26.
493 Incredibly, R. Schneur Zalman of Liadi explains in *Tanya* (Ch. 27) that a person should not become disheartened by their inability to achieve total righteousness, because even if they spend their entire life battling their inclinations, "perhaps this is the entire purpose of their existence and this is their life's work—to perpetually overcome the opposing side."

Indeed, according to the *Tanya* (Ch. 15), more important than *being* righteous is the work the person invests into *becoming* righteous. As the *Zohar* (II:128b) teaches: "When the 'other side' is suppressed, G-d's glory is revealed in all worlds." The effort itself brings more joy and satisfaction to G-d than the actual achievement, status, or saintliness of the person.
494 Indeed, the third Rebbe of Chabad, R. Menachem Mendel, known as the Tzemach Tzedek, once asked his grandfather, R. Schneur Zalman of Liadi, the founder of the Chabad Chasidic movement: "What is the ultimate point of Chasidut?" R. Schneur Zalman replied: "The entire point of

Chasidut is that one should transform the nature of his character traits (*middot*)." (*Likkutei Dibburim*, p. 128.)
495   See *Likkutei Sichot* Vol. 2, p. 409.
496   Job 31:2.
497   See *Sotah* 3a.
498   Laws of Divorce 2:20.
499   Indeed, our Sages teach that one's Jewishness is not a matter of choice or circumstance; rather, it is an indestructible essence. An example of this is a Jew who chooses to convert out of Judaism; they are nonetheless still regarded as a Jew in the eyes of Jewish law (See *Shulchan Aruch, Even Ha'ezer* 44:9).
500   *Sanhedrin* 44a.
501   This can be read as a repudiation of Christianity's replacement theology, which mistakenly links the special connection between G-d and the Jewish people to their behavior rather than to their essence.
502   Genesis 1:27.
503   See *Tanya*, Ch. 26.
504   *Torat Menachem—Hitvaaduyot* 5742 Vol. 1, pp. 109-110.
505   Interestingly, the Greek word synagogue reflects the meaning of the Hebrew. Etymologically, it implies a space of "meeting" or "bringing together," emphasizing the importance of the people and their gathering rather than the innate holiness of the place.
506   *Sanhedrin* 39a.
507   *Sukkah* 51b.
508   A story is told about the synagogue in the town of Nevel, where, before prayers each morning, the local townspeople would exchange their daily experiences of small *shtetl* life and discuss each other's challenges in livelihood.

Once the prayers began, however, all conversation ceased. The people blocked out all distracting thoughts and worries, and they immersed themselves in prayer. Once, at a gathering, R. Michoel the Elder elaborated on the sanctity of a synagogue. "It hardly seems appropriate to speak about your sources of livelihood, from cows to horses, in this holy place," he said. The people agreed, and they decided that from then on they would not speak about mundane matters before or after their prayers. They adhered to this resolution with the utmost respect. About a month later, R. Michoel ascended the podium one morning and requested the congregation's attention. "I suggest that we no longer pay attention to the resolution we made. From now on, we may talk about mundane matters in synagogue before the prayers begin, as we used to. Needless to say, this should not be done during the service itself."

In response to the many questioning looks, R. Michoel continued, "Although we had proper intentions, it seems that this resolution caused more harm than good. Before the resolution, we shared our daily difficulties with each other. We knew when a person needed a loan to replace his cow that had stopped producing milk, or when another person's horse grew old, and he needed funds to purchase a new one. When we stopped talking before the prayers, we lost touch with each other and were unable to show our care (for one another)."

509 See *Pri Etz Chayim, Shaar Olam Ha'asiyah* ch. 1; *Likkutei Sichot* Vol. 1, p. 201.
510 See *Brachot* 21b.
511 Ibid. 8a.
512 Chasidic sources (*Sefer Hama'amarim 5672*, p. 1457) explain that a *minyan* is composed of ten because ten is a "whole" or "complete" number, representative of a fully formed set or structure. Throughout Jewish literature and mysticism, the number ten appears in moments and matters of utmost significance, from the "ten utterances of creation" to the ten *sefirot* of the Kabbalistic Tree of Life to the Ten Commandments, and the list goes on. Ultimately, the number ten implies the manifest presence of various, necessary constituent parts required to make up a whole body or system. This is true for a *minyan* as well.
513 In fact, there is a principle in Jewish thought based on the verse, *G-d's splendor is found in the multitudes* (Proverbs 14:28), which teaches that the greater the gathering of G-d's children, the greater the honor given to G-d.
514 *Kikar La'aden* (Chida), Ch. 7 (explaining *Avot* 2:4).
515 *Bava Kama* 92a.
516 Job 42:10.
517 See Rashi *Chagigah* 16a s.v. *Umevarchin*.
518 Indeed, the *Zohar* cautions that if a particular *kohen* cannot achieve true love (or if he is engaged in any sort of conflict with a member of the congregation), he should abstain from participating in the Priestly Blessings, because the animosity in his heart at that time can affect him negatively!
519 See *Tanya*, Ch. 32, et. al.
520 Exodus 19:2 (from *Mechilta D'Rabbi Yishmael* ad loc.).
521 *Vayikra Rabbah* 89:9; *Derech Eretz Zuta Perek Shalom*. See also *Tanchuma Yitro* 9.
522 *Uktzin* 3:12.
523 Leviticus 19:18.
524 Deuteronomy 6:5.
525 https://www.chabad.org/library/article_cdo/aid/359588/jewish/Morning-Prayers-and-Torn-Shoes.htm.
526 *Likkutei Sichot* Vol. 2, p. 404.
527 *Likkutei Sichot* Vol. 2, p. 410.
528 See *Keilim* 3:5; *Torah Ohr, Terumah* 79d.
529 Genesis 30:8, see Targum and Rashi ad loc.
530 I Kings 19:12.
531 See Isaiah 16:3, ibid. 28:7, and Job 31:28.
532 *Tanya*, Ch. 13.
533 *Kuzari* 3:5.

534　https://www.orayta.org/orayta-torah/orayta-byte-parsha-newsletter/189-sparks-vayechi-rabbi-david-aaron.html.
535　Genesis 48:11.
536　https://www.forbes.com/sites/forbesagencycouncil/2017/08/25/finding-brand-success-in-the-digital-world/?sh=209922e6626e.
537　Interestingly, the word appreciate describes both the *recognition* of value, as well as its *growth*, conveying the fact that the two are deeply interconnected.
538　See Exodus 16:22.
539　Ibid. 34:21.
540　*Shabbat* 49b.
541　*Beitzah* 13b.
542　In *Thank You for Being Late: An Optimist's Guide to Thriving in the Age of Accelerations*.
543　*Tanya, Igeret Hateshuvah*, Ch. 10.
544　*Beitzah* 16a.
545　The book *The Sabbath* eloquently expresses this vital shift in consciousness.
546　Zechariah 8:18; Ezekiel 46:9; Nehemiah 10:34, et al.
547　Exodus 27:21 et al.
548　See *Metzudat Tzion* to Isaiah 14:13.
549　*Taanit* 29a.
550　*Amidah* for Festivals.
551　*Bereishit Rabbah* 48:12; Rashi's commentary to Genesis 18:10.
552　Indeed, a deeper look at the program and rituals of the Pesach Seder reveals that it is designed to disrupt our senses, as expressed in the Four Questions, which begin with the words, "Why is this night different from all other nights?" The *Zohar* states that everything is done differently on this night because in the heavens the Divine energy flows differently, skipping the protocols that are in place throughout the rest of the year. The Seder's "disruptive/disorienting" practices were thus designed to reflect and channel the positive "disruptive" and transcendent heavenly energies available only on this festival.
553　See *Tanya, Iggeret Hakodesh* 14.
554　See *Torat Menachem* Vol. 2, pp. 57-62.
555　See, for example, Judges 20:16 and I Kings 1:21.
556　*Sotah* 3a.
557　An amygdala hijacking describes the emotional response to stimuli that hijacks the rational part of the brain. You can read more about an amygdala hijacking here: https://www.healthline.com/health/stress/amygdala-hijack.
558　See *Derech Chaim*, Ch. 8, et al.
559　*Brachot* 10a.
560　See *Zohar* III: 16a; ibid .13b; see also *Ma'amarei Admur Ha'emtza'i Hanachot 5577*, p. 302.
561　Genesis 4:7.
562　*Gittin* 45a.

563 See *Tanya*, Ch. 26.
564 Notably, in addition to encouraging preventative action rather than using guilt and shame as tools of deterrence for sin, Judaism's ultimate method for inspiring righteous behavior is its focus on the profound impact of our actions. A powerful example of this can be found in the Talmudic discussion relating to witnesses who are called upon to testify in a capital case. The Mishnah asks (*Sanhedrin* 4:5): "How would they admonish the witnesses?" Meaning, due to the severity of a capital case, where there is an extra need to discourage witnesses from testifying falsely, what would be said to the witnesses to discourage them from lying? The Mishnah says that, among other things, we tell them that "each and every person is obligated to say, '*Bishvili nivra ha'olam,* for my sake was the world created (and I must therefore do the right thing).'" (See *Mishneh Torah*, Laws of Sanhedrin 12:3 with *Lechem Mishneh* ad loc.)

Simply put, when seeking to inspire ethical behavior, our Sages' method of choice was to inspire a sense of agency, purpose, and empowerment.

565 One way to ascertain whether your feelings of compunction derive from a noble impulse or from a deceptive influence (i.e., the *yetzer hara*) is to look at their end result. Do your feelings of failure and inadequacy impel you to improve your behavior, or do they keep you stuck in self-defeating patterns and block your path forward? If they are holding you back, then such feelings themselves are "sinful" according to the Jewish definition, because they cause you to continually "miss your mark." As the early Chasidim would say: "Depression is not a sin, but it can take you lower than any sin can take you." See *Beit Aharon, Seder Hayom* 4b.
566 See *Yoma* 86b; *Tanya*, Ch. 7.
567 *Brachot* 34b; *Mishneh Torah*, Laws of Teshuvah 7:4.
568 However, there is an important caveat to this equation. One cannot reap this benefit of Divine intimacy by sinning deliberately in order to return, as the Mishnah (*Yoma* 8:9) teaches: "One who says, 'I will sin and then return' is not afforded the opportunity to return." Gaining the spiritual advantage of becoming a *baal teshuvah* only works retrospectively for those who have already sinned, not for those seeking shortcuts to G-d.
569 Deuteronomy 30:19.
570 *Brachot* 18b.
571 *Yalkut Shimoni, Mishlei* 942.
572 *Etz Chaim, Shaarei Kedushah*, et al.
573 In explanation of how these holy sparks fell into the captivity of the *klipot*, Kabbalah teaches that G-d created a world before this one, based purely on the quality of *din*, judgment. This was a world that had no room for mistakes whatsoever. Moreover, communication and flow of energy between entities in this world was impossible, because everyone and everything was judgmental of everyone and everything else. This resulted in the closing down of all channels of sharing and receptivity. There was therefore no circulation within the system, causing the structure of this world to simply shatter once it reached a critical mass of tension. In this

state, there was no available mechanism of healthy release or realignment. As a result, the holy animating sparks of pure energy that went into creating this first world "fell," so to speak, and were scattered throughout the next iteration of creation, our world, founded on the counterbalancing quality of *rachamim*, mercy and compassion. Those Divine sparks from the previous world are now strewn about and hidden within our current creation.

574 *Tanya*, Ch. 8.
575 Related to this process of continuing illumination and revelation of G-d's light, our Sages teach: "G-d did not create a single thing in vain." In the Jewish view, every object that we possess, person with whom we come into contact, and experience that we have—everything we witness, hear, or do—throughout our lives is a deliberate part of this grand scheme. It is our job to uncover its inherent inner significance, because this recognition and resulting right relationship is what "unties" whatever "knot" by which it (or we) may have been constrained. As such, we are instructed (Proverbs 3:6) to *Know G-d in all your ways*. But how can we do this? The Sages explain that it is through our own consciousness and intention that "All your deeds shall be for the sake of heaven."
576 See *Reshimot* 44.
577 https://www.chabad.org/library/article_cdo/aid/421911/jewish/The-Ruin-in-the-Forest.htm.
578 *Pesachim* 76b.
579 See *Shnei Luchot Habrit, Chayei Sarah*; *Midrash Talpiyot "Chazir"* citing R. Bechaye; et al.
580 Deuteronomy 14:6.
581 Leviticus 11:7.
582 *Yalkut Shimoni*, Psalms 830.
583 See Rashi, Genesis 26:4.
584 Laws of Temperaments 2:6.
585 *Brachot* 28a.
586 *Yoma* 72b.
587 Source: https://www.chabad.org/library/article_cdo/aid/218787/jewish/The-Two-Way-Mouth.htm.
588 *Sotah* 3a.
589 E.g., Sforno on Genesis 3:1.
590 *Sanhedrin* 107a.
591 *Bava Batra* 16a.
592 *Bereishit Rabbah* 9:7.
593 Genesis 1:31.
594 *Zohar* I:14a; *Bereishit Rabbah* ibid.
595 II:163a.
596 *Keter Shem Tov* Vol. 1, 115.
597 *Zohar* ibid.
598 Isaiah 11.
599 *Tamid* 7:4.

600 *Likkutei Torah, B'haalotecha* 35c.
601 *Pardes Shaar* 12, Ch. 2; *Reishit Chochmah Shaar Haahavah*, Ch. 6 s.v. *V'hamargil*; *Shnei Luchot Habrit* 89a; ibid. 189a; *Chacham Tzvi* 18; *Tanya, Shaar Hayichud V'ha'emunah*, Ch. 6; *Likkutei Torah, Re'eh* 22b.
602 *Etz Chaim* 1:2, et al.
603 2:14.
604 30:20.
605 Ibid. 40:5.
606 Isaiah 2:4.
607 Leviticus 25:8-16.
608 Ibid.
609 Jeremiah 17:8.
610 See R. Bechaye to Leviticus ibid.
611 See *The Road to Character* by David Brooks.
612 See Abarbanel to Leviticus 25:1.
613 *Avot* 5:21.

Acknowledgments

I would like to express my heartfelt gratitude to the following individuals for their part in making this book possible.

Firstly, to the Lubavitcher Rebbe, my Rebbe, whose wisdom and teachings continue to shape and inspire my life and thinking. I hope this book makes you proud.

To Rabbi Mendel Kalmenson for conceiving the vision for this book and for turning to me as a collaborator to assist in bringing his idea to life. Your eloquent demeanor, keen understanding of people, and refined insight is inspiring. I will forever treasure our exchange of ideas that led to the creation of this work.

To my dear wife and life partner, Leah, for your continued loving support and encouragement over the time-consuming process of working on this book.

To my dear children Chana, Mendel, Frayda, and Chaya, you are my light and joy.

To my parents, siblings, and all of my teachers and friends for your roles in shaping who I am and for your teachings that inspire me daily.

To the various editors who worked on this book, and to the teams at Chabad.org and Kehot Publication Society for your efforts in bringing this manuscript to the world.

Most of all, to G-d Almighty, thank You for the gift of life and for the Torah that gives life meaning and purpose.

Zalman Abraham

I would like to acknowledge the following individuals:

My co-author, Rabbi Zalman Abraham, whose knowledge, integrity, and demeanor have made collaborating with him on this and other projects a privilege and pleasure.

Rabbi Zalman Shmotkin, the executive director and driving force behind the legendary Jewish website, Chabad.org, for his support for this book.

My gifted editor, R. Eden Perlstein, a man of many talents, whose unique ability to crystalize and contextualize has enriched this book immeasurably.

Rabbi Meir Simcha Kogan, director of Chabad.org, for his constant wisdom and patience.

The editorial team at Kehot Publication Society for their rigor and professionalism. In particular, Rabbi Dovid Olidort, and Rabbi Mendel Laine, for his dedication and editorial expertise.

Chanie Kaminker of Hannabi Creative for the creative cover design. This is our fourth book together, and I look forward to future collaborations.

My dear esteemed friends, Sacha and Tanya Gaydamak, for dedicating this book in honor of our mutual distinguished friends, Vadim and Stella Aminov. I am profoundly grateful for and deeply blessed by their friendship.

My dear brother, Yekusiel, whose constant friendship and support is a great source of joy and blessing.

My wife and life partner, Chana, whose unwavering dedication helped facilitate this book, and whose clarity and companionship is one of life's greatest blessings.

I would also like to express our gratitude to G-d for our beautiful children, Geula, Dov, Ester, and Zelig, who bring unlimited joy to our lives.

My dear parents, Rabbi Yosef Yitzchak and Hindy Kalmenson, my beloved grandmother, Sara Shanowitz, and my dear father- and mother-in-law, Rabbi Yosef and Tamara Katzman, for their constant counsel, love, and support.

I would also like to pay tribute to my paternal grandparents,

Rabbi Yekusiel and Batsheva Kalmenson, of blessed memory. My life and that of my family is greatly enriched by their living example of Jewish and Chasidic values.

Last year, my maternal grandfather, Rabbi Sholom Ber Shanowitz, of blessed memory, returned his soul to its Maker. His love and passion for Torah study and his zest for life were legendary, and his memory serves as a constant source of inspiration to our entire family, who aspire to emulate his example.

My dear brothers and sisters, Chanie, Nechama Dina, Menucha, Yekusiel, and Moishy. I feel so blessed to have you in my life.

Lastly, I would like to express a profound sense of gratitude to the Rebbe, of righteous memory, whose living wisdom, example, and teachings continue to inspire and guide me daily.

Mendel Kalmenson

More Titles by Mendel Kalmenson

Seeds of Wisdom I
Seeds of Wisdom II
A Time to Heal
Positivity Bias